# LORD OF THE ISLE

For Vanessa

# LORD OF THE ISLE

*The Extravagant Life and Times of*
## Colin Tennant

Nicholas Courtney

BENE FACTUM PUBLISHING

*Lord of the Isle*
*The Extravagant Life and Times of Colin Tennant (Lord Glenconner)*
Published in 2012 by
Bene Factum Publishing Ltd
PO Box 58122
London
SW8 5WZ
Email: inquiries@bene-factum.co.uk
www.bene-factum.co.uk

ISBN: 978-1-903071-64-9

Text © Nicholas Courtney

A CIP catalogue record of this is available from the British Library

Cover and text design: www.mousematdesign.com

Printed and bound in Malta for Latitude Press

## PICTURE CREDITS

Julian Barrow, 36a; Bonhams, 41, 107–8, Colin Tennant Collection, 3–12, 14–8, 20–2, 24–33, 35, 36e–7, 39–40, 42, 45–6, 50, 55, 65–7, 70–1, 74, 76, 82, 102, 105, 112, 115, –8; Nicholas Courtney, 36 b, c and d, 53–4, 56, 69, 75, 81, 86, 96, 112–4, 117–8; Colin de Chair, 23, 103; Lady Glenconner, 34, 38, 43, 47–9, 51–2, 57–60, 62, 64, 68, 72–3, 77–9, 84–5, 89–9, 92–5, 98, 104; The Glen Collection, 1–2, 116, 119–22; Sarah Henderson, 61, 87–8, 91, 97, 109–10; Lawrence Lawry/*Hello!*, 83, 101; Patrick Litchfield, 63; Ivar Massar, 19; Tony McGee/*Hello!*, 46, 99–100; Lord Montagu of Beaulieu, 13; Ariana Roger, 80; Brett Walker, 111; Wartski, 101; Michael Winner, 106. Front cover photograph by Patrick Litchfield, back cover photograph by courtesy of Bonhams.

# CONTENTS

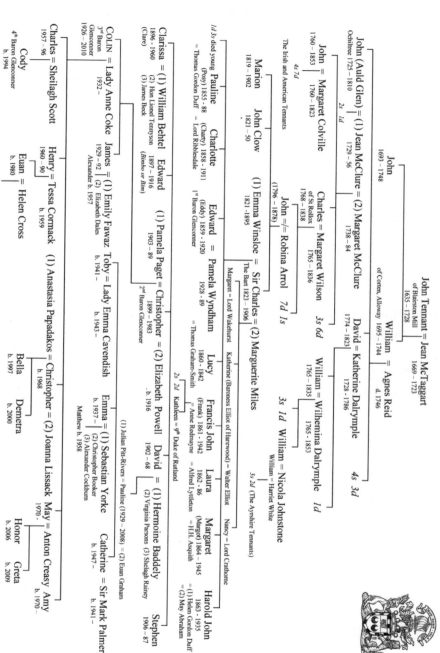

# AUTHOR'S NOTE

To thank everyone who has helped me in the writing of this book individually would be a lengthy task – even dangerous in that I might inadvertently omit someone. But, in the words of the sergeant-major, 'you knows who you are' and all have my grateful thanks. However, I acknowledge my grateful thanks to Lady Glenconner who has been of inestimable help, not least in allowing me access to, and use of, her fine collection of family photographs. Also in reading the text for errors and enlarging on various topics. It is undoubtedly a better book through her input.

Colin Tennant and I were working on his autobiography which was woefully incomplete when he died in 2010. He appointed me his literary executor and so I have carried on where we left off. As I have used transcripts of his tape recording throughout the text, it would be repetitious to acknowledge each quote. Thus, unattributed passages within quotation marks have come from Colin.

Be not afeard: the isle is full of noises,
Sounds, and sweet airs, that give delight, and hurt not.
Sometimes a thousand twangling instruments
Will hum about mine ears; and sometimes voices,
That, if I then had wak'd after long sleep,
Will make me sleep again: and then, in dreaming,
The clouds methought would open and show riches
Ready to drop upon me; that, when I wak'd,
I cried to dream again.

*The Tempest*, 3:2. 148 – 156

# PROLOGUE

It is so typical of Colin Tennant, the 3rd Baron Glenconner, that a biography of him does not end with his dramatic death outside the hospital in Souffrière in St Lucia for, as in his eventful life, his story twists and turns in many diverse and unexpected directions.

For the funeral in early September 2010 I joined the immediate family of Anne, his wife of fifty-four years, the twins, Amy and May, the daughters-in-law, Tessa Tennant with her son Euan, and Sheilagh with her son Cody (then a strapping lad aged 16 and now the 4th Baron Glenconner and 5th Baronet), along with Joshua Bowler, Colin's recently discovered son, on the Virgin Atlantic flight to St Lucia. It was not a particularly mournful journey, as no one really believed that Colin would not be there to greet us at the airport. But when the white-clad figure was missing from his usual corner, from where he could espy the disembarking passengers, it finally dawned on us that he really had gone forever.

We went straight to the optimistically named Lazarus Funeral Home. While I said farewell to my friend of over forty years, Anne and the girls were choosing the coffin. The choice was not difficult, for the single plain one in oak stood out amongst the array of white, shiny plastic versions with 'silver' rococo handles and stable-door type lids to show off the deceased. At Beau, Maharukh Desai, who had aided Colin's passion for collecting antique Indian jewellery, was waiting for us, having flown in from India that morning. It was all very strange with no Colin there to organise us, and Kent Adonai, his factotum and friend for thirty years, was still very weepy. But there was much to do. Various politicians and local dignitaries called on Anne: we called on the Roman Catholic priest of Our

Lady of Lourdes in Choiseul to discuss the funeral service – even though Colin, if he was anything, was lapsed Church of Scotland. The tiny priest, who came from India, had his own format and we only just managed to include two Anglican hymns in the order of service. I gave an interview 'down the line' to the BBC's *Last Word*. It was all very poignant. I said that one of Colin's greatest legacies was how he had changed the lives of countless numbers of people, myself included. One night we all dined with Lyton and Eroline Lamontagne at Fond Doux, Lyton being another of Colin's protégés.

At dawn on the day of the funeral, I showed my fellow pall-bearers the clip on *YouTube* of the Irish Guards carrying The Queen Mother's coffin out of St George's Chapel. Josh and his son Patrick, Sheilagh's sons Cody and Matthew Scott, and Euan and I practised the slow march with a couple of teak loungers around the swimming pool. Euan, at least six inches taller than the rest of us, threw the 'bier' at an impossible angle, so I suggested that he went before us with a large bunch of heather that he brought from Glen, the seat of the Tennants in the Borders. Meanwhile Kent had dressed Colin's body in a magnificent Indian coat, gold-embroidered shoes and a silk wedding *kurta* with *churida* (trousers), along with a golden crown and the Tipu Sultan white jade amulet he always wore.

The Mustique contingent flew up for lunch and, as St Lucia tradition dictates, the mourners filed past Colin's coffin in the Great House only with the lid closed. The coffin turned out to be solid oak, so heavy that we pall-bearers could barely carry it to the hearse, a converted black pickup truck with an illuminated cross on the roof. At Choiseul all the townsfolk were about in the street, while the members of the local chapter of *La Woz*, a historic Creole cultural society of The Rose, who mark every important happening on the island, were seated under a canopy. There were the king and queen, prince and princess, doctor, magistrate, policemen, nurses and soldiers, all dressed in white and red satin, with red sashes denoting their rank.

The church was full. There had been many wakes for Colin in the villages around Souffrière, and one representative from each attended the funeral. The service was traditional. An octogenarian altar boy removed the flowers, St Lucia flag and Colin's hat from the coffin and replaced them with a pall. The local Member of Parliament, Marcus Nicholas, gave the address; the hymns were sung with gusto, prayers were intoned. Bryan Adams, the Canadian rock singer-songwriter sang the traditional folk song *He Was a*

*Friend of Mine*. It was indeed appropriate as he was so fond of Colin.

The service over, the St Lucia flag and Colin's hat restored to the coffin, we pall-bearers then struggled to put it on our shoulders to march out of the church. We staggered up the hill through Choiseul, then down to the cemetery to the grave (carefully sited in view of the sea) Colin had bought a decade earlier. The coffin was lowered into the grave, gleaming white for the twins had painted it the day before. Hardly had the coffin touched the deep bottom before wet mortar was slapped onto the top edge and large concrete slabs sealed the tomb. The committal was a happy affair, with the members of *La Woz* dancing with the other mourners. The 'doctor' even took her stethoscope to Kent: it was the first time he smiled since Colin had died. The dancing and the drinking continued in Choiseul until the tiny hours of the morning, and when the party was over, 'Mr Tennants' had finally gone.

# Chapter 1

# ADMIRAL'S HOUSE

'I'm the *Horrible* Colin Tennant!' was how the 4-year-old son of the second Baron Glenconner innocently described his Honourable status to strangers. Few murmurs of dissent were heard, especially from his nanny. His mother, Pamela Paget, had perforce married Lord Christopher Glenconner at Wells Cathedral in 1925, in a lavish ceremony designed by the bridegroom's brother, the epicene Stephen Tennant, who dressed the bridesmaids in colours taken from the cathedral's stained glass, and turned up with a snake and tortoise concealed in his pockets. Colin was born the next year, on 1 December, at their home 76 Sloane Street, Chelsea, in the heart of London.

His birth was the cause of much rejoicing, not to say expense. Lord Glenconner rewarded Pamela with an exact replica of her engagement ring from Cartier that had flown from her finger as she threw sticks for her lunatic red setter, Netta, to retrieve from the Serpentine in Hyde Park. The original 'tutti-frutti' ring, set with a wonderful cabochon emerald, faintly tinged with blue and bounded by small emeralds and rubies, is presumably still buried somewhere in the mud of the lake. Pamela never wore the replacement and, seventy years later, Colin took the ring back to Cartier to have it stamped and hallmarked. The expense also reached as far as the tenantry and employees of Glen and Kirk House, the twin Glenconner houses in the Borders, who handsomely anted up for a Scottish silver quaich.

In a scene worthy of a P. G. Wodehouse novel, Evan, the name of Lord Glenconner's prize and favourite shorthorn bull, was seriously considered for the infant Tennant; as was Marmaduke, an alternative suggested by his great aunt, Margot Asquith, who declared it 'her favourite name'. Finally 'Colin' was chosen after the full-length portrait of Lady Gertrude Fitzpatrick, daughter of the 2nd Earl of Upper Ossory, by Sir Joshua Reynolds that hung in the drawing room at Glen. The girl is standing on a little hillock, or *collina*, behind Fermyn Woods Hall in Northamptonshire, which gave the painting its title.

And so the day before Christmas Eve Colin, dressed in the family christening robe trimmed with Valenciennes lace, was launched on society at his christening at Holy Trinity Church, Sloane Street, where the faithful housekeeper, Tilly, had decorated the font with white heather brought down from Glen. His godparents, who included Sir Ian Colquhoun of Luss, appear to have taken no further part in Colin's life once they had renounced the sins of the flesh at the font and given him the additional names of Christopher, after his father, and Paget in deference to his mother's family, along with a tiny silver tankard. Colin's solitary nursery life ended dramatically with the arrival of his brother James in 1929, but typically Pamela could not remember whether the birth was on the fifth or sixth of March as she was staying with friends at the time.

Soon after the birth of James, when Colin was 5, the family moved into Admiral's House, situated at the highest point in Hampstead. This imposing eleven-bedroom house had been built at the end of the eighteenth century for Fountain North, an eccentric naval officer with high-ranking aspirations. Like Admiral Boon's house in *Mary Poppins*, the roof was divided into facsimile main- and quarter-decks of a frigate, complete with cannon, which he fired on George III's birthdays and to celebrate British naval victories. Immediately below the quarter-deck were North's quarters, built like the captain's cabin in the stern of a ship-of-the-line. In the 1-acre garden was a tunnel that came out on Hampstead Heath which, according to local legend, was the escape route of the highwayman Dick Turpin. The architect George Gilbert Scott once lived there, although he complained that the lofty elevation was 'too cold for him'. John Constable recorded the house twice.

For Colin and James life in the nursery situated in the former cabin of Admiral's House (or Adho as the family called it) appears to have been harmonious, well ordered and prosperous. There were servants everywhere, including Pringle the butler, and the aforesaid Tilly the housekeeper, who had been inherited from Lord Glenconner's mother (also named Pamela) when, after being widowed, she married her second husband, the former Foreign Secretary, Viscount (Edward) Grey of Fallodon. The daughter of a porter at St Pancras station, Tilly became the major force within the family. Not young when she arrived in 1922, she was to stay with Colin's mother until the day she, Tilly, died aged 97, devoting her life to the service of the family. When she was 70, for example, she broke her hip but insisted on continuing her work. To lay the table she would tie a length of string round her waist and crawl along the passage to the dining room. There she would drag the tray laden with plates and cutlery and place them piece by piece on the table above her. Payback time came when Pamela nursed the bedridden Tilly for the last ten years of her life. Tilly's toothy ally was Doris, the cook. The full-time gardener was appropriately called Mr Green. There was an oft-changed nanny and a nursery maid, or two, to look after the boys.

Every day in term time, and wearing their respective uniforms, Birley, the chauffeur, would sedately drive Colin in the new 8-litre Bentley down Fitzjohn's Avenue to Arnold House, his day school, and collect him in the early afternoon. Holidays were spent either at Glen or sometimes on a lavish trip abroad. In the spring of 1931, for example, Pamela took the boys to stay in Lausanne, but their visit coincided with the crash of the London Stock Market. Pamela's immediate reaction was to vacate the luxurious Paris Hotel and take a house in the town, which was cheaper. The devastating collapse of the money markets at home, on top of the Wall Street crash of 1929, was to change their lives forever. However, up to that time, harmony reigned in the lofty nursery and the servants' hall in the basement, but all was not well with Christopher and Pamela on the floors in between. They clearly never should have married and a dark cloud was to form on Colin's otherwise sunny childhood sky.

In the long, lonely evenings of later years in St Lucia, Colin spent many hours poring over the visitors' book from Wilsford, his paternal grandmother Pamela's house near Salisbury, where she had lived with her second husband Edward Grey. Colin would delight in the names of the fashionable, the intellectual, and the family members who visited Wilsford, then piece together the frequent house parties hosted by Pamela. Many of these were to introduce her handsome, rich and eligible sons, Christopher and David (though not Stephen, who was gay) to a succession of equally beautiful and eligible young girls – the likes of Alice Astor, granddaughter of William Astor of New York City, and Cary Brand, scion of Viscount Hampden. Nancy Mitford and her sister Diana were also visitors.

While Pamela Grey applied her considerable energies to finding suitable wives for her marriageable sons, she was also on the lookout for a husband for her goddaughter and namesake, Pamela Paget. Her father, Sir Richard Paget, always known as Artie, had been an admirer of Pamela before she married Edward Glenconner, and the close friendship extended to his wife, Lady Muriel Finch-Hatton. The visitors' book reveals that the Pagets often came to Wilsford before the First World War, their house at Cranmore in Somerset being just far enough away to warrant an overnight stay. After the war they were always accompanied by their daughter Pamela. It is clear that she was unofficially being groomed to marry, though the paucity of eligible men after the First World War made the task considerably harder. In the meantime she joined her sister, Sylvia, at Newnham College, Cambridge where she read Anglo-Saxon history. Soon after her arrival she was surprised to receive a visit from Christopher, who had been dispatched by his domineering mother to sound out the possibility of her marrying his brother David. It was typical of Pamela Grey to think that just because she was fond of Artie Paget and Lady Muriel, her son would be happy with Artie's daughter. Christopher knew that his debonair brother was heavily involved with the ingénue Hermione Baddeley (whom he later married after the birth of their daughter Pauline), and therefore was most certainly not romantically interested in the provincial, blue-stocking Pamela, nor she, most likely, in him. 'I had no one as it happened' she once confided to Colin. In the end, Christopher carried off this ewe lamb and proposed to Pamela himself. Her acceptance was solely motivated by what she thought was expected of her, laced with a heavy dose of parental pressure. It was not a propitious start to any union.

Christopher and Pamela could not have been more different. The catalyst was, of course, Pamela Grey and when she died in 1928 her considerable influence on Christopher and her protégée Pamela died with her. The couple's relationship deteriorated over the next few years until Christopher felt that he could take no more of his wife and moved out of 'Adho'. Amongst other things he could not cope with her attitude to wealth. When he passed through a difficult time at the head of the Tennant financial empire she would remark what fun it would be to be poor – he did not think it fun at all.

There was no one else involved in the ensuing divorce. Universal condemnation was heaped on Christopher for his defection but, in his defence Pamela was, as Colin was to admit, 'terribly, terribly difficult, with a temper as well'. The decree absolute was granted in 1935 when Colin was barely 9. He had a clear recollection of his mother coming into his bedroom while he was resting after lunch to tell him that she was no longer married to his father. He just said 'Oh!' but the news struck him very forcibly. Both he and James were far more affected by the divorce than they realised and, by his own admission, it taught Colin thereafter never to rely on other people's affections. He overcame the trauma by 'being outward and ambitious to get on'. He became irrepressible, but as he said 'what was being repressed was very damaged [and] quite neurotic'. When it was suggested that Colin should see a psychiatrist to help cope with his neurosis, his father was furious, declaring that no son of his 'was going to be psychotic'. The neurosis that began with a traumatic childhood only increased over the years.

# Chapter 2

# WICKHAM'S, ETON

Colin's parents' divorce meant that he and his brother, James, were brought up almost exclusively within the sphere of, and influenced by, the Paget family. The brothers did see their father on occasion, but at that time Colin remembered Christopher as a distant figure: 'There was never any intimacy with my father. I cannot recall him ever hugging or kissing, or even touching me at all. He just held his hand out – I was always surprised that the boys Charles and Henry rushed forward to kiss me. He was very undemonstrative, and we saw so little of him.' He recalled being taken by his father to the Ritz for dinner just once, but his step-mother, Elizabeth, Lady Glenconner, remembers otherwise. They met always in the holidays and during school exeats. Years later Colin flew into an abject rage when he showed his cousin, John Chancellor, a letter from his father that was signed just 'Yours, Daddy'. It can only have been a momentary aberration as all other surviving correspondence invariably carries the valediction 'with love from Daddy' or 'Best love, Daddy'. Colin kept the book he was given by his father for his eleventh birthday that had been signed by his secretary: 'To Colin from Lord Glenconner. Christmas 1937.'

Neither did Colin's mother show much tangible affection: according to Colin, she never kissed or cuddled her sons. Pamela did, however, devote her life entirely to them. Having no inkling that Christopher was leaving her, she was totally overcome by the divorce when it came. But she never stopped loving Christopher and was grateful to Elizabeth, his second wife as, unlike her, she made him happy. For some time after the divorce Pamela appeared somewhat 'scatty and uncoordinated'. As Elizabeth Glenconner said: 'She was terribly unhappy, and you don't behave very well when you are unhappy.' Pamela was finally saved by the advent of the Second World War which gave her something useful to do when, among other voluntary projects, she worked in a munitions factory.

Despite the trauma of the divorce, life at Adho continued very much as before. Christopher had settled an extremely generous £5,000 a year on Pamela which, with her modest and careful nature, was more than enough to run the house with a full staff that by then included a governess, Stella Toy (Colin never forgot her address, a boarding house in St Ives '1 Clodgy View'). Indeed Pamela created an enchanting, if alternative, environment for her sons. She was pretty and although marriage had prevented her from finishing her degree at Cambridge she was highly intelligent. She introduced Colin to the delights of algebra and Latin. In true Paget fashion, conversation was on anything and everything, particularly at mealtimes. Pamela spoke in a precise, witty manner somewhat reminiscent of her great aunts, Camilla and Louise Rice, who were Jane Austen's great nieces. Pamela thought of them as 'very auntified aunts'. She would often embark on some wild story that lasted throughout the meal, going off at tangents, but always coming back to the key point before they had finished eating. Another Paget trait was to sing songs at mealtimes.

Colin's school holidays were generally spent either at Glen, with his father and step-mother and their children, Emma and Toby (Catherine was born after the Second World War) or at Cranmore when Pamela, the only Paget with any money, used to rent the house from her parents. Lady Muriel, her mother, was rarely there, having 'usually just left for Latvia'. However, when illness anchored her to Somerset, to her obvious delight Colin and James visited her. She wrote to Artie: 'Children are the most delightful companions. Colin *v.* clever & thinks things out to their logical conclusions. He bought some sweets for old Mrs Birch yesterday & said, "You see, if I am kind to old people when I am young, young people might be kind to me when I am old."'[i]

Pamela's grip on Colin was loosened when, in 1936, he was sent to Scaitcliffe, a preparatory school set in a commodious, red-brick Victorian house on the edge of Windsor Great Park at Englefield Green in Surrey. The school was owned and run by the ferocious Ronald Vickers, son of Col. Tom Vickers who had been Chairman of the armaments manufacturers of the Maxim machine-gun and, later, battleships. Mr Vickers was very good-looking with a classical appearance, noble brow, and big round eyes. The feminine element of the school was provided by Mrs Vickers and their two unmarried daughters who had once been ravishing beauties. It was said that the Duke of Sutherland had been interested in Rosemary [May] who was 'really pretty, big eyes [and a] big round face'. There were also three nurses: Nurse Major, Nurse Minor and Nurse Minimus. Colin remembered Mr Vickers as ruling the school with a rod, if not of iron at least of cane. He had a ferociously explosive temper, and had been tutor to the Duke of Albany or one of the younger princes. Mr Vickers had a very unusual system. Every morning at assembly, he rattled off twenty questions – Latin or Greek words, a paradigm or whatever – 'so fast that we did not have time to write the answers down on a chitty of paper. The head boy collected up the papers and threw them straight into the waste paper basket'. He then gave out full marks to the senior boys – even if they hadn't written anything at all – going down the class to the last boy in the class who was given the lowest marks, whereupon Mr Vickers exploded with rage and dragged the wretched child into his study where he was soundly beaten. There was no way out of the routine.

Colin claimed that he never minded the system or that Mr Vickers despaired of him. Even when he was soundly beaten, two minutes later he would meet the headmaster in the passage and greet him warmly with: 'Hello Mr Vickers'. As he maintained, he was always a very cheerful child, 'sociable and never shy'.

Colin's life at Scaitcliffe was very much the same as at any other preparatory school of the time. There were baths twice a week. The masters were mostly failures of one kind or another, save for Mr Owen, who was obviously clever and taught Latin and Greek. Colin shone at Latin and could recite long passages from the Epic Poets. He always maintained that he was more a Paget than a Tennant and by this time he was tall for his age and bean-pole thin. He was 'springy light [with] strong legs' and in his time he won the long jump and the 100 yards. The boys were allowed home most weekends and Birley the chauffeur would collect Colin and deliver him back on Sunday night whether Pamela was there or not.

Academically, Colin was very clever – 'as bright as a button' was how he described himself. For two years he was in the top form at Scaitcliffe, and was Captain of School the whole of his last year. But even as head boy he never exerted any influence on anyone or the school, nor did he try. By his own admission, exams were never a problem as he 'was always able to answer the questions immediately'. Being so clever and good at exams, it is surprising therefore that he did not try for a scholarship to Eton. Throughout his life Colin would quote widely and accurately, often pieces that he had learned as a child and not thought of since, just like his great-grandfather, Sir Charles Tennant who, at the age of 81, could recite all 224 lines of Burns' *Tam o' Shanter* perfectly.

For Colin and James the holidays were always full of interest and excitement, and were different. Pamela organised frequent trips abroad that often lasted for two months. There was skiing in the winter holidays, often to Château d'Oex in Switzerland, where she would sometimes spend the whole winter with James, whom she claimed to be delicate.

In 1936 Pamela took Colin and James to Garmisch-Partenkirchen, near Munich, for the Winter Olympic Games. There Colin saw Hitler, 'admittedly in the very distance', although a more lasting memory was of being parted from his mother and hugged by a huge white polar bear, the symbol of the Games: 'much more exciting than seeing Hitler', he later recalled.

Another year they went to Switzerland, which triggered Colin's deep and lifelong love affair with the media, particularly of photographers and of acting up in front of the camera. There he witnessed the filming of the World and Olympic figure-skating champion, the Norwegian Sonja Henie, playing herself in a feature film, *Thin Ice*. It was Tyrone Power's debut film: Colin's too. For a few seconds he is visible behind Sonja Henie, wearing a red woollen hat, skating on one leg with arms outstretched.

That summer of 1936 they had planned to join Lady Muriel in Leningrad, but at the last minute she decamped to Latvia so they all went to Finland instead. There they stayed with a friend of Colin's grandmother's, Madame Hella Wuolijoki, a great power in the country and one-time head of the Communist Party. As a propaganda stunt whilst in Helsinki, Colin and James were photographed sitting on a sofa with the Soviet Ambassador's children. The family then moved on to a log cabin on Hella's estate in the middle of a large forest to the north of the city. There, they were looked after by an old Russian peasant woman who, to their grave suspicion, fed them black bread, and yoghurt, which they had never seen. Hella, a very inventive and clever woman, was also enormously fat, weighing at least 20 stone. Colin and James were intrigued by this naked bulk witnessed in its entirety in the Finnish sauna and later in the icy waters of the lake. Whenever Colin discovered Finns, particularly in his bar on St Lucia, he would amaze them by singing a popular part-song in Finnish with them.

For the summer of 1937 they went to the Island of Oronsay, on the West Coast of Scotland. They travelled with old family friends, Sir Kenneth and Lady Barnes, and their son Michael. Ken Barnes had a very amusing mind. He was the founder and Principal of RADA and had two famous sisters, Dame Irene and Dame Violet Vanbrugh – the Vanbrugh Theatre is named after them. Oronsay was a magical holiday. Colin caught a giant lobster in a rock pool and forever after kept the claw in his various bathrooms for the rest of his life. Another year, Pamela took them all to Ireland for a typically different and exciting holiday. She rented a long two-storeyed, lime-white house on a little island in Tully Lough, Co. Galway. Besides the house 'there was a heronry [where] otters barked around it in the early mornings'.[ii] The lough was part of Renvyle House and Estate that belonged to the Irish poet, Oliver St John Gogarty. At that time Gogarty ran Renvyle as a hotel where his distinguished friends, the likes of Augustus John, W.B. Yeats and Lady Lavery, mingled with the guests who had paid.

Among the various holidays were the two to three weeks spent by Colin and James with their father and their new step-mother, Elizabeth at Glen. From the very beginning Elizabeth found Colin 'an attractive-looking boy, polite and with good manners' although she recognised a 'nervous and temperamental disposition', but she 'liked him more and more as he grew up'.[iii] She was, after all, only ten years older than Colin and they were to become great friends throughout their lives. Although Colin was devoted to his mother he was deeply fond of his step-mother, declaring, often, that she made his childhood bearable. Towards the end of his life, she would always telephone him on his birthday, 'one of the best birthday presents' he declared every year as he listened to her crystal-clear voice.

Whilst at Glen the boys, still in the nursery, would don their kilts and lace jabots at 4 o'clock each afternoon and wait in an anteroom beside the drawing room until it was time to go in for afternoon tea. Polite conversation followed and, when tea was over, they scuttled back to their enchanted life in the house and around the estate. As a second son who had never expected to inherit the estate, and whose adolescent years were spent at sea, Christopher was totally ambivalent about Glen – he even put it on the market in 1932. Fortunately it attracted no bidders. But for Colin the house and estate were very different. Every day was spent outside: his friends were the children of the estate staff and the villagers of Innerleithen. Sometimes, when there was a large house party at Glen in which they took no part, he would be billeted on the under-keeper and his wife, Jimmy and

Elizabeth Alvares, or on Mr Robson and his wife, Grace, in the garden house. Less successful interaction with the staff and locals came in the form of little plays that he and James were made to perform in front of them, since this audience thought it not right to laugh at the young masters.

Colin became fascinated by natural history, an interest initially fostered by his step-grandfather, Lord Grey. In the spring he could 'read' a field and work out where a plover would lay her eggs, then lift them for the family to eat. He would not take them if the pointed ends were facing inwards as he knew these were close to hatching. He was adept at collecting mushrooms and would identify them from a book: wild flowers too, which he would press or draw in a sketch book. 'Don't ask me anything about gardening, but [regarding] wild flowers, I am teeming with knowledge' he would boast.

Fishing, too, was an abiding love. Colin would lift the York stone slabs on the terrace to collect worms then fish the burns. Once he caught a hundred trout in a day. There were also rabbits and vermin to shoot. Although he started shooting as a boy he became an adequate, but never a good, shot. In the winter when the lochs froze there was ice hockey.

Sir Charles Tennant had collected a great library of around 10,000 books which Colin would pick through whilst at Glen. Much of his early knowledge, particularly of natural history, came from these works. At one stage, when he was interested in falconry, he found a sixteenth-century treatise on the care and flying of raptors in the library to study. At the outbreak of the Second World War, Pamela took Colin and James to live at Glen, where they remained for the whole of what became known as the 'phoney war', just long enough for Colin and his mother to catalogue the library. Consequently he was familiar with the names and works of scores of authors, but not with their works in any detail.

Soon after his thirteenth birthday Colin went to Eton for the Easter Half, having been put down for Mr A.K. Wickham's house at birth. Being clever he went straight into Upper Remove but, as he was not a King's Scholar, he had to remain in Lower School for the obligatory year. Lord Montagu of Beaulieu was part of the same intake and, although in a different house, remembers his first sight of Colin: 'He was the most glamorous person I had ever seen. He literally stood out in the crowd. He was extrovert and of course terribly clever.' Colin's first cousin, John Chancellor (his Aunt Sylvia's son) was an exact contemporary and confirmed that Colin was greatly admired for his good looks and debonair attitude, although he tended to ignore his cousin, treating him as a poor relation (as he did for the rest of their lives).

Even at this age Colin had a great artistic flair, filling his room with the works of Alexander Nasmyth and a then obscure Victorian painter, Atkinson Grimshaw. Being rather dreary (usually wet) night scenes, these were an odd choice for one so young.

On arrival at Eton Colin was given the nickname of 'Pamela Molly Blitch' when it was discovered that his mother's name was Pamela – just as Gregor McGregor of McGregor was known as Anna after his sister. Blitch was a brand name of a make of blotting paper. Colin recalled his Eton schooldays (1940–44) with little pleasure, 'for at that time the College, and particularly Wickham's, was not very glorious. No one in my house was in Pop, and anyway I did not aim in that direction. I have never been socially ambitious. It is just that I am very good at it. I have never been a climber, as I was born at the top. Nor do I aspire to go any higher or fall any lower – I am perfectly happy with my exact station in life'.

One contemporary in Colin's house was a boy from Norfolk called Michael Pratt. In early December 1941 two bombs fell on Eton. One landed on the house of the Precentor, Dr Henry Ley, who was fortunately unhurt when it exploded, while the other hit Upper School. This second bomb failed to detonate and the bomb disposal squad could not defuse it, so merely sandbagged it to limit the damage. Colin's room virtually overlooked Upper School and the unexploded bomb. For some unexplained reason, the unfortunate Pratt, whose room overlooked the safety of Keat's Lane, was made to change rooms with Colin. Notwithstanding the ticking bomb outside Pratt 'slept contentedly and unconcerned all night long',[iv] but was woken early next morning to see the destruction of half of Upper School when the bomb finally exploded. As Michael Pratt wrote later: 'Whether I was considered more expendable than Colin we shall never know.'

Even at Eton, Colin was very well off, being sent £8 every half by his father's secretary. His Maternal grandfather, Artie Paget, sent him cheques for his birthday, but with the warning that his 'tariff of 1s. a year of age does not extend beyond the age of 21 years'. The cheque for 16s. was accompanied by the comment that the 'failure of British policy after 1918 has been due to the utterly unconstructive education of Eton and the other great public schools'.

Colin was well cared for at school by his respective parents' servants. Eggs were sent a dozen at a time by the keeper's wife from Glen and there was a standing order for a brace of grouse a week during the season – later he wrote to the keeper that they be first sent to Admiral's House for his mother to cook 'owing to the difficulty and expense of getting grouse cooked at Eton'. Tilly would admonish him regularly for not sending back the boxes in which she had sent some fruit.

Academically Colin shone throughout his time at school. Although he could have kept just the best reports, his surviving essays bear such glowing comments as: 'There is a good deal of reflection here', 'Good, you have aimed high', 'This is the best thing that you have done this half'. He scored top marks in his German papers – French too, although in later life he was not noted as a linguist. He never forgot his Latin. Years later in the mid 1970s he used a line from Horace: '*Non cuivis homini contingit adire Corinthum*' ('It is not everyone's lot to go to Corinth') for an advertising campaign to attract clients to Mustique.

But it was on the river and the field where Colin really excelled. As a 'wet-bob' he was one of the 'choices' (he rowed at bow) in all his House boats and gained his lower and upper boats (colours in the form of a distinctive cap). He rowed at number 4 in *Victory*, immediately behind *Monarch*, the lead ten-oared boat in the Procession of Boats on the Fourth of June, and ahead of *The Prince of Wales*, that year captained by Hugo Money-Coutts, a lifelong friend and subsequent Mustique business partner. Colin played football for his house and ran extremely fast, being an 'athletic choice' – that is, running in the first team for the college.

After four years at Eton, Colin was near the top of his tree. He was in the Library (the equivalent of a prefect) but never aspired to Head of House. He had also made some good, lifelong friends, the likes of Hugo Money-Coutts, Tony Berry, who became an MP and was killed in the Brighton bombing, Michael King, the son of Cecil King, the owner of the *Daily Mirror*, Robin Kenyon Stanley, John Bevil Rudd (who was later to spend six months in prison for sleeping with a black snake dancer in apartheid South Africa), and Tim Mosley.

While the rest of the school sat for the Oxford and Cambridge Examination Board's School Certificate, Pamela insisted that both Colin and James took the Scottish examinations as they were considered more difficult. Again Colin's photographic memory came into play: 'I could see a Greek text and its English translation and the next day recall both perfectly', he reminisced. In the event, both he and James gained open exhibitions to Oxford University: Colin's was worth £30 a term. However, it was to be three years before he could take up his place because, leaving Eton at the end of the Michaelmas half of 1944, he was immediately drafted into the Army. Thus, with school behind him and the Second World War still being fought in Europe and the Pacific, Colin was launched into an uncertain world.

# Chapter 3

# 7 ORIEL STREET, OXFORD

'Where the fuck do you think you are – the bleedin' Ritz?' Sergeant Brown yelled at Guardsman Tennant, 360691, and his new friend, Peter Rees, as they made up their bunks, one on top of the other, with crisp, white, monogrammed linen sheets, pillowcases and under-blankets. The rest of the twenty-two recruits hugely enjoyed the cabaret as they threw their rough, grey Army blankets on the standard palliasses set on the wooden slats of their own bunks.

Colin had left Eton two weeks after his eighteenth birthday, spent Christmas with his mother and James in London, and had joined the Scots Guards that he claimed was his 'family regiment' shortly after New Year's Day, 1945. For his basic training he first went to Pirbright, then on to Lingfield, the training depot of the Irish Guards in Surrey, as Caterham, the Scots Guards' depot, was full at the time. There he joined many of his contemporaries (not necessarily friends) from school. As one who revelled in the past, particularly his own, Colin filled in the names of half of his Brigade Squad on the platoon photograph over sixty years after it was taken. He identified Peter Gardiner-Hill, the great cricketer, Michael Keeling, Robert Goff, the distinguished High Court Judge, and Michael West de Wend-Fenton, a passionate and impulsive figure later to be known as 'Beau West' after he joined the French Foreign Legion when Margaret Lygon refused to marry him. But Colin's real and lasting friend was Peter Rees. Peter had been to Stowe where he had been voted the most unpopular boy in the school for two terms running just because he was 'so extremely bright and inquisitive'. Colin and Peter took to each other instantly, recognising their common intellect, backgrounds and trials (real and supposed) at the hands of their respective parents – Peter's father was a martinet of a general. Both were physically slight.

Colin survived his six weeks basic training although, according to Peter Gardiner-Hill, compared to the other recruits he was considered somewhat 'effete and a bit soft'. He was patently not used to that kind of life and the course was extremely tough, made even tougher with the extreme cold and six inches of snow on the ground. Colin coped adequately and was generally well-liked, but gone was the swagger of his school days. In its place was an almost shy, and reserved, young man. Clearly he knew exactly how to play the system to succeed as an Army recruit where extrovert behaviour was rewarded by cleaning the latrines with your toothbrush.

From Lingfield the whole platoon moved up a notch and was transferred to Pirbright, the Guards' pre-OCTU (Officer Cadet Training Unit) in Surrey for a ten-week course. During his time there the Allies formally accepted the surrender of Nazi Germany on V-E Day (8 May1945) and the whole depot was given a 24-hour leave pass. Colin scooped up ten of his friends and headed for London by train. Lord Monteagle of Brandon recalls the whole party of cadets travelling in the luggage racks, there being no other space on the crowded train. Colin treated them to dinner at The Gargoyle, his Uncle David's nightclub, then took them to his mother's home at Phillimore Gardens where they dossed down on the floor before returning to Pirbright in time for the final parade of the day.

Again, Colin survived Pirbright and was selected to go on for officer training at Mons Officer Cadet School at Aldershot. There he and the rest of his intake were subjected to the legendary Sergeant-Major Brittain, Coldstream Guards. Known as 'The Voice', Brittain could strike fear into any Officer Cadet, whatever his background, and was credited with the line 'I calls you sir, you calls me sir. The only difference is that you mean it, I don't!' Colin went on the large exercise on Snowdon, where the Welsh farmers made huge claims for compensation for sheep killed, or supposedly killed, by the Officer Cadets using live ammunition. For some unexplained reason he completed his training three months after the rest of his platoon, who were all commissioned into the Scots Guards in September 1945. By the time Colin came to be commissioned at the end of the year, the Scots Guards were not taking any more officers, so instead he went into the Irish Guards. He returned to Lingfield where he was reunited with Sergeant Brown, who had transferred to the Brigade of Guards Armoured Training wing.

However, all was not lost for Colin with the Scots Guards. After a spell at Windsor and Pirbright in the Irish Guards training battalion, Colin was sent to join one of their companies attached to the 2nd Battalion Scots Guards in Northern Ireland, stationed at the Palace Barracks in Holywood on the outskirts of Belfast. Their principal duty was to mount the guard at Hillsborough Castle, the official residence of the Governor of Northern Ireland, who at that time was the Earl Granville. Granville was married to The Queen Mother's eldest sister, Lady Rose Bowes-Lyon, a godmother to her niece, Princess Margaret. The Governor was the King's representative and as such treated as Royalty. When Captain of the Guard, Colin often dined with the Granvilles, thus giving him his first brush with 'Royal' life. Gerald Monteagle, who joined the company a little after Colin, recalls it as 'not a very arduous posting, and often quite fun'.

For the five months of his service in Northern Ireland Colin found himself in a distinguished position and, as an eligible bachelor, he was much in demand from both inside, and outside, the castle. He shot with the owners of the neighbouring estate; there were dances and hunt balls. Paul Spurrier recalls Colin telling his brother officers to wear a little dab of carmine in the corner of their eyes to enhance their colour, and to always wear white gloves with their Blues when dancing. The makeup was something Colin had learned from his homosexual uncle, although Stephen Tennant employed it 'to seduce the rank and file'.

Dublin, with its lack of rationing, was not far away and easily accessible for Colin and his brother officers on weekend leave. One acquaintance at that time was Lady Sarah Stuart, the totally beautiful 18-year-old daughter of the Earl of Moray, who was staying for the summer on Lambay Island in Dublin Bay. When Sarah and Colin lunched in a Dublin restaurant it was, as she recalled, 'wonderful to have a full menu, not the grim 1s. affair with a single choice for each course we had back at home'.[v] She remembered Colin as 'exotic, beautifully dressed, with wonderful manners'.

When his time in Northern Ireland was nearly up, Colin wrote to his friend Piers Nibenham, ADC to General Kirby, asking to be transferred to his staff in the Finance Division of the British Headquarters in Berlin. He was turned down on the grounds that he was too young. Soon afterwards Tim Mosley wrote to him from the Coldstream Guards' barracks at Sidi Bishr, outside Alexandria, Egypt, giving news of their Eton friends who were serving overseas – Michael Barnes was in Greece, John Rudd and

Michael Pratt were in Palestine with Tony Berry and Rupert Strutt, while Peter Rees was in Trieste and Hugo Money-Coutts in Germany at the time when Colin was stuck in Northern Ireland on ceremonial duties.

A posting finally came for Colin, but not to join one of his friends abroad as he hoped, but to Caterham as a platoon commander training up recruits. He ended up in Chelsea Barracks in London, which was more to his liking, although the soldiering was dull, with continual ceremonial guard duties at Buckingham and St James's Palaces, the Bank of England, and the Tower of London.

After three years, in January 1948, Colin was released from his service to King and Country. Along with countless others of his ilk he was de-mobbed with the gift of a suit and the grateful thanks of the nation. It was typical of Colin to keep his Army Book 439 with the Inset IV: *Record of Issue of Services Handkerchief Certificate*s the only memento of his military career.

After Eton and his military service, and all that it entailed, it is hard to see Colin being socially gauche, or, as he put it himself, 'still very simple and not yet broken into London life'. He was, after all, only just 21 years of age and living in London with his mother and James in his Aunt Dolly Gladstone's house in Phillimore Gardens. An early solecism was to mistake the M of 'Alice Mary' as a D, so he replied 'Dear Mrs Dary' to an invitation from Princess Alice [Mary] of Athlone to dine at Kensington Palace before her granddaughter, Anne Abel Smith's, coming-out dance. Soon after this, one of the King's Private Secretaries was commanded to invite him to stay at Sandringham. Colin was flabbergasted and made up some feeble excuse as to why he could not go. According to him the real reason he declined was that he did not own a pair of pyjamas and had no money. He always regretted not going as he would have encountered Queen Mary.

Colin left the Army just in time to take up his Open Exhibition at New College, Oxford for the Hilary Term. Out of the blue an Eton contemporary, Lord Montagu of Beaulieu, wrote to him inviting him to share his rooms in College. As he had made no other arrangements, Colin accepted gratefully and moved in at the end of January. Colin recalled his social life that first term: 'Edward [Montagu] knew everybody and I knew no one. He was on every conceivable list, including the Royal Family's, and I was on nobody's'. He had tons of stiff invitations all the way down the mantelpiece while I had one flimsy one for some debating society in Oxford.'

For some unexplained reason Colin decided to read PPE – Politics, Philosophy and Economics – none of which interested him. He thought politics were 'uninspiring', philosophy beyond him, and economics was 'completely out of date and hopelessly impractical'. After struggling for two terms he wrote to his father telling him that he wanted to give up PPE and switch to history. Christopher replied, characteristically giving sage advice:

> I think that you are probably right to give up PPE. Philosophy is not a subject of practical use and except in a case of a very few, it is something to which one is more likely to come in later life.
>
> Economics is important if one is to understand politics and what is going on in the world. It is bound also to be of value in business life.... It is, however, much better to concentrate on one subject, like history, and do it well than to attempt too much and do it badly. And if you can find time to do some serious reading on economics over the next few years so much the better.[vi]

The letter was typical of Christopher's sound wisdom. Although Colin did not take his advice over the economics, he was doubtless grateful to have his blessing to switch courses and read modern European history. With so many returning servicemen at that time, Oxford offered a series of truncated two-year courses which Colin took, having already spent a couple of terms reading PPE. He chose a very narrow period, 1898 to 1904, of Diplomatic History, solely as he felt that he knew nothing of the causes of the First World War. 'It was not very helpful', he later claimed. Typically he cited that his interest in Russia was heightened because of his grandmother, Lady Muriel Paget (see Appendix I), just as his fascination in the Tudor period was fostered by his forebear, Sir Christopher Hatton, Lord Chancellor and favourite of Queen Elizabeth. Colin always professed never to have gone to a single lecture, nor done any work, which is certainly not true. He had to pass his exams at the end of each year, and obviously would have been missed by his tutor, David Ogg, during weekly tutorials if that were the case. After three years he obtained a 2:2 in history, mainly by reading the peripheral books to his course as opposed to the set books. He saw himself as 'not particularly well read but well informed'.

For his first vacation, Easter 1948, he was joined by Michael Barnes and Peter Rees for a short course at Tours University. Every day they hired bicycles and visited the great châteaux of the Loire. Colin, aware of his good looks wrote: 'At Valençay with a peacock' beneath the photograph of himself posing below a column in the grounds of the château. He and Peter Rees teamed up again that autumn for six weeks, driving 5,500 miles around Europe. They went in Colin's car, *La Gloire Noire*, a Triumph Gloria built specially for the 1934 Monte Carlo Rally, travelling mostly at night as they were too tired to rise early in the mornings. Their route took them through France to Cannes and Monte Carlo, then on to Portofino, across Italy to Trieste, still in the Anglo-American Zone, where they stayed at Miramart, the residence of the Military Governor, Lt.-General Sir Terence Airey. Peter had been his ADC when in the Welsh Guards. On the return journey Peter, an expert on the *Almanach de Gotha*, plotted the route to take in the grandest families in Austria and Germany. They arrived, often unasked, to stay at a succession of unreceptive castles. At one particularly fine *schloss*, Wasserleonburg, near Noetsch in south-east Austria (where the Duke and Duchess of Windsor had spent part of their honeymoon), Colin claimed that he was visited by a succubus as he slept in a distant turret. He and Peter arrived home two days after the Oxford term had started.

But Oxford gave Colin far more than a secondary education. He avoided all organised sport, but his great athletic prowess was invaluable to the Oxford University Drag Hounds for laying the trail. His friend, Vivian Naylor-Leyland, was whipper-in. He also avoided the multitude of societies, except for the Oxford Union Debating Society: 'Give me a donkey and I will talk its hind leg off!' he would say.

To his delight Colin was joined by a nucleus of close school and Army friends, Peter Rees, Euan Graham, Milo Cripps, Christian Carnegy, John Baring and Hugo Money-Coutts. Though all comparatively well-off and aristocratic, none was a member of the legendary Bullingdon Club, described as: 'the acme of exclusiveness at Oxford; it is the club of the sons of nobility, the sons of great wealth; its membership represents the *young bloods* of the university'.[vii] Even in post-war austerity, the Bullingdon dinners were famous for their drunkenness and extravagance. Edward Montagu was elected to the 'Buller' in his first term and said that Colin was jealous of his membership. Colin, however, always maintained that he never aspired to the club, as 'being far too individual to be part of a pack'. Certainly the club uniform, the dark blue tailcoats with ivory facings and mustard-coloured waistcoats, would have appealed to the peacock in Colin.

During his last year at Oxford, Edward Montagu was to regret his election to the Bullingdon. In a scene reminiscent of Evelyn Waugh's *Decline and Fall*, his fellow members 'piqued that he preferred a pansy party to their meeting, decided to break up his rooms, which was rather discouraging for Edward. They broke most of his things and returned to break the last of his glass collection'.[viii] Colin was 'rather sorry for him' and glad he was not there.

Although Colin and Edward shared rooms, they led different lives in different sets. Their respective friends occasionally came together when they hosted joint breakfast parties. Large and expansive cooked breakfasts were served in their rooms, Colin having had the milk sent down appropriately by the 'milk' train from Glen especially for the occasion. The frequent breakfast parties were men-only affairs, but such was their success they later hosted afternoon strawberry parties with champagne, to which girls were invited as well. Margaret West de Wend-Fenton remembered Colin at that time as being 'a wondrous figure, still and silent, but greatly admired'. She found him rather a solitary soul, despite being surrounded by his many good, and true, friends. She felt that being so much in command of himself, he appeared somewhat aloof to the casual observer. She also noticed that he was very observant, examining everything at a party she gave in her parents' flat. Her contemporary and friend, Sarah Macmillan (who was the daughter of Harold and Lady Dorothy Macmillan, although it is now acknowledged that she was the result of Lady Dorothy's thirty-year affair with Robert Boothby) always thought of Colin and James when singing the line *'Two, two, the lily-white boys, Clothèd all in Green, Ho, Ho'* from 'Green Grow the Rushes O'.

After a term Colin moved out of Edward Montagu's set of rooms in New College into a house, 7 Oriel Street, Oxford, close to Oriel College, Christchurch and Corpus Christi. Typically he furnished his room with pictures he had bought, or purloined from Glen: a classical scene by William Etty that hung over the fireplace, a collection of plaques of Roman Emperors after Rubens on the chimneypiece, and a drawing of a reclining *putto* from the seventeenth-century Bolognese School.

For the rich and well connected in the late 1940s, Oxford, London and the country were very jolly places to be. There were parties galore. Billy Wallace, an Oxford contemporary of Colin's, and later confidant of Princess Margaret, gave a grand dinner in the summer at Brympton Grange, a fine

Georgian house near Montacute in Somerset, to which Colin was invited. Apart from his own racy set from Oxford, there were many other acquaintances, such as Ludovic Kennedy, Ian Gilmour, Mickey Brand, the Marquis of Blandford (known as Sunny, who became the Duke of Marlborough), Henry Porchester, who later inherited the title Earl of Carnarvon, and John Synge. All were to become friends, or at least remain on good terms with, Colin. Women also began to play a serious part in his life.

At that time Colin had many women friends who were not necessarily girlfriends, but all part of his set. He caught the eye of Lady Caroline Thynne, daughter of the Marquess of Bath, and Elizabeth Lambert greatly enjoyed his company. Colin often stayed at Chatsworth at the invitation of Lady Elizabeth Cavendish, daughter of the 10th Duke of Devonshire. Another particular ducal friend was Lady Caroline (Montagu Douglas) Scott, daughter of Walter, the 8th Duke of Buccleuch and Mary Lascelles, known as 'Midnight Molly'. Caroline and Colin remained close for many years until she married his friend and contemporary, Ian Gilmour, in 1951. Doubtless armed with innumerable pairs of pyjamas, full evening dress and a dinner jacket, Colin was a frequent guest at all four of the Buccleuch houses – Boughton, Drumlanrig, Bowhill and Dalkeith. Inspired by a visit to neighbouring Bowhill, a Glen house party played a game after dinner where each had to make up a rhyming couplet about a Paris dress designer. The winner was Colin's mother, Pamela, who came up with:

*Molineux a thing or two*
*When she married Walter Buccleuch.*

Caroline Scott was in the party of six that Colin organised to visit Spain in the summer of 1949 – the others being Christian Carnegy, Mark 'The Chimney' Chinnery, Zoë d'Erlanger and Xan Fielding. They flew to Madrid (where they were joined by the Duc de Lerona) and hired a car. So soon after the war, Spain was at that time still very primitive. It was a wonderful holiday where they combined the magnificence of the southern Spanish cities of Toledo, Jerez, and Seville with a visit to the Tennant mines at Tharsis near the Portuguese border. In Madrid they went to a nightclub at midnight and emerged at noon the next day.

Not long into his second year at Oxford, Colin gravitated to London for all his entertainment and was on all manner of lists, including the foreign embassy circuit. He was first taken up by the Spanish Ambassador, the epicene Duque de San Lucarla la Mayor, Vizconde de Marblas. After lunching together they would repair to a small room where the Duque would lie on a chaise longue gazing at Colin. Nothing untoward ever took place, nor did Colin see anything wrong in introducing him to Pamela who 'rather enjoyed this amusing man of the old school'. Throughout his life there were those who suspected that Colin was bisexual. He was certainly not part of Edward Montagu's self-professed, but covert, homosexual coterie but, as Lord Montagu put it, he 'would not have been surprised to learn that Colin was bisexual at Oxford, but no more so than was normal for the product of a major British public school, the Army and Oxbridge in the late 1940s and early 50s'.

At one of the many ambassadorial lunches and dinners Colin met the 2nd Earl Haig and the widowed Duchess of Kent. The Duchess was a very great beauty and figure in London society who had fallen in love with 'Dawyck' Haig, and he with her. He was not the easiest person, socially or emotionally, but their relationship found approval in Royal circles. There was a possibility that he might have made her happy. Colin was surprised to receive a telegram from Dawyck, whom he had met only briefly at a lunch, asking him to dine. Colin accepted immediately, thinking that it would be great fun. He arrived at Dawyck's small flat in Eaton Place early and waited in silence until the Duchess of Kent was shown in with her Lady-in-Waiting, Mrs Campbell Preston. They were standing around, not saying much, until they repaired to the ABC Cinema in Oxford Street that was showing *Le Diable au Corps*, a film about an older woman falling in love with a much younger man. Dawyck, at 29, was ten years younger than the Duchess.

After the agonising performance of the film, they all went on to The 400 Club in Leicester Square, where they again sat without conversation. Colin tried his best but, being very young and new to London life, he struggled to find a mutually interesting subject. To brighten up the evening Colin said one could always tell if a sapphire was genuine if it kept its colour when immersed in water. To demonstrate the theory, he asked the Duchess for her enormous sapphire ring and dunked it in his water glass, whereupon the stone went completely transparent. He never saw Dawyck and the Duchess together again.

The trips to London in the week and the house parties at the weekends soon took their toll on Colin. He was in danger of being rusticated. A certain standard was required of an Exhibitioner, so he resigned his scholarship, worth £30 a term, which just covered his battels. Leading a giddy life, coupled with his gambling debts (mostly the horses – Ladbrook & Co. had threatened him with the bailiffs over an unpaid account of £81 1s. 3d), took a serious toll on his finances. To tide him over until his next allowance was paid into his bank account, he opened another, with a generous overdraft facility, at the Midland Bank in Oxford. Years later, when a Director of C. Tennant, Sons & Co, he had a secretary named Madame Personier: 'A bold piggy-faced woman with black hair in perhaps her early forties. She was of unknown origin, but probably married to a Frenchman.' Colin noted that she would come in admirably early, but it turned out that she was, in fact, going through his mail and extracting the letters that came from the Oxford Branch of the Midland Bank, advising him that his overdraft limit had been far exceeded, was rising daily, and asking what he proposed to do about it. One day Madame Personier was late and Colin opened the latest pleading missive. The bank manager was summoned to the office and it was discovered that Madame Personier had found the temporary arrangement in Oxford and milked it for all it was worth by forging Colin's signature on his cheques. She was duly arrested, charged, convicted of fraud and sent to prison. At her trial it transpired that she was an habitual offender and been to prison many times before. She had used the money to fund a boy band and attended 'raves' up and down the country. Colin never heard of her again.

During the Michaelmas term of his last year at Oxford, Colin suffered a nervous breakdown. He was staying with the Dowager Duchess of Devonshire at Hardwicke Hall, in Derbyshire, who was delighted with his plight as it 'gave her something useful to do'. Colin found Hardwicke a fascinating place in which to be ill, everything in the house being exactly where it had been placed when furnished in 1599. According to the Dowager, even the blankets on his bed had been bought in Spain, probably before 1589. Confiding in his cousin Pauline Jones, the daughter of David and Hermione (Baddeley) Tennant, Colin admitted that 'there is something rather shameful and ridiculous about nervous breakdowns', but in other correspondence the illness was referred to as 'influenza' caused by sleeping under sixteenth-century blankets, no doubt described as Spanish 'flu. He consulted a psychiatrist and spent a month with his father at Glen over Christmas to recuperate.

Returning to Oxford for the Hilary term, Colin found that many of his friends had either gone down without taking their degrees, like Edward

Montagu, or had been rusticated, like Vivian Naylor-Leyland. He lamented their loss and decided 'not to try to find new friends' but to work for his degree instead. Apart from his breakdown Colin was also suffering from a slow heart, as had his Uncle David, which sapped his energy and made him lethargic. As a result of the two medical conditions (and possibly attending the party of the wife of the French Ambassador, Madame Odette Massigli, in London mid-exams), he came down with his moderate degree which, in the early 1950s, appears to have been acceptable – two decades later, 'time spent on a second-class degree is time wasted'.[ix] His tutor, R.S. Creed, wrote to him: 'I am delighted to see how completely you have falsified the gloomy forebodings by some of the prophets ... I always thought that you might spring a surprise on them', while A.K. Smith, the Warden of New College, wished him well, congratulating him on 'so creditable class as a Second'. He added that although Colin was handicapped 'by ill heath, in other circumstances [he] might have gained a First'.[x]

To celebrate the end of his exams and his formal education, Colin left for Venice to meet up with a striking Italian beauty, Charis Vivante, then followed her to Forte du Maroni, a converted tower on a rocky promontory near Viareggio. He travelled in a rickety old bus that took all day and most of the night. When he arrived he thought that he was going to die from exhaustion and was taken to hospital to recover. He stayed with Charis for a few days and returned with her to Venice and her cerebral friends. She was part of a group who took their name from an uprising of intellectuals in the 1820s, the *Intelligencia de Resolve de Mental*. Beautiful and intelligent, Charis was to be typical of a succession of Colin's girlfriends.

And so armed with a not very impressive degree, a healthy overdraft and a grand and overflowing address book, Colin embarked on the next stage of his life. He began by buying a terrace house in Belgravia, 6 William Mews, behind Lowndes Square, which he invited his Eton and Oxford friend, Euan Graham, to share. They lived in great comfort and style, with an Italian live-in maid to look after them, although Euan was not there often as he was pursuing Pauline Pitt-Rivers (née Tennant) whom he later married.

Christopher Glenconner had secured for Colin what would now be called 'work experience' (he was unpaid) for a year at Hambros Bank of which he, Christopher, was a Director. As a learner going through the departments Colin thought it 'very good training as they are merchant bankers while we are merchants'. How much he learned in his year is unclear but his knowledge of the banking world can only have been limited by the fact that he was out every night, more often than not for lunch as well.

The experience Colin gained at Hambros Bank was taken a year later to the family firm, the metal brokers and chemical traders C. Tennant, Sons & Co., where his father was the well-respected Chairman. The company, though highly profitable, was a mere shadow of the vast empire that successive generations of Tennants had built up over the previous 150 years. (see Appendix II)

*Chapter 4*

# 6 WILLIAM MEWS

It is said that you make your friends in the first year at university and spend the second year losing them, but for Colin the change came after he left Oxford as he moved into a wider, different society. He always liked to say that he drew his friends mostly from within his family: 'My primary interest in my life is my relations. Practically every one whom I invited to my sixtieth birthday party was a relative, because I have always sought my friendships or social contacts from amongst my relations. I rarely make close friends with people outside my family; fortunately there are plenty of them representing every aspect of life'. Typical of this large family network was Francis Wyndham, who became a confrère from the early 1950s when Colin was living 'reluctantly' in Phillimore Gardens with his mother and James. Francis, the distinguished author and former *Sunday Times* journalist, was the son of Guy Wyndham (Pamela Glenconner's brother) and his second wife, Violet, thus Colin's first cousin once removed. From the very beginning Francis was captivated by Colin, recalling him as 'dazzling and very good-looking' – at that time he had the nickname 'Joy' as in the line from Keats' poem: '*A thing of beauty is a joy forever.*' Unlike his 'poor' relationship with John Chancellor, Colin always said that he and Francis greatly enjoyed each other's company and that of their many mutual, intelligent friends, who later included the likes of Lucian Freud. He described Francis as 'a literary lion' with the unique capacity of 'giving his considered opinion in two or three words … listening to him speak in the simplest possible terms at the time one hardly realises his genius'.

Although he would never admit it, Colin's greatest gifts – the art of conversation and flair for giving wonderful parties – were inherited directly from his mother, Pamela. Consciously, or subconsciously, Colin copied the way she spoke. Often his sentences were punctuated with a little laugh that accentuated their whimsical nature. By that time Pamela had moved to Hill Lodge, a grand, commodious house in Kensington with a huge garden where there were so many family and friends living as paying guests that Colin renamed it 'Hill Lodgings'. Aunt Sylvia Chancellor, and occasionally John, lived in the basement: Lord Northland's daughter and her friends lived in a wing. Colin suspected that his mother only lived in London as it was where she thought he and James would be happiest. But she lived, and entertained, as if she were in the country, taking a great interest in the local church and school, doing the garden herself – and most of the decorating in the house. She loved what would have been the London equivalent of the village people, and through this attachment Colin would claim that his true friends, too, came from the village. But that was towards the end of his life and a far cry from his hedonistic days of the early 1950s.

Colin was taken up by another cousin, Anne Charteris, one of the great *salonières* of the twentieth century, who was married to the author Ian Fleming. Colin was a frequent guest at her literary luncheon parties in Victoria Square, behind Buckingham Palace, in London, and also at their cottage at St Margaret's Bay, on the south coast between Dover and Deal where Noël Coward was their nearest neighbour. As Colin recalled: 'She simply took me as a young relation [a third cousin], whom she could beckon and bid as she chose. I was eminently biddable'. It was through her that he learned the art of conversation and, as he admitted later, he never looked back: 'It was in those days I took up talking and ever since have never stopped. I would wonder why people would listen to me endlessly. Sometimes I imagined it was because I was amusing. But I can now see it was because I was rich and I was oblivious of that at the time'. At the end of his life talking remained his 'principal fascination', even though it was often limited to his 'personal trainer'.

Colin compared Anne Fleming's salon to the great centres of conversation of the eighteenth century, such as that those of Lady Holland and the Duchess of Devonshire. On one visit to the house in Kent, Ian Fleming had just finished the typescript of his first James Bond novel, *Casino Royale*, which Colin remembered vividly:

He [Fleming] did not care for our social chat and sat in his study after dinner with the door open, but within earshot of the sitting room where we all sat around the fire. There were a number of us, and Anne asked Cyril Connolly in her usual scathing voice to read out from the typescript. All these intellectuals fell about laughing over these idiotic descriptions – there was something about a 'black triangle' referring to a girl's crotch in the first chapter. We all shrieked with laughter thinking how funny it all was. Of course we learned better later.

After he married, Colin maintained that he regretted that he was summarily dropped by the literary circles of his bachelor days. He blamed his new wife Anne for restricting the conversation to those on either side of her as opposed to letting the conversation flow around the whole table. Francis Wyndham, however, disputes Colin's claim that he missed these gatherings. Although he, Colin, could generally hold his own in any conversation, he could certainly not be classed as the leader of, or to shine in, such august company – the only position he would countenance. He was content to leave that to others more qualified. He remained on an intellectual fringe, however, through his step-mother, Elizabeth Glenconner. An intellectual herself, she was close friends with such luminaries as Derek Hart and Cyril Connolly. Once Connolly was staying with her and Christopher at Glen, when he was given breakfast in bed and used a rasher of bacon as a bookmark!

From William Mews Colin conducted a series of affairs. He was to profess: 'I was never promiscuous, nor indeed was promiscuity the moving spirit of my relationships. Sex is not my driving motive. I am not predatory. I was fortunate to have had relationships with very fascinating and beautiful girls'. His first serious affair was with Pandora Jones, the daughter of the Hon. Sir Bede Clifford, the youngest of the three 'Clifford beauties', the other two being Atalanta, and Anne, who married Viscount Norwich. Pandora was the prettiest girl he had ever seen. She had been married to Timothy Jones, who had one leg, the son of Sir Roderick and the remarkable Lady Jones (the authoress Enid Bangold who, amongst other works, wrote *National Velvet* and she had worked for the roué Frank Harris, her first lover). Sir Roderick, on the other hand, was eminently respectable. During a long and distinguished career he had been head of Reuters and before that, head of the telephone system in South Africa when Colin's mother had been staying there as a child. Hearing the news of his knighthood, Pamela composed the couplet:

*For fixing up our telephones,*
*He was created Sir Roderick Jones.*

As part of his training in C. Tennant, Sons & Co., Colin was sent briefly to the New York office and allowed to return on the *Queen Mary*, travelling in first class. There were many passengers he knew, including David and Diana Naylor-Leyland, who were on their honeymoon. It was there that he first met Pandora, who was travelling with her parents. On the last night they dined together, but she left to pack, leaving Colin with another young passenger in the main saloon. They were approached by a man who asked if he could join them, then by another stranger. They chatted for a while and then one of them suggested that they play cards. Colin readily agreed and, after a small amount of money passed hands, he received a message from the steward outside who advised him 'not to sit with those two gentlemen, and on no account play cards with them'. When Colin returned, his travelling companion had been cleaned out of all his money. The professional cardsharps ambled off but, when the luggage was outside their cabin prior to docking, Colin rifled through their cases and retrieved the man's money.

For Colin, his affair with Pandora was all too short-lived and she moved on to several other affairs, including Lord Andrew Cavendish (the Duke of Devonshire) and the artist Lucian Freud, before Michael Astor, whom she married. Samantha Cameron is her granddaughter.

Another serious beauty with whom Colin had a prolonged liaison was the model Anne Gunning Parker, known professionally as 'Anne Gunning' after the legendary and beautiful Gunning sisters from Ireland of the eighteenth century. (The Gunning Sisters were born to impecunious Irish parents who launched them on Irish society at a ball in Dublin in 1748. Elizabeth married the Duke of Hamilton; Maria the Earl of Coventry.) 'Rather a Gainsborough girl, charming and very modest', Anne Gunning was the top model of her day (the early 1950s) and a favourite of fashion photographers such as Norman Parkinson. Colin even accompanied her around London as the male model for a feature for the French *Au Jardin des Modes*, later to feature in *Paris Match*. The affair did not last and subsequently she married Sir Anthony Nutting as his second wife.

Another top model and cover girl who was briefly part of Colin's life was the utterly beautiful Ivy Nicholson, known as the 'beanpole from Arkansas'. Much later she transferred her affections to Andy Warhol, believing that 'she could change him'. She fell from grace and ended up penniless in San Francisco.

Although she could not be described exactly as a beauty, a nonetheless exceptional woman in Colin's early life was Lady Jeanne Campbell, daughter of the notorious 11th Duke of Argyll, and the adored granddaughter of Lord Beaverbrook. Tall, vivacious, somewhat buxom and the possessor of sparkling eyes, Colin's affair with 'Jeannie' was lively: 'You never knew where she was going to be next. The only way to find out if she was even in the country was to go to her flat in Eaton Square and ask the maid if her passport was in the cupboard'. It was a bizarre flat, where he once met Brigitte Bardot. Colin claims that Jeannie married Norman Mailer at his instigation. As he said: 'She did not know what do about Norman. I am always rather willing to give advice, and put it to her that her grandfather, Lord Beaverbrook, would not like it if she did not marry him. After all, she could always marry and divorce him later', which is exactly what she did. In fact Jeannie was pregnant by Mailer and her grandfather advised her to have Mailer's baby but *not* marry him. After they parted, Mailer depicted her as the bitch in his fourth novel *American Dream*, and later was to describe her as 'a dear pudding of a lady' and 'a remarkable girl, almost as interesting, complex and Machiavellian' as himself. But Mailer was just being typically vindictive, for Jeannie was bright and clever, and possessed an original mind and a ready wit. She began as an actress, appearing at the Old Vic, then worked for her grandfather on the *Evening Standard*. Lord Beaverbrook later appointed her as the paper's New York correspondent, in which role she famously covered the funeral of John F. Kennedy. Afterwards she worked for *Time-Life*. As one of her numerous lovers, Colin was in august company: over the decades the formidable list included Oswald Moseley, Randolph Churchill and Presidents Kennedy, Khrushchev and Castro which, according to James C. Humes, a speechwriter for many American presidents, were amazingly all in the same year. She and Colin remained the greatest of friends up to the time she died in 2007.

In the early 1950s Colin spent the summers in the south of France where, during this time, he was often accompanied by the Lady Elizabeth Cavendish, daughter of the 10th Duke of Devonshire. They stayed in his father's house in the hills behind Nice, or at the Carlton in Cannes. Colin loved gambling and was once in the casino where King Farouk, one of the richest men in the world, was losing heavily on the tables. He heard the king say to an aide behind his chair: 'If I were a rich man, I would never lose.' On one of his forays to Nice he met a bold American divorcee, Norma Clark, a woman 'of Norwegian extraction with ash-blond hair and the most wonderful skin, almost like velvet'. She had married the leading athlete on her campus, followed by a conman called Monroe. They would go to parties and she would cosy up to rich men. 'In those days very rich people married any number of times as you could not have a relationship without being married.' Norma had managed to attract the attention of Alfred Clark, who was very rich indeed, and married him as his fifth wife. The marriage lasted just four months and Colin met her as she raced through her $400,000 divorce settlement, a fortune in 1952. She divided her time between Colin and the Duke of Marlborough at Blenheim Palace.

Colin's affair was intense and alternated between Biarritz, Paris and London: she once wrote to him from Claridges telling him to 'get lots of rest' as she would be waiting for him there. To Colin 'part of her charm' was that in some ways she was rather prim, and once admonished an advance in the afternoon with 'I never make love until 6 o'clock!' They parted amicably, she going after some richer prey.

Another year Colin and Lady Elizabeth Cavendish stayed at Eden Roc in Cannes with Pamela Harriman, the great '*horizontale*' whom he had met with Violet Wyndham, and Pamela's young son, Winston Churchill. Later he stayed with her in her apartment in the Tokyo Avenue in Paris at the time she was beginning her affair with Elie de Rothschild. Colin was given a maid's room off the kitchen but had the use of the flat until 6 o'clock in the evening, when it was out of bounds. If he wanted to go out he had to use the back stairs.

Colin was having a high old time, not that he was ever 'high' because he never used drugs, although he remained a heavy smoker for many years. He eschewed alcohol as he 'never had time to drink' as he was enjoying himself to the full. At dances he would not sit out 'gloomily' as he danced with 'great glee most of the time until it was time to go home'. There were dances galore during the Season, usually at the Hyde Park Hotel or 23 Knightsbridge, the site in front of the present Berkley Hotel. Colin was ever-popular, with a reputation of being 'a sparkling figure' who would make a point of dancing with plain girls, as 'his streak of compassion made him unable to bear the plight of wallflowers. They could always count on one prestigious whirl'.[xi]

Such gadding inevitably took its toll. He once woke up in a panic and ran barefoot in his pyjamas from Williams Mews to the out-patients at St George's Hospital (the present Lanesborough Hotel) nearly half a mile away and complained: 'My heart has stopped.'

Every day he managed to go to Upper Wimpole Street to see Dr Goldman for his vitamin B injection, where he often ran into David Somerset (the present Duke of Beaufort) 'the handsomest man in England'. Dr Angus Blair, who was married to Colin's cousin Elizabeth Paget, confirmed that these injections were 'fashionable with the gentry' but had absolutely no beneficial effect, except possibly psychologically. Colin recalled the visits with:

*Oh! Wondrous Wizard, who wields a syringe,*
*With a flick of the wrist that's surprisin',*
*On your skilled diagnosis, who dares to impinge,*
*Who scoff at your aureomycin\*?*
*So if ever you're seedy, or feel rather low*
*Just telephone up WELBECK 2230!*

\*Amongst other things aureomycin is used to treat conjunctivitis in cats.

But this constant gadding, charming exterior, and quick, witty repartee belied a far deeper and infinitely more sinister side to Colin's character, and that was his very unattractive and uncontrollable temper. Whilst not seen by those who knew him well (the likes of Francis Wyndham never witnessed an outburst in all the years he knew him), the explosions when they came were quick and terrifying. They were generally triggered by something trivial or irrelevant and were heralded by a small vein twitching in his right cheek. The incandescent anger that followed often lasted for only a few seconds, then vanished as quickly as it came. Colin always maintained that people did not mind, which was certainly not true. He forgot very quickly but the recipients did not. As Simon Blow pointed out: 'There was, indeed, an element of rage in all Pamela's [Colin's Wyndham grandmother] children. Clare's tempers were legendary and some said that a reason she never grew old came from her instant ability to express rage'.[xii]

Often the fits were accompanied by violence, and there are many accounts throughout his life of the subject of his ire being struck, kicked or worse, bitten. At Oliver Messel's funeral in Bridgetown in Barbados, for instance, Colin's party was late as they went to the wrong church and he was therefore greatly flustered. As they arrived at the right church Messel's coffin was being taken out of the back of the hearse and the police waved the taxi on. The driver naturally obeyed and drove on only for Colin to scream for him to stop, and to reinforce his command he sank his teeth into the wretched man's arm. The party leapt out of the car and ran for the church to beat the coffin. The taxi driver was waiting for Colin after the service and money was pressed into his bloodied palm. Often objects would be thrown during the rages. Nevill Turner, who worked for Colin in the Bahamas, recalls his first visit to Mustique:

> It was a management meeting my second day on the island that included Colin, Nicholas Courtney [the island manager], and myself. The subject of electricity and generators came up. Colin said he would not discuss it, and it must not be mentioned again. Of course it was the most vital item on the agenda. Each time it was mentioned, Colin screamed and hurled a coffee cup [that] smashed against the wall above my head. Eventually he ran out of ammunition. I thought it was rather odd.[xiii]

Throughout his life certain words, like 'electricity', would trigger an explosion. At Glen, he would go into an abject rage at the mention of 'wine' as in 'Can you get some wine out for dinner?' Consequently the white wine was never chilled, nor the red opened early enough to breathe.

Another spectacular tantrum, with more money changing hands, came at a hotel near Souffrière in St Lucia. Colin flew into a rage when he was kept waiting for a drink and threw all the tables and chairs over the balcony into the sea. In the early days the rages were generally reserved for those he considered his social inferiors, particularly colleagues and employees. It was well-known at C. Tennant, Sons & Co. that his secretary was paid a handsome bonus for working for him, although at that period of Colin's life she was further compensated by not being overtaxed with work from her oft-absent chief. The rages probably reached their zenith when he gave up smoking. In a particularly anxious moment he kicked in a plate glass window in his office and cut an artery in his leg. He was lucky to survive. Later, those at the receiving end of his towering rages widened to his wife and family, which naturally made for an uneasy relationship. Colin's wife Anne once asked him why he shouted at, and abused, people, to which he replied that he greatly enjoyed seeing them squirm.

Colin was all too aware of his uncontrollable temper. In the 1950s he was being driven by Clarissa Eden to a ball at Cliveden. Going through Wimbledon he became rather agitated and asked her to stop the car, whereupon he leapt out and walked up the street out of sight. He returned a few minutes later, perfectly calm. Clearly he did not want Lady Eden to witness an explosion.

Amongst all his friends of his bachelor years, the two most influential were unquestionably the great artist Lucian Freud and Judy Montagu. Colin met Lucian through the purchase of the portrait he painted of his wife, Lady Caroline Blackwood, which he had seen illustrated in an old copy of *Vogue* whilst in Trinidad. To Colin: 'It was a ravishing picture, by far the loveliest picture Lucian ever painted. She was lying in bed. One wrist is resting on her left ear; her hair falls down straight. And her huge Jersey cow eyes give her a startled expression'. He knew Caroline well and instantly wanted to buy the oil painting. On his return to London he tracked Lucian down and found that Cyril Connolly had bought the painting for £200 but had not been able to come up with the money. This was no problem for Colin who was given a generous allowance by his father on top of his salary from C. Tennant, Sons & Co. The purchase was to change his life.

After the acquisition Colin would go down to Dorset to stay with Lucian and Caroline in a little woodland house near Shaftesbury. The famous picture *Two Figures* by Francis Bacon (nicknamed *The Buggers*) hung at the top of the stairs and formed part of the joint exhibition (with Ben Nicholson) of the three painters in the main room in the British Pavilion at the Venice Biennale in 1954.

It was during one of these visits that Colin decided to ask Lucian to paint his portrait and, once commissioned, he devoted several years of his life to fostering his friendship with him. Lucian lived his life very much in separate compartments, and Colin fitted into one of them. They would lunch together, usually at Wheelers, two, three, sometimes four times a week, then return in the afternoon to Lucian's house in Delamere Terrace overlooking the canal in Little Venice. Each sitting took hours as Lucian painted Colin, looking 'slightly away from him'. He started with the corner of his subject's right eye, whereupon 'it spread out across the canvas like a disease'. He painted 'laboriously and meticulously'. The result was very dear to Colin and was one of the last of his treasured possessions to be sold.

It was bought by Michael Lynton, Chairman of Sony Pictures Entertainment, who resides in Los Angeles.

But over the six months that Colin sat for the portrait the sittings and the subsequent meetings developed into an obsession as he became totally absorbed by Lucian. They were in fact totally unalike, with very little in common. Lucian had been brought up in Berlin where the images from his childhood were completely different from Colin's background. Lucian's friends were mostly drawn from the intelligentsia 'and entertaining people of Jewish extraction', far removed from Colin's more conventional companions. Years later, during the long and lonely nights in St Lucia, Colin worked out why Lucian and his friends, mostly of European origin, were 'totally enraptured by the aristocracy of England'. They never ceased to be amazed that the country should be run by a group of 'banal chinless wonders, with no real education'. They believed that the aristocracy were members of some kind of secret society, the Establishment, made up of men like the Archbishop of Canterbury and the Prime Minister, such as Harold Macmillan, who were always drawn from the upper classes. To them, the aristocracy still retained some kind of mysticism, and they thought that to succeed, the Jewish intelligentsia had to become part of that society. Lucian joined that society when he married Lady Caroline Blackwood, daughter of the Marquess and Marchioness of Dufferin and Ava. Colin was embraced by Lucian as he, too, was a significant part of that world.

After the portrait was finished they still met on a regular basis where Colin was patronised by Lucian, just as he became Lucian's patron by buying and commissioning paintings. He introduced Lucian to other like-minded collectors, and it was through his introduction to Lady Elizabeth Cavendish that her brother, the Duke of Devonshire, began his collection of Freud's work.

Their relationship began to wane when Lucian changed his painting style after he fell in with the likes of Lady (Bindi) Lambton, and he moved to rather more 'dashing kind of pictures'. Colin gradually became aware that he 'was not intellectually educated, and never had been'. As a result he began to change his 'friendships to a rather more entertaining and challenging group of people', amongst them 'unquestionably the most exceptional person' he had ever met: Judy Montagu. Their relationship was to change his life yet again in a new and exciting direction.

Colin's affair with Judy began in 1952 and it was to her that he owed the greatest possible enjoyment of his bachelor days. To him she had that 'crazy talent for friendship that has never been equalled', sentiments echoed by Patrick Leigh Fermor:

> Judy Gendel [her married name] was full of contradictions. She wasn't remotely like anybody else. Intelligence and flair and an innate competence at almost everything – except, sometimes her own interests – were gifts which, even when she was very young, impressed Prime Ministers, presidential candidates and heads of colleges.... Feelings of early isolation, perhaps, set the companionship of friends higher than anything. She loved them and lived for their company.... They sprang up spontaneously from affinity or contrast, from the delights of reciprocal stimulus in conversation, from loving warmth and romantic impulse; and all of them wrapped in a snowballing mythology of private humour and back reference, were fostered by a genius for the comic and the odd.[xiv]

The lives of Colin and Judy were also inextricably linked though their families, friendships and the Liberal party. She was the only child of Edwin Montagu and Venetia Stanley. The son of the international financier and Jewish activist, Samuel Montagu, first Baron Swaythling, Edwin, who was left £1 million by his father in his will, was 'intellectually brilliant, morally scrupulous, fashionable, rich in money, but poor in physical looks'.[xv] Venetia Stanley was the daughter of the 4th Baron Sheffield, who came from a family of intellectual, faintly eccentric, aristocratic Liberals. Venetia was 28 and the best friend of Violet Asquith when she formed a totally platonic friendship with Violet's father, Herbert Asquith, the Prime Minister, then a man of 62. Asquith was by then married to Colin's great aunt, Margot Tennant.

Colin first met Judy in their late teens when on a skiing holiday to Zurs, in Austria, organised by Elizabeth Glenconner shortly before the war. Judy was there with her mother, Venetia, and her cousin, the accomplished Clarissa Churchill, with whom Colin was to remain a life-long friend. After Judy's affair with Mark Bonham-Carter ended, she and Colin became what he described as 'an item': she called him Clovis after Clovis Sangrail, the eponymous hero of the Saki short stories, so named as he was 'so appallingly frank'. For the next two years they had the greatest possible fun together and, through Judy, Colin met a different set of more interesting people, doing more amusing things, than he had known in the past. Colin remembered her as: 'the most wonderful, inspirational *chatterer*. Not a chatterbox, but the most marvellous chatterer that anyone could possibly hope to meet. She had made more friends instantaneously than anyone I knew, spent money more carelessly. She gave everything she had, until nothing was left'. She would have been even richer had she not had an aversion to opening brown envelopes, many of which contained dividend cheques or money drafts that she threw into the wastepaper basket unopened.

Colin and Judy were the most marvellous double act: they were 'literally dazzling' and 'terribly amusing' together. Francis Wyndham, who was very much part of her set, tells how they sparked each other off with wit and clever repartee. With their quick, original and clever minds, Colin and Judy greatly enjoyed each other's company, and had a great following. They developed a rather simple humour of their own. A typical aphorism of what was thought screamingly amusing ran: 'Friday night is mother's night. Anyone wishing to become a mother, turn up. And don't be late. Last week we had to start without you'! They loved tongue twisters which Colin would oft repeat:

> If Moses supposes his toeses are roses, then Moses supposes erroneously;
> For nobody's toeses are poses of roses, as Moses supposes his toeses to be.
> Well, I don't know about poor old Moses, but my toeses are roses – I've just had a pedicure!

Their wit was spontaneous. Colin and Judy always went for the whole summer to the South of France (and later on to Venice for the season) where they were joined by a succession of friends, and friends of friends. One such was Claus von Bülow, born in Denmark of Danish-German noble origins. He has been teased that, as he rarely appeared before dusk, he must be a vampire. When it was suggested that he join Colin's group of friends for dinner, Claus declined, saying that he had a date. 'So who's the lucky corpse?' inquired Judy. In the early 1980s he was famously acquitted of trying to murder his heiress wife.

Throughout his life, Colin's wit and quick repartee never left him. Years later, for instance, he was walking in Mustique when he spied a chaise longue lying in the ditch with a broken arm and a leg missing. 'Ah!'

says Colin, 'a chaise no longer!' Always nervous, he was forever fiddling with his metal watch strap. One day his watch was in his hand when Diana Heimann, a friend and house owner, asked him why he was holding his watch: 'Because the boy who normally holds it has the day off', replied Colin. When Patrick Lichfield took a group photograph of the residents and employees of Mustique, Colin, recalling his remark, had Chico, a young black boy from the village, seated on the chaise longue holding the most enormous pocket watch.

One perennial joke oft-told by Colin, often with such peals of laughter that he could hardly get it out, was 'Fetch me a crocodile sandwich, and make it snappy!' He was later to recall with much pleasure some guests to Mustique from the North Country. They hated everything about the island and complained vociferously, even damning the harmless geckos as 'bloody miniature crocodiles scampering all over the walls!'

Most of Colin's witty remarks were made entirely off the cuff; others were *esprit d'escalier* and passed on with glee. When Tony Blair's spin doctor, for example, complained that he himself was subject to spin, Colin came up with the line 'more spinned than spinned against!'

Colin always professed that he, Judy Montagu, Mark Bonham-Carter and a few other friends were the last reincarnation of the 'Souls' and, knowing their children, he also felt close to them. The original Souls were 'a group of men and women bent on pleasure, but pleasure of a superior kind, eschewing the vulgarities of racing and card-playing indulged by the majority of the rich and noble, and looking for their excitement in romance and sentiment.'[xvi] Their nomenclature came from Lord Charles Beresford who, at a dinner held by Lady Brownlow in 1887, scoffed that all the gang (as they preferred to be called) did was to 'sit and talk about each others' souls'. They were at their zenith in the 1890s and lasted a little over a decade longer. 'The impetus of the Souls' romantic and intellectual activities' had come from the Tennant sisters, Laura and Margot, who crystallised this 'group of leisured but sensitive country-house people'. The sisters were inseparable and had grown up wild and uninhibited under the free, but watchful, eye of their father, Sir Charles. Margot had been a 'venturesome child', roaming the moors, climbing to the rooftops of Glen by moonlight, although he drew the line at allowing her to ride her horse into the house. The originality and verve of the two girls set London society alight. They frequently used Glen as the rendezvous for members of the Souls, where the guests were all their great friends and relations.

In a sense, Colin was not far off in equating himself with his (and Judy's) forebears insofar as the gatherings and house parties of the Souls, with their hives of 'animated talk, word games and romantic fancy', were what they and their friends were all about. However, the Souls had also had a political agenda (not least the Irish Home Rule debate), which was certainly lacking in Colin's set at that time. That said, he did make the briefest foray onto the public stage when he agreed to join a Brains Trust to kick off Barbara Cartland's campaign as a Conservative candidate for the Hertfordshire County Council elections. Colin and Barbara Cartland were joined by her daughter, Raine Legge (the present Dowager Countess Spencer), Sir Jocelyn Lucas MP (who bred the Lucas terrier) and Mark Chapman-Walker from the Conservative Central Office. The *Daily Express* reported that Colin 'was speaking publicly for the first time and lived up to the Tennant family reputation for strange Scots wit. Like his [great] aunt Lady Oxford [Margot Tennant] he had the audience in screams of laughter over nearly nothing, while golden-haired Mrs Legge, lovely in an electric-blue dress and a bouquet of pale pink roses, insisted that Britain was not a dirty nation'.[xvii]

One of Judy's particular friends was Princess Margaret who, like scores of others, had been captivated by her from the beginning. Far cleverer than the companions chosen for her by her parents, Princess Margaret was drawn instantly to Judy and her amusing, fun-loving and intelligent friends. Through Judy she had a new take on life and it was then that she realised that, against this sparkling group, she was woefully ill-educated – while Princess Elizabeth was tutored in such subjects as constitutional history, her sister was given no more than a good educational grounding by a not overly proficient governess. But what Judy did for Colin, to his lasting pleasure, was to rack his friendship with Princess Margaret up onto a different, and far closer, level. Colin had, of course, known the Princess for many years. He had first met her at a drinks party for Elizabeth Lambert, daughter of the Regimental Colonel of the Irish Guards, Field Marshal the Earl of Cavan, popularly known as 'Fatty Cavan'. As Colin recalled:

The Cavans were establishment people. I was in the Irish Guards, and this was probably Princess Margaret's first London party. She arrived in a ginger fur tippet [a stole], terribly old-fashioned and obviously lent by her mother at the last minute. It must have been dragged out of some cupboard as it was reeking of mothballs. I used to see her after that in '48 and '49 when we met quite often at house parties like Drumlanrig, [Lady Caroline Montagu Douglas Scott was her great friend] where there were invariably many other, and much more attractive, young men than I.

It was said that Colin introduced himself to Princess Margaret at that drinks party as '2nd Lieutenant Tennant of the Irish Guards'. After that initial introduction, they would meet fairly frequently at dances and balls; they often coincided at house parties, as with the Duke and Duchess of Buccleuch. At one tremendously grand house party at Boughton, their Northamptonshire seat, Colin met Margaret Vyner (née Heathcote), who was to remain a close friend for the rest of Colin's life. Besides Princess Margaret the guests included the most glamorous couple, the newly-married Ludo Kennedy and the ballerina Moira Shearer, Rosie Churchill, and Lady Anne Lumley, daughter of the Earl of Scarborough. Margaret, who was reading English at Cambridge University at the time, had been taken to the party by her friend, Rory McEwen, the folk singer and botanical artist. Being young, she was nervous in such company and remembers Colin being 'incredibly nice' to her. They were the only two in the house party not to go to church. Other times that Colin's and Princess Margaret's paths crossed were at St Paul's Waldenbury, the home of her aunt, Lady Rachel Bowes-Lyon, and again when Lady Hambledon asked Colin to stay at the same time as Princess Margaret as she thought that 'it would be a great help to have him there to entertain her.'[xviii] But it was only when Princess Margaret encountered Colin with Judy that she saw him in a totally new, and exciting, light. From that moment on, they were to become close, and were to remain lifelong friends. The timing was right too.

Princess Margaret's life had formerly revolved around her father, King George VI. She was the only one who could control his 'gnashes', his fits of uncontrollable rage: he was her *raison d'être*, just as she made him extremely happy. But when her father died in February 1952, her world turned upside down. She was downcast and bereft.

Turfed out of Buckingham Palace, Princess Margaret went to live with her mother, The Queen Mother, at Clarence House. It was there that she famously turned to the Comptroller of her mother's Household, Group Captain Peter Townsend, the older father-figure and divorcee. The story of their romance is too well known to bear repetition but, by the time Princess Margaret decided not to marry him, the nucleus of her men friends (what was euphemistically called 'The Princess Margaret Set') had fragmented or married. There had been the tall, red-haired Johnny Dalkeith, later 9th Duke of Buccleuch, whom the King would have liked her to marry but he, like most of her other suitors, was too conventional for her, although they remained lifelong friends. In a similar vein were David Ogilvy, later Earl of Airlie, and David Burghersh, who was to become the 15th Earl of Westmorland. Colin always maintained that 'of all her early consorts, the one she would have liked to have married was Sunny Blandford [the present Duke of Marlborough] but he was snapped up by Sue Hornby. She [Hornby] had wanted Ian Gilmour, but he married Caroline Scott so she turned her attentions and got engaged to Sunny'. Colin also believed that the marriage between Sunny and Princess Margaret 'would have been very successful'. At that time all Princess Margaret wanted 'was a loyal circle of friends and to be soothed by the crowd. After her experience with Townsend, she wanted to forget about marriage and have a jolly time'.

It was an amateur production of Edgar Wallace's play *The Frog* that cemented Colin's friendship with Princess Margaret. Judy was the prime mover in its production and she chose the play as it had an enormous cast of between thirty and forty people. Colin had long since cut his teeth in amateur theatricals. At Christmas in 1948 he had played the Dauphin in a masque put on by the Duchess of Buccleuch for charity at the Assembly Rooms in Edinburgh. There he danced a stately pavane, taught by an old lady from Peebles, with Caroline Scott who played Mary Queen of Scots. He then appeared in a play called *Lord and Lady Algy* put on, again for charity, by Judy Montagu, with Henry Porchester in the lead. It was a flummery plot where a husband and wife could not live together as they could not smoke the same brand of cigarette, or back the same horses, but the play did have the advantage that the cast could dress up in eighteenth-century costume for a fancy dress ball in the last act. All the cast of *Algy* (and many more) went on to *The Frog*.

Quite soon after they met, Judy invited Princess Margaret to direct the play, but with so many rehearsals it was not possible, so she became the assistant stage director instead. The leading actors met for extra private rehearsals in Tony Berry's flat, which meant that Colin began to meet Princess Margaret on a more regular basis, as opposed to the odd house party or the occasional dinner.

When Princess Margaret met Judy, her close friends changed overnight. Judy had a far wider social outlook than Princess Margaret's former set, some of whom seemed more admirers than true friends. For the Princess, Judy and her associates were the opposite – a circle of friends, but not necessarily consorts. It was more relaxing for her to be with Judy's followers who were all ages – people like the enormously rich Welsh landowner, Sir Michael Duff, Maureen Dufferin (the Marchioness of Dufferin and Ava), the American songwriter Elsa Maxwell and Henry Porchester. They were mostly older than Princess Margaret, but 'she threw herself into their lives with glee'.

Judy cast Colin in the title role of *The Frog,* a serial killer whose identity was a secret until he was finally unmasked. He appeared and disappeared at critical moments having committed a heinous crime, wearing, for some mysterious reason, a Second World War gas mask. At one point, he abducted the lead, Raine Legge into a cupboard while she was singing, and was finally exposed for an instant by Henry Porchester, who played a Cockney detective sergeant, the male lead. (When not the frog, Colin was a rather timid little clerk, shuffling in and out.)

There were two performances of the play at the Scala Theatre in Charlotte Street, and it was considered, by the cast and the audience (which included The Queen, The Duke of Edinburgh and The Queen Mother), to be a great success, although the play itself was not up to much. The players, the likes of Viscount and Viscountess Norwich, Douglas Fairbanks Jnr., the Duke of Devonshire and Lord Plunket, were recognisable to the audience, either personally or through the gossip columns, and invariably drew shrieks of laughter whenever they appeared on stage. Colin loved it: 'So many people came on and off it was like a constant *Hellzapoppin* parade.' Francis Wyndham, who played Boris, said that the only one who showed any talent at all was Elsa Maxwell who was, after all, a professional songwriter.

After the first night the cast repaired to Milroy Club in Hamilton Place to await the reviews which, when they came, were dire. The critics loathed it. Noël Coward, although a great favourite of the Royal Family, was scathing about the production. He wrote in his diary:

The whole evening was one of the most fascinating exhibitions of incompetence, conceit and bloody impertinence I have ever seen in my life. With the exception of young Porchester, who at least tried to sustain a character, the entire cast displayed no talent whatsoever....

It was a hilarious evening on the whole, if only it hadn't been so irritating. It was certainly a strong moral lesson for all of us never to be nervous again on opening nights. Those high-born characters we watched mumbling and stumbling about the stage are the ones who come to our productions and criticise us! They at least displayed no signs of nervousness; they were unequivocally delighted with themselves from the first scene to the last, which, I may add, was a very long time indeed.[xix]

Coward claims to have found Princess Margaret backstage 'complaining that the audience laughed in the wrong places' whilst eating *foie gras* sandwiches and sipping champagne, a reference that upset her: in her annotated copy of his diaries she has written 'I don't like *foie gras*.' Notwithstanding the rotten reviews, the play made £10,000 for the Invalid Children's Aid Association, a massive sum at a time when the agricultural wage was £6 12s. a week.

After the frequent rehearsals for *The Frog*, Colin, Princess Margaret, Judy and Billy Wallace would go on for dinner, then repair to a nightclub – habitually The 400 or Les Ambassadeurs – usually until 4 o'clock in the morning. The 400, 'the night-time headquarters of society' was one of Princess Margaret's favourite haunts. She and her party were always seated at the same table known as The Royal Box beside the small band that played softly to avoid drowning out conversation. Cabaret entertainers, like Danny Kaye, who admired Princess Margaret very much, often joined the table after their performances.

There was a minute dance floor and food, but no menu. If guests wanted to eat, they simply ordered whatever they wished and it was served promptly. This was no mean feat in post-war London. If you were still there at dawn, breakfast was offered. There was a minimum charge of one guinea, and drinks were sold only by the bottle. In 1957 the *400* Club dropped its dinner-jacket-only rule, but manager Gaudent Rossi always wore his, as did Princess Margaret's escorts.[xx]

The summer of 1954 was very enjoyable for Colin when he slowly drifted into being Princess Margaret's preferred escort. It was not deliberate on his part, or hers; they 'just found it was more fun being together ... [they] sat up later, talked more, and laughed more'. It also coincided with her relationship with Billy Wallace going off the boil, not that it was ever that strong. Tall, gangling and utterly charming, 'with his chin receding into his neck', Billy was known by his friends as 'Old Faithful', being her ardent suitor and constant companion. He regularly proposed to her and was always rejected. But he was unwise enough not only to have an affair with the daughter of a Canadian philanthropist, but also to tell Princess Margaret about it on his return. She did not appreciate it, so she drifted away from him as number one suitor towards Colin, possibly because he 'was less involved with her past' and 'had never been part of that set'. The *Daily Express* summed up his position when they wrote that Colin: 'used to be rather apart from the others – with them but not of them'. Never backward in coming forward, Colin summed up his appeal: 'Quite frankly, I was newer and funnier than they had ever been. And possibly better looking too. Nor was I a serious admirer, someone angling for her attention, or wanting to become her boyfriend. We were just having a very good time.'

To Princess Margaret and Colin it seemed only natural in August to ask each other to stay in their houses in Scotland. Colin simply invited her up to Glen, as he would invite any of his friends to stay in the country, but the Press saw their friendship in a different light and took the visit as tantamount to an engagement. Readers were regaled with the news that the visit added 'fresh colour to the swelling whisper that she will soon announce her engagement to the 28-year-old Colin Tennant'. A proposal had certainly not been remotely behind the invitation, and even less evident in Princess Margaret's acceptance. As Colin put it: 'We were simply close friends insofar as you can be friendly with someone of that distinction.' Yet the headlines persisted, causing Colin to travel on *The London Express* (train) under the assumed name of Archie Gordon. A highly stylised, fictional account of the visit appears in Colin's sister Emma's novel, *Waiting for Princess Margaret*.

After a few days at Glen they moved on to Balmoral, the Queen's castle in the Highlands. For the first two days Princess Margaret and Colin were the only guests, and were then joined by The Queen. As the sisters went riding each morning, and did not return until just before lunch, Colin felt that it was pointless getting up to eat breakfast with the Equerries at a quarter to nine, leaving nothing to do between then and a quarter to one, when they gathered for lunch. As he had been sitting up talking with Princess Margaret in her own bedroom, the White Heather Room, until 3 o'clock each morning, he could see no point in coming down to breakfast early. The next evening he took a card and wrote 'Please do not wake me until 10 o'clock' and stuffed it in the nameplate on his door. Notwithstanding the instructions, the page came and banged on Colin's door at 8 o'clock as before. The following evening he crossed out the words 'until 10 o'clock'. It was not appreciated by the Household and was counted as a definite black mark against him.

Slowly the castle filled up with family and friends and, to the press, Colin's long stay at Balmoral was absolute proof of his engagement. Every morning the newspapers were laid out on the sideboard carrying the headline: 'Will there be a proposal today?' The Royal correspondent of the *Daily Express* reported that, on the day of Princess Margaret's twenty-fourth birthday, her rooms were filled with 'red roses, white gladioli and pink carnations' (her least favourite flowers) from British and American well-wishers. To Colin's great relief, nothing was said, nor were there jibes from other members of the Royal Family, guests or members of the Household to make him embarrassed: in Royal circles if a thing is unpalatable then it has never happened, and therefore cannot be discussed. The only reference that was made to the speculation was that one night after dinner family and guests made up topical verses to be sung to the music of *My Darling Clementine*. The Queen Mother's and Dennis Dawnay's version has survived with such verses as:

*Oh my darling, oh my darling Margaret*
*She's the pride of old Balmoral, for the nicest girl I've met.*
*In the summer, in the summer, o'er to Germany flew she*
*To see the Army, and the Airforce and the good old Rhine Navy.*
*On her birthday, on her birthday the whole Press behaved like hell,*
*When she went out on a picnic, they all thought they'd come as well.*
*Oh my darling, oh my darling, our darling Margaret*
*She's the pinny girl of Fleet Street, she's Beaver's\* little pet.*

[*Lord Beaverbrook, proprietor of the *Daily Express* and *Sunday Express*]
When it came to the turn of Princess Margaret and Colin, they sang their own version with the refrain:

*Oh Balmoral, Oh Balmoral, British women's eyes are glued,*
*Every time you have a friend there, an engagement is construed!*

The Press speculation, however, totally changed the relationship of Princess Margaret and Colin. As he was to admit, seeing the constant reports written in the papers that were 'staring him in the face, it did raise the possibility that maybe I should [propose]'. The 'engagement' was also the hot topic of his friends. Anne Fleming wrote to Patrick Leigh Fermor: 'Judy thinks that nothing will come of the situation but I believe that Colin is serious and would enjoy being a Prince Consort.'[xxi] Afterwards, Colin went on to stay as planned with Judy Montagu in Venice where her Venetian friends begged the question '*Est ce qu'on lui fait déjà la révérence?*' The Press saw his visit as a man fleeing from the rejection of Princess Margaret. Colin summed up their relationship: 'I do not think that Princess Margaret ever expected me to propose to her – that was not the purpose of our friendship and quite possibly, that is why our friendship has endured. Neither of us was rejected.' But that is only a small part of the explanation of their close and lasting friendship. Although they indulged in what Colin described as 'heavy petting', they never had a serious affair. As he said: 'If I had actually been more of a lover and less of a companion, we would not have remained such friends'. In that way he was delighted that she never found him physically attractive as he was not at all her type, unlike 'Peter Townsend, and then Tony [Armstrong-Jones] and then Roddy [Llewellyn]. They were smaller, foxy, talkative men ... I was her support, really'.

Throughout their lives, Colin was totally committed to Princess Margaret. He was often accused of 'toadying' up to her and, as later with Mustique, of using her and her Royal position, but their friendship was genuinely founded on mutual respect. While she admired his better qualities, which included a rich and generous nature (particularly where she was concerned), he admired her greatly.

Princess Margaret was ravishing, terribly funny, and such good company. She had two completely different sides – one was Royal, the other was bright, clever, quick and endlessly attractive. Surrounded by young men, she was surrounded by fun. We used to talk and talk and laugh. She had an original mind and in all the years I knew her, she never said the same thing twice. She used to flirt and flirt at parties, but never with me. Although she did not have a very good singing voice, like a professional singer, it was a good 'music hall voice'. But she did have the most charming speaking voice, very brightly (*sic*); in fact I have never met anyone who spoke more clearly. She didn't wave her hands about and was never histrionic.

Princess Margaret was my familiar in some ways, although I was never familiar with her. I was always there for her and she relied on me in private, though not in public.

There is another rational, yet lesser-known, reason why Colin and Princess Margaret should have become, and remained, such good friends. Returning to Colin's habit of poring over the visitors' book from Wilsford (his paternal grandmother Pamela's house near Salisbury) he noticed that one of the 'suitable' girls brought in for her sons was Lady Elizabeth Bowes-Lyon, who signed herself modestly 'Elizabeth Lyon' in the book.

Born in 1900, the Lady Elizabeth was a year younger than Christopher Glenconner. Because of the First World War she did not 'come out' until 1919, when she promptly fell in love with the Hon. James Stuart, the dashing son of the 17th Earl of Moray and descendant of the Bonny Earl O'Moray and Robert the Bruce. In March 1922, however, whilst in New York, Stuart received a letter from Lady Elizabeth which upset him greatly. She told him that 'the most extraordinary things have happened to me in the last 3 weeks'.[xxii] Later that same day Stuart received a letter from another source which told him that his beloved Lady Elizabeth 'and Glenconner are seldom apart',[xxiii] from which he assumed, as it turned out rightly, that Christopher had supplanted him in her affections and was the new man in her life. The other 'most extraordinary' thing was, most likely, that, for the second time, she had turned down the marriage proposal of the Duke of York. Nothing therefore was to come of the relationship between Stuart and Lady Elizabeth, and later he was to transfer his affections to Lady Rachel Cavendish, daughter of the 9th Duke of Devonshire, whom he subsequently married in 1923. It was a shrewd move on the part of the politically ambitious Stuart as ducal sons-in-law, like Harold Macmillan, generally made it to Cabinet rank and beyond.

When apart, Elizabeth and Christopher wrote to each other constantly, she from Glamis, he from Wilsford or Glen. In a letter to her former governess, Beryl Poignand, she confided: 'I have been having a wonderful soulful correspondence with Lord Glenconner! He does write most excellent letters, & <u>most</u> highbrow – so funny.'[xxiv] They were to meet in Paris in late May when his business trip coincided with her visit to comfort her friend, Diamond Hardinge, who had been seriously ill. Christopher and Lady Elizabeth had lunch together, and then went to Versailles where it rained heavily throughout the afternoon. Nine years later Christopher wrote to her recalling every detail of the day and how deeply in love he was with her. The visitors' book shows her staying at Wilsford for three days (a 'Saturday to Monday') in June 1922 on her own with Christopher, although undoubtedly Pamela Grey was also in the house. He then went to shoot partridge at Glamis (a poor day because of the wet) in early September in a party that included the Duke of York, before leaving for Venice at the start of its season. It was then that things began to go wrong.

The large party in Venice organised by Christopher included a Bright Young Thing with the androgynous name of Peta, and an American, Henry Channon, known to all as Chips, who was at Christchurch, Oxford at the time, and already on the way to being something of a celebrity. He later became a Member of Parliament, but is best remembered for his revealing diaries of the time that were published posthumously. Chips adored 'London society, privilege, rank, and wealth, [where] he became an energetic, implacable, but endearing social climber'.[xxv] For some unexplained reason Chips wanted to make trouble and reported to Lady Elizabeth that Christopher had had an affair with someone called Peta whom she naturally assumed was a man. When Christopher returned to England his letters were unanswered and telephone calls were neither put through nor returned. The real story must have come out as Lady Elizabeth clearly forgave him, as he was one of the first to call at her London house to congratulate her on her engagement to the Duke of York.

Although Colin knew of the brief relationship between his father and Lady Elizabeth Bowes-Lyon, he never mentioned it to Princess Margaret. She, on the other hand, knew all about it and several times during the 1970s suggested that her mother and Christopher should meet again. Nothing ever came of it and Colin doubted that his father, never one to dwell on the past, had ever thought about it again. Christopher died in 1983 at the age of 83 when Colin was in the United States and was buried before he was able to return. However, that November Colin was asked to shoot at Royal Lodge, the home of Queen Elizabeth The Queen Mother in Windsor Great Park as Princess Margaret's guest. That Friday night Colin was seated on the right of The Queen Mother and, towards the end of dinner, she leaned towards him and said: 'I am so sorry to hear about the death of your father, but that Christopher, he used to bully me so', to which Colin, greatly surprised, managed to stammer: 'Oh Ma'am, I'm sure not.' The Queen Mother was not to be put off: 'You see, I was the youngest in a large family and I was very shy. He used to say "Let's go to the party. You must come to the party. We must go out."' She told Colin that he frequently went to southern Spain, where he was a Director of a sulphur mine, and had once brought her back a pair of long, white kid gloves: 'I have them now in my drawer upstairs', she confided quietly. Clearly she had never forgotten Christopher.

*Chapter 5*

# HOLKHAM HALL

Early in 1955, Colin was invited to a dance given by Lord and Lady Northbourne for their daughter, Susan, at the Ritz. Lady Northbourne (who was of partial American-Indian descent) could have invited Colin through their connection with Colin's cousins, the Rices, who lived at Deene, close to Northbourne Park in Kent. It is more likely, however, that the invitation came through Susan herself, who was one of the debutante lodgers in the basement of Hill Lodge, 'where they stitched up their dresses'. Although he had known her for some time (and indeed had been to her ball at Holkham Hall in Norfolk), it was at this dance that Colin 'clicked' with Lady Anne Coke, the beautiful 23-year-old daughter of the Earl and Countess of Leicester.

For the Countess of Leicester, the prospect of Colin as the *inamorato* of her eldest daughter, the Lady Anne Coke, cannot have filled her with much joy, for before she had ever met him, she certainly had heard of him. And what she had heard was not good. His reputation had long preceded him through the Royal Household grapevine when she, as a Lady of the Bedchamber to The Queen, had been fully apprised of his antics on his visit to Balmoral the previous summer by Sir Arthur Penn, Deputy Comptroller of the Household. Reports of his behaviour during the weekend of her daughter Anne's dance at Holkham had also failed to impress. Later, she and her middle daughter, Carey, had met him on a boat in Nassau, where they failed to take to him.

Colin had been asked to stay for that weekend by Lady (Billa) Harrod, who had the prettiest small country house in Norfolk just outside Holt. It was a large house party that included, amongst many others, Lady Caroline

Blackwood and the novelist, Venetia Murray. Colin recalled the weekend: 'We arrived frightfully late and no doubt behaved very badly.' The house party went back to Holkham Beach on the Sunday after the dance, where Colin continued in the same vein by taking off his clothes and walking semi-naked across the wide sands into the sea. When he was finally reunited with his clothes, the others had left for the lunch party. Colin arrived, late and dishevelled, and was barred by the servants from entering the house. His summary of his initial standing with Lady Leicester was somewhat understated: 'I could see that she was not likely to take very kindly towards me when I was drawn to Anne.'

Lady Leicester's first impressions notwithstanding, Colin and Anne's romance began well, for just as he was 'drawn' to her so, according to him, he was right for her. The timing was exactly right too.

At the age of 18, Anne had met Viscount Althorp, or Johnnie as he was known throughout his life, when he was asked to shoot at Holkham. He was a captain in the Royal Scots Greys and an Equerry to The Queen. The eldest son of Earl Spencer, he was heir to the Althorp estate in Northamptonshire and a large chunk of Norfolk that marched with the Holkham and Sandringham estates. Anne thought him 'very good looking, amusing in a quiet way, and charming'. As the Leicesters did not have a London house, Anne stayed with another Norfolk neighbour, Lady Fermoy, in Wilton Crescent for the Season. Johnnie would call for her there to take her out to dinner. On one occasion, Lady Fermoy's precocious 15-year-old daughter, Frances, came in. According to Anne:

> She seemed to be very taken with Johnnie. Frances was very grown up for her age. She knitted him a pair of shooting stockings. He was very touched. I wasn't. One night after a dance he invited me into the gardens outside and he asked me to marry him. I said yes and we told our parents. Mine were very pleased. But some months later, the romance just fizzled out. We hadn't announced the engagement. He didn't apologise. I was so in love with him and it broke my heart.

The postscript is well known. Frances, encouraged by the scheming Lady Fermoy, engineered for Johnnie to transfer his affections from Anne to herself. They married two years later in the summer of 1954. After the wedding Frances went back to her old school, West Heath, to give a lecture

1. The happy couple. Colin's parents, Lord Glenconner and the former Pamela Paget leaving Wells Cathedral, 1925. The guard of honour was provided by the Mendip Stave Dancers.

2. 'Collina', Joshua Reynolds' portrait of Lady Gertrude Fitzgerald, after which Colin was named. It hung in the drawing room of Glen, the Tennant seat in Peeblesshire.

3. The infant Colin in the cup won by his father's prize shorthorn bull, Evan, after whom Christopher Glenconner wanted to name his eldest son.

4. Pamela Glenconner with her two sons, Colin and James, at Glen. As with the basket saddle, Colin and James were diametrically opposed to each other all their lives.

5. Admiral's House, Hampstead, Colin's childhood home. The top floor was built like the deck of a frigate by an eccentric naval officer.

6. Colin and James before their father's Bentley at 'Adho'.

7. Tilly, the devoted housekeeper. She was to remain with Pamela Glenconner for the rest of her life.

8. Pencil drawing of Colin aged 6 by the accomplished artist, Violet, Duchess of Rutland, 1932. She was a cousin by marriage of the Tennants.

9. Colin competing in the long jump at Eton where he finished third and narrowly missed winning the 100 yards, Summer Half 1944. An 'Athletic Choice', he also ran for the College.

10. A 'leaver's photograph' of the Hon. Hugo Money-Coutts. He and Colin were to remain friends all their lives as well as business partners in Mustique.

11. Lt. Colin Tennant, Irish Guards, an instructor at Caterham Barracks, Surrey. 1947.

12. Stephen Tennant, *(left)* Colin's epicene uncle. He was a great influence on Colin, even advising him to wear a dab of carmine in the corner of the eyes to enhance their colour.

13. Shades of *Brideshead Revisited*, Colin photographed by Lord (Edward) Montagu. They gave breakfast parties at their rooms at New College, Oxford, where Colin had the milk sent down from Glen.

14. Collage of guests at Billy Wallace's dinner party, Brympton Grange, Summer 1948. Amongst the party, who remained lifelong friends, are (clockwise from centre outside left) the Duke of Marlborough, Tony Berry, Martha Firestone, Marigold Cory-Wright, unknown, Zoë d'Erlanger, Ian Gilmour, unknown, Theo Hokant, Hamish Wallace, Henry Porchester, Rosie Churchill, John Synge, Sarah Birkin, Marigold C-W (again), Rose Grimston, the US Ambassador's daughter, Sharmain Douglas, John Synge (again), Mickey Brand, Sue Hornby, unknown, Ludovic Kennedy and Felicity Warburg.

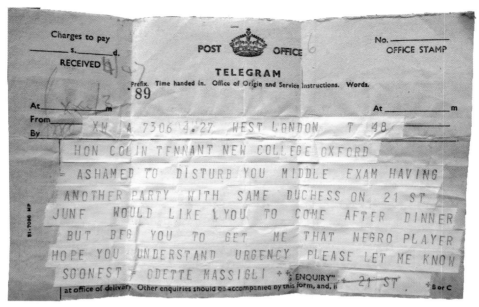

POST OFFICE

**TELEGRAM**

Charges to pay — s. — d.
RECEIVED

No. — OFFICE STAMP

Prefix. Time handed in. Office of Origin and Service Instructions. Words.

89

At — m    At — m

From

By    XW A 7306 4.27 WEST LONDON T 48

HON COLIN TENNANT NEW COLLEGE OXFORD

= ASHAMED TO DISTURB YOU MIDDLE EXAM HAVING
ANOTHER PARTY WITH SAME DUCHESS ON 21 ST
JUNE WOULD LIKE YOU TO COME AFTER DINNER
BUT BEG YOU TO GET ME THAT NEGRO PLAYER
HOPE YOU UNDERSTAND URGENCY PLEASE LET ME KNOW
SOONEST = ODETTE MASSIGLI + "S ENQUIRY" + 21 ST
+ B or C

at office of delivery. Other enquiries should be accompanied by this form, and, i

15. Telegram from Odette Massigli, wife of the French Ambassador. The mid-exam revels can only have contributed to Colin's poor results.

16. The Hon. Sir Clifford Bede playing chess with his daughter Pandora. She was Colin's first serious girlfriend.

17. Ivy Nicholson, known as the 'Beanstalk from Arkansas', was another of Colin's glamorous girlfriends in the early 1950s.

18. Feeding time in St Mark's Square, Venice. Judy Montagu, (centre) with Colin for the autumn festival. Judy had a 'crazy talent for friendship that has never been equalled'.

19. It would appear that all three in the Triumph TR2 have been to the same hairdresser. Lady Jeannie Campbell with her husband, Norman Mailer, and friend in the South of France. She led Colin 'a merry dance' throughout their relationship.

21. Amateur theatricals – the cast of Lord and Lady Algy. (left to right) Mark Birley, Liz Hoyar- Millar, Henry Porchester, Colin Tennant, Tony Berry, Raine Legge, Romona von Hofmonnsthal, David Metcalf, Judy Dugdale and Gerry Noel. May 1954. This production was followed by The Frog by Edgar Wallace, which raised £10,000 (a considerable sum in 1952) for charity, although it was slated by the critics.

20. Rumours were rife of the engagement of Princess Margaret and Colin after he stayed at Balmoral for her 24th birthday. Although the newspapers were full of the speculation, no one within the castle walls made any reference to it other than in specially composed songs.

22. Colin the businessman in New York.

23. The magnificent Palladian Holkham Hall, Norfolk, was built in the early 18th for the 1st Earl of Leicester by William Kent. It was the childhood home of Lady Anne Coke.

24. Colin and the new Lady Anne Tennant after their wedding St Withburga, the church in the park of Holkham.

25. 'All aboard' at the start of Colin and Anne's six-month honeymoon to France, Cuba and the United States.

26. Marcia Rokes the 1953 Carnival Queen of Trinidad. Colin managed to persuade his fellow judges to choose a black contestant for the first time.

27. Mrs Stanhope Lovell, known as 'Hellfire Jack', was the manager of the Tennant's Ortinola Estate in Trinidad. She so impressed Colin that he named the new village in Mustique after her.

28. One of the former owners of Mustique, Elmer Maingot (née Hazel) with her husband Ever. Her family had owned the island for a hundred years before selling to Colin.

to the senior girls on how to secure a rich, titled husband. Their third child was Lady Diana Spencer.

Anne was devastated when Johnnie, the love of her life, dropped her, and soon left on the *Queen Elizabeth* for the United States, 'ostensibly to sell Holkham pottery, but really to get over it'. It was there that she received the invitation from The Queen to be one of her six Maids of Honour to carry her train at The Coronation in June 1953.

As dynasties go, the Cokes and the Tennants could not be further apart. Even though the Tennant fortune was founded in the late eighteenth century, their considerable wealth came from manufacture and trade (see Appendix II). Notwithstanding that past members of the family had married into the nobility and landed gentry, were landowners themselves, and had a baronetcy and a peerage, to the old aristocracy like the Cokes, they were still *nouveaux riches*. The Cokes derived their wealth from a more acceptable, more ancient source, the ownership of land: all 46,000 acres of it.

Anne is descended from Thomas Coke, the 1st Earl of Leicester of its fifth creation. The Cokes had held land in Norfolk and Suffolk since the fifteenth century and had acquired Holkham in 1609 through Sir Edward Coke, a particularly skilled lawyer. He chose an ostrich holding a horseshoe as his crest, for just as the ostrich can digest anything from stones to bits of iron, so Coke could absorb and digest the most complicated laws.

Coke held high office under Queen Elizabeth I, Kings James I and Charles I, and became Speaker of the House of Commons. As Attorney General he presided over the trial of Sir Walter Raleigh and the Gunpowder Plotters, rising to Chief Justice of the King's Bench division in 1613. When he died, aged 83, his widow declared 'We shall never see his like again, praises be to God', which can be taken two ways.

It was Sir Edward's descendant, Thomas Coke, who became the 1st Earl of Leicester and built Holkham Hall, one of finest examples of the Palladian revival style of architecture in the country. It was designed by William Kent and assisted by Lord Burlington, whom Leicester had met in Rome while on the Grand Tour between the years 1712 and 1718. The considerable collection of works of art that Coke amassed filled the new house. Amongst these treasures was the 'Codex Leicester', the most famous of the thirty known scientific journals by Leonardo de Vinci. In this seventy-two page document, written in his characteristic mirror writing, Leonardo explores the link between art and science, and the creativity of the scientific process, namely the properties of water and rocks, air and celestial light. Whilst at home, Anne's only task was to dust the Codex. It was sold by the auctioneers Christies in 1980, when Colin was greatly relieved that his own opening bid was below the reserve of £2 million. There were no other bids. The Italian Government wanted to buy the Codex, as did the French, but as there had been a serious earthquake in southern Italy it was thought imprudent to spend the money in the wake of the disaster. In the end it was sold after the auction to Armand Hammer, the American industrialist. It changed hands again in 1994 for $30.8 million when it was bought by Bill Gates of Microsoft.

As the first Earl's son predeceased him, Holkham passed to his nephew, Wenman Roberts, who changed his name to Coke. It was his son, according to Burke's *Peerage* (what Colin called a 'book of deference' as opposed to 'a book of reference') who was the 'well-known and popular Mr Coke of Norfolk, the great politician and agricultural reformer'. He was created yet another 1st Earl of Leicester in 1837. From there on, the Cokes have lived in grandeur at Holkham, managing their estates and serving their country in the Army, and their Sovereign in one capacity or other. Anne's father, Thomas, the 5th Earl, was Equerry to The Duke of York, then King George VI and the present Queen. His sister, Lady Mary Harvey, was a Woman of the Bedchamber to The Queen Mother, while Anne's mother, Lady Elizabeth Yorke, daughter of the 8th Earl of Hardwicke was a Lady of the Bedchamber to The Queen.

The Leicesters not only served their members of the Royal Family, but were close friends too. King George VI and The Queen Elizabeth attended Anne's coming-out dance at Holkham, along with Princess Margaret. Anne was asked to Windsor Castle for Ascot Week (unusually twice), where she was described as having 'eyes of cornflower blue … hair …like golden corn'.

But Lady Leicester was not content to confine her life to being just the chatelaine of Holkham and working for The Queen. When, during the Second World War, a detail of German prisoners of war was billeted at Holkham, one of them, a potter in civilian life, discovered a special clay on the estate and began 'throwing' pots. After the war Lady Leicester set up the Holkham Pottery, producing contemporary and commemorative pieces, some designed by her second daughter Carey, from this source of clay. These were then sold in the gift shop attached to the house, and to wholesale stores. Their chief saleswoman was Anne, who travelled throughout Britain and the United States.

Compared to Colin's giddy whirl, Anne's life was somewhat tame. She was not encouraged to take friends home to Holkham, 'a vast house standing in fleeting isolation where everyone had sniffling colds from September until after Easter', where virtually the only entertainment was the shooting parties throughout the winter. However, once Colin had met her parents properly (he 'always got along very well with Lady Leicester, who got on well with everybody'), he was well accepted. Lord Leicester treated him 'as he would anybody who was a guest in his house'. Pompously reminiscing, Colin believed that for Anne he 'was rather a good choice ... [he] was infinitely glamorous and at that point on the verge of considerable wealth and was socially adept'. Also, he had reached the age of 29 without 'serious entanglement'.

But once it was established that Colin and Anne were an item, they were the beautiful couple to the Press, to be photographed and written up wherever they went. Their life was a mid-1950s version of Evelyn Waugh's *Vile Bodies*, with 'such a lot of parties' – there were balls and dances, cocktail parties and dinner parties, house parties and villa parties in the South of France. Anne was invited by Christopher and Elizabeth Glenconner to Glen for August, along with a succession of Colin's friends and relations, the likes of David and Simon Blow, Lords Christopher and Valentine Thynne, Anne's fellow Maid of Honour, Lady Jane Willoughby, and Henry Vyner, the owner of Studley Royal and Fountains Abbey. Colin introduced Anne to his London friends, whom she liked greatly, particularly his cousins Susanna (Zanna) Chancellor and Ingrid Wyndham. Now that Colin's affections had transferred to Anne, his relationship with Princess Margaret was naturally less intimate, although he and Anne, whom she had known all her life, continued to see her. In time, Anne became her most trusted friend, although typically Colin took all the credit.

It came as no surprise when, on 16 December 1955, a simple notice appeared in Court Circular in *The Times*: 'The Engagement is announced between Colin, eldest son of Lord Glenconner and Pamela, Lady Glenconner, and Anne, eldest daughter of the Earl and Countess of Leicester.'

Shortly after the announcement of the engagement, Lord Leicester wrote to Colin telling him that he expected him to continue calling his wife 'Lady Leicester', notwithstanding the fact that she was a mere fourteen years his senior. She was Lady Leicester to Colin for the rest of her life.

Colin and Anne decided on a spring wedding and were married the following April by the Bishop of Norwich at St Withburga, the Coke family church in the centre of the Holkham Estate. Invitations went out and presents arrived. The Queen and the Duke of Edinburgh sent a silver inkwell, while the village subscription, limited to 10s. a family, went to buy an 'electric kitchen mixing machine'.

The day of the wedding (21 April 1956) was on 'one of those rare and magical days of spring where the sun shines unceasingly in the cloudless blue sky'.[xxvi] The special train chartered by Lord Leicester for 'several hundred pounds' took 200 of the guests from London King's Cross to Hunstanton, where buses were laid on to take them on to Holkham. Two coaches in the train were reserved for the forty staff of C. Tennant, Sons & Co. There was a buffet car where a cold lunch cost 10s. 6d. a head and Louis Roederer champagne 1945 was 47s. 6d. a bottle, although some cheaper wines were provided. Guests came to the wedding from far and wide. The tenantry and estate workers from Glen arrived in a specially chartered bus – the account of their trip, recorded in the charming letter of thanks from the head gardener, C.T. Robson, made no reference to the hilarious party in the Victoria Hotel given by Anne's aunt, Lady Sylvia Combe, where they danced until dawn. Some Belgian friends of the Leicesters landed in the park in a private plane, while The Queen Mother and Princess Margaret flew to the local RAF base, had a sandwich at Sandringham, and then came over to the church. Special staging had been constructed so that at least 450 of the 700 guests could be accommodated.

The wedding itself was a wonderful affair. Colin chose Lord Tennyson as his best man as he and his brother James (the brothers having had a difficult relationship since adolescence) were by then totally estranged. Anne arrived in 'a gown of white organza with silver embroidered lace with silver lace on the skirt' and wearing the important Coke necklace and a pair of earrings given to her by Lord Glenconner. The dress was designed by Norman Hartnell and came by road with one of his fitters, arriving just two hours before the off. Anne appeared relaxed saying, 'I'm not really worried, but I will be happier when I see it.' The reception was a tremendous affair where 'weather-beaten estate workers in their Sunday best rubbed shoulders with Society guests'.

There was one, however, who was a great deal less happy at the wedding and that was the young society photographer, Anthony Armstrong-Jones, always known as Tony. Colin had commissioned him earlier in the year to take some portraits of him, as he had admired the photographs Tony had taken of his half-sister, Emma. The photographs of

Colin, interestingly signed 'Anthony Jones', are exceptionally good. Other than providing a list of the guests he wanted invited, the choice of Tony was the only contribution Colin made to the arrangements of the wedding. Long before the days of the 'photographer Earls', to Lady Leicester the wedding photographer ranked alongside hairdressers, caterers and florists and such people were classed as tradesmen, whatever their background. Lord Leicester referred to him as 'Tony Snapshot'. While the estate and office staff and the villagers were considered guests and served champagne in the state rooms, Tony was relegated to tea in the servants' hall – the fact that he was an old Etonian, coxed the winning Cambridge eight in the University Boat Race of 1950, and was godson of their great favourite, Sir Michael Duff, counted for naught. There was always bad blood between Colin and Tony, which Colin believed stemmed from that unintentional slight at his wedding, which was, in fact, none of his doing. Tony always referred to Colin as 'that shit',[xxvii] and when telephoned by the author for an interview he exploded 'I *loathed* the man. I want nothing to do with his biography' and slammed the receiver down.

The first part of the honeymoon was spent in Paris, where Colin totally stunned his new wife with an explosive rage soon after they arrived in the honeymoon suite of the Hotel Lotti, near the Place Vendôme, as there were just two single beds. Colin's violent tantrum, not witnessed by Anne before, came as a terrible shock to the new bride. When he recovered, Colin went down to reception, where he raged at the night porter. The porter knew that there was a double bed in the basement, but as he was on his own, he and Colin lugged the mattress up the three flights of stairs (it was too big for the lift) to the suite, waking all the other guests in the hotel as they went. By the time they had brought up the base, Colin was exhausted and went straight to sleep.

At Le Harvre, Colin and Anne joined the RMS *Queen Mary* for New York. Anne always slept with her bedroom window open, so opened the porthole of their cabin and closed the curtains. That night a large wave splashed against the liner's side and drenched Colin, who was fast asleep. He blamed Anne for the heavy cold he suffered for the rest of the voyage. They continued to Havana. May is one of the hottest months in Cuba. Anne was unused to the heat and the humidity and, with her fair hair and fairer complexion, she suffered dreadfully. But worse was to come when they attended a cock fight. The first pair, enormous cocks with vicious steel spurs, were shown to each other as the large crowd placed their bets. As the handlers let them go the two birds flew together, flapping wildly as they savaged each other with beak, claw and spur. One of them spied Anne's hair and, mistaking it for straw, flew onto her head and buried its feet and spurs in her tresses. There was blood everywhere, Anne was in shock, and the punters blamed her for losing their money. The Yellowstone Park in Montana was less stressful. The planned six-month honeymoon was cut short as Anne was pregnant.

Despite the fairytale aspect of the courtship and the wedding, all was not as it seemed. Colin saw himself as being 'very charming, attractive, rich, good looking and much sought-after through his connection with Princess Margaret, and as such, a good catch'. Throughout his life, Colin needed to work from a 'blank canvas' whatever the project, and especially in his marriage. He dismissed Anne's first real love, Johnnie Spencer, as a mere eighteenth-century dynastic understanding between two aristocratic families with vast landholdings. Anne was certainly in love with Colin – she would not have married him otherwise – but whatever she gave, it was never enough for him. But Anne was resolute. Four decades later, in a documentary about Colin, *The Man Who Bought Mustique*, she revealed that soon after they were married he said: 'I'm going to break you.' But she was determined not to be broken and, consequently, was always on her mettle. Despite her pretty, soft exterior, Anne is made of sterner stuff. She is full of resolve and, in her, Colin had certainly met his match. Conversely, with his complex state of mind, Colin was simply not capable of conventional love. He was certainly glamorised by Anne, whose Coke grandeur appealed to his snobbish side.

Colin and Anne returned from their honeymoon to their first London marital home, a small flat behind Eaton Square in Belgravia. Although the flat had a fashionable address it was too cramped and not a satisfactory place from which to start their married life. As Colin said: 'The whole summer was hot and bothered. Well, we were bothered.' Despite the heat and the cramped conditions those first months of marriage settled down into a routine. Colin's father had made him a Director of C. Tennant, Sons & Co. with a view to encouraging him to take more interest in the business. Two other directorships followed, The London Tin Company and the state-run British Metal Corporation, where he was often seated next to a fellow Director, Field Marshal Sir Gerald Templer, whom Colin said (as he frequently did about all kinds of men) was in love with him. Later, he was a Director of the London Metal Exchange. With the responsibility of marriage should have come responsibility in the family firm, but it was not to be.

Colin and Anne's first child, the son and heir, was born at the Welbeck Hospital in London in the middle of February 1957. At his christening (with heated water) he was given the names Charles Edward Pevensey by his godparents – Lord (Patrick) Plunket, Euan Graham, Evelyn de Rothschild, the Countess of Arran, Ingrid Wyndham (who by that time had married Jonathan Guinness) and Elizabeth Lascelles. Soon after Charles was born, the family moved to a very agreeable little house in Knightsbridge. After the monthly nurse had departed they hired, and soon fired, an unsatisfactory Swiss girl before engaging Nanny White. Nanny White was a large, spare kind of woman with big bones and a faded, whitish yellow skin, a sharp beaky face and dyed black hair. She was not particularly pleasant, and rather fierce. But she instantly fell completely and totally in love with Charles, which made it increasingly difficult for Anne to look after him herself in such a small house.

Despite Nanny White's attentions, Charles grew up into 'the most rewarding and beautiful child that you could imagine, and had made a lot of progress in life'. Happiness reigned. He was 3 when Anne, expecting her second child, went into hospital. Whilst she was away Colin sacked Nanny White, with the most disastrous effect on Charles: in retrospect Colin believed that this was when he suffered a nervous breakdown. The crisis in Charles' life coincided with the birth of Henry in 1960. There were to be three more children; Christopher who was born in 1968 and the twins, May and Amy, in 1970.

Over the next few years, Charles was alternately better or mildly psychotic. By the time he was 7, Colin had moved his family to Old Park Farm near Cheshunt in Essex. There was nothing old, or farm-like about it, except that it was in Theobald's Park. He added a small wing where Charles and Henry were looked after by a nanny, Brenda, and 'a succession of either forbidding or benevolent nursery maids'. But Charles' problems had already started when he refused to eat or go to sleep. He went to the local dame school, where he was well-liked and well-received, but one day it was discovered that he had a collection of drawings of the Nazi Army stashed in his desk. Charles even went so far as to boast that his grandfather, Christopher, had been a Nazi general during the Second World War, and was still wanted for war crimes. Even at that tender age he was obsessed with Hitler. Later, in an interview with *Woman* magazine, he admitted that his problems really started when he was about 5 years old: 'Suddenly I started to suffer from incredibly vivid and terrifying nightmares. They used to haunt me, especially the one when I'd go up to my father or mother and they'd suddenly rip off their faces and turn into witches.'[xxviii]

Colin sent Charles off to a child psychiatrist for counselling and he returned much better. At 10 years of age he was packed off to a boarding prep-school. Charles begged his father not to send him away but Colin was determined that he should be like other boys of his age and class and to 'give it a go'. Charles later admitted that he was so unhappy that he seriously thought of committing suicide. Realising his plight he was sent to Westminster Under School, in London where, to please his father, he set to and worked hard. Charles had been put down for Eton at birth but failed the entrance exam by a single mark. He failed again by the same margin the next term 'which sent him over the edge. It was very damaging to Charles'. But by that time, Colin had embarked on the project that was not only to make his name, but to dissipate his fortune too. And that was the Island of Mustique.

Chapter 6

# ORTINOLA, TRINIDAD

In March 1958 Colin, as a Director of Tennant's Estates (1928) Ltd., was sent by his father to Trinidad to inspect and advise on their holdings, the oil leases and the Ortinola Estate. He had worked in Trinidad five years earlier. 'Being weary of tasting tea and broking cocoa in the Combined Produce Department of C. Tennant, Sons & Co.', he spent two months working at the brokerage firm of Alstons head office in the capital, Port of Spain. He had 'swapped positions with Mr James Alston, of Trinidad'[xxix] who worked in London. Colin went by way of New York and Nassau, then had a gruelling journey south, being caught in Kingston, Jamaica, which he 'thought vile, dirty and dull', for two days without his luggage, which was in Montego Bay. In Trinidad, he was met by the eponymous Colonel Alston, the senior partner of the firm that Tennant's had been 'associated with over the last seventy-five years'.

By chance, Colin's visit coincided with the near centenary of the Tennant involvement in the West Indies. He always maintained that the ownership of their estates was the result of a bad debt from a distant Tennant cousin, an Excise officer from Leith, who had been involved in sugar speculation that had gone wrong. In fact the estates came through Sir Charles (the Bart), who had invited his third cousin from Ayrshire, William Tennant, to be his partner and manager of the London agency, C. Tennant, Sons & Co., and gave him a sizeable participation in the firm. Not wishing to restrict their activities to the mere factoring of St Rollox chemicals, and being situated in the merchanting quarter of the City of London, it was inevitable that Will Tennant should seek to expand their fortunes by dealing and speculating in commodities. Sugar was one such product. Emancipation had been granted to the slaves in the West Indies in 1834, but in Trinidad, as elsewhere, they had to work out their 'apprenticeship' for a further four years. As a result the sugar estates soon collapsed. However, with the advent of indentured labour from India, the signs looked good for the recovery of the price of sugar, which tempted many brokers, including Will Tennant, into speculation. He advanced considerable sums to the Jewish sugar broking firm of Bernstein & Co. who operated in Trinidad. In the early 1850s, the price of sugar plummeted, leaving Bernsteins with immense margins to pay. In his despair, Will Tennant turned to Sir Charles, who unhesitatingly came to his rescue by writing out a cheque for £100,000 from his personal bank account. The Tennant partnership was saved and Bernstein & Co., being insolvent, then handed over the mortgages of the sugar estates, totalling 10,000 acres, to the Bart. And so began the long association of the Tennant family and the West Indies.

To Sir Charles, these West Indian properties were merely an extension to his massive holdings in Great Britain. He sent out managers, usually from Scotland, to look after the estates and appears to have taken no further interest, other than what he gleaned from the balance sheets as their fortunes waxed or waned through the fluctuating price of sugar. There were five estates, centred around the Oroponche Lagoon near San Fernando on the leeward coast, with the romantic names of La Fortunée, Bonne Adventure, Buen Intendo, Plaisance, and Pluck. There was a sixth estate, Ortinola, not far from Port of Spain, in the densely tropical Maracas Valley. It had long been held that Trinidad had the ideal conditions for growing cocoa. Seeing the potential, Tennants bought the Ortinola Estate sometime in the 1870s from Hypolite Borde as the demand for chocolate increased. C. Tennant, Sons & Co. then agreed to supply Cadbury Brothers of Bournville with all the cocoa from their estates. In the late 1880s a young Glaswegian, J. P. Bain, was sent to Trinidad to resuscitate Ortinola. Bain set about clearing 220 acres at the head of the valley and building a fine house for himself and his family. Known as 'Cocoa' Bain, he was to stay there for the rest of his life, a loyal and devoted employee of the Tennant family.

Eddy Glenconner visited the Trinidad properties twice. He had no head for business and treated Ortinola as an extension of his Scottish estate, Glen, to be indulged in one of his passions, forestry. With great foresight he was one of the first in the Caribbean to plant his land with mahogany trees. He also pioneered the grapefruit in Trinidad – when Colin first went out he saw a vast tree beside the house with 2,000 grapefruits hanging from its branches. There is a fine photographic record of Eddy's visit in 1911. Prominent is the eldest of the three high-spirited daughters, Janet, who had married a merchant seaman called Jack Stanhope Lovell. She was later to play a large part in the Tennant fortunes.

When Eddy died the Trinidad properties were divided equally btween his sons, Christopher, David and Stephen. In 1922, Christopher went out to view his patrimony. By that time 'Cocoa' Bain had died and the mantle had passed to his son-in-law, Jack, but the real power on the estate was his daughter Janet, so much so that the two were known as 'Jack' and 'Hellfire Jack'. There was also a neighbour at Palmiste, the agronomist and former Liberal MP, Sir Norman Lamont, who kept an eye on the estates. Christopher's visit was not a success. He stayed at Government House in Port of Spain, where he contacted a high fever, and his pulse when down to 30. It was no wonder that he took a jaundiced view of the island and the Tennant operations. He never returned. He did, however, manage to collect some tiny caimans (alligators) as a present for his youngest brother, Stephen. The brutes were kept on the hotplate in the dining room at Wilsford and would snap at visitors as they helped themselves to eggs and bacon at breakfast. They – the caimans not the guests – were always escaping and Tilly, the housekeeper, spent her time flushing them out from under the sofa with a broom. In the end they were sent to a zoo where, to Stephen's great disappointment, they failed to recognise him.

With the reorganisation of C. Tennant, Sons & Co. in 1928, the Trinidad properties and the merchanting operation in San Fernando were divided, the land going into a separate company, Tennants Estates (1928) Limited. No sooner had all this been ratified than the rumblings of the slump were felt. Much of Christopher's inheritance was entailed in trust from Sir Charles' will, while his free and private fortune was rapidly depleted. Recalling with distinct distaste his experiences in Trinidad he resolved that the estates should be the first of his assets to be liquidated. It is also likely that they were a considerable financial drain in those depressed times. He sent out his personal assistant to negotiate the sale. Working with the general manager, Paul Sheldon, the estates were sold for £72,000, an unbelievable £7 2s. an acre. Much of the land, including Inverness, part of La Fortunée, where he lived, was bought by Sheldon himself. He sold on the land around Pointe à Pierre to Texaco, where they eventually built their refinery. Another farm, Usine St Madelaine, was bought by Tate & Lyle. But it was a different story at Ortinola where

'Hellfire Jack' (Janet) held out, telling Sheldon, 'You sell this place over our dead bodies'. It remained unsold.

However, this catalogue of intrigue and total disaster was marginally saved by the wisdom of Sir Norman Lamont. Lamont had long held that one day oil would be discovered in Trinidad and thus advised that the oil and mineral rights should be excluded from the sale of the land. At his instigation, a company, Associated Trinidad Oil Rights (ATOR) was formed, combining his own land with the Tennant's land, making a total of 15,000 acres in two blocks. Again, Sheldon negotiated the deal in return for 25 per cent of the Tennant revenues and 2.5 per cent for his lifetime. By 1935 the declining agency, Tennants San Fernando, was sold to Alstons. Mrs Lovell did, however, agree to two of the remaining cocoa estates being sold to Cadburys at the beginning of the Second World War. It was also at this time that an agreement was made with Kern Oil (later absorbed by Texaco) to lease the oil rights from ATOR. The lease was for twenty-five years, starting at BWI$1, rising to $10 an acre. The leases were then sold for a 'notional amount' so that the royalties were treated as repayment of capital and thus free of the 40 per cent Trinidad tax. Oil was eventually found and the tax-free income proved invaluable. But Sir Norman, a rich man already, did not enjoy the royalties for long as he was gored to death by his prize bull in 1949.

By 1953, the year of Colin's first visit to Trinidad, the revenue from the oil rights was gushing in and Ortinola was not losing too much money. At Alstons he was mentored by Rupert Alexis 'an elderly coloured man in charge of the cocoa and coffee department', and then moved round the various divisions. To escape the flood of inevitable invitations Colin went to stay with the Lovells at Ortinola at the weekends, which he greatly enjoyed. He found it 'very curious to get into bed and see TENNANTS inked on the sheets'[xxx] which, with the blankets, towels and everything around the house, were ringing with the humid damp. He commended the Lovells for their 'everlasting loyalty and for jealously guarding their interests for so long with so little recognition'. He admired Janet Lovell greatly, and when Henry was born he was given the middle name of Lovell in her honour, and the new village in Mustique bore her name in her memory, when it was built in 1968.

In such a small society as Port of Spain, Colin developed something of a celebrity status and was invited to judge the beauty queens at the Carnival. His fellow judges were an eclectic lot – Chief Justice Perez, of

Portuguese origin, Prince Alexander of Yugoslavia, who was a British West Indian Airways pilot, the Canadian Trade Commissioner and Mrs Ward, the Indian High Commissioner and Mrs Akow, of Chinese origin. Since its inception, the official Carnival (as opposed to the Calypso Carnival) had been the preserve of the white community and thus the Carnival Queen had always been white. To Colin this was entirely wrong and, in a scene not unlike Henry Fonda in the film *Twelve Angry Men*, he managed to persuade his fellow judges to choose, for the first time, a black contestant, Marcia Rokes, as the Carnival Queen.

Events in the oil business in Trinidad had moved on considerably when Colin returned in 1958. Oil had been discovered on ATOR land which was earning royalties at BWI$.25 a barrel on top of the acreage payments. But labour was a problem at Ortinola and the redoubtable Janet Lovell, by now drawing a pension, was losing heart. Her grandson, Jasper, under the guardianship of Ernest Tennant (another of her admirers) had been sailing with three friends off the north Norfolk coast in England when the boat capsized and he was drowned. She had always dreamed that he would take over the running of the estate. But as the estate was making around £2,000 a year it did not warrant, nor could it afford, a European manager. Mrs Lovell not only said that she would not mind if the estate was sold, but also suggested a buyer, the Hon. Bhadase Maraj, the leader of the Democratic Labour Party, the opposition party he founded, who might like it as a country retreat. Colin went to see him at his garish white villa, where he lay in bed between two women and several outsized teddy bears. Although somewhat preoccupied, Bhadase seemed receptive to the idea of the purchase and Colin was asked to return at a more suitable time.

The squandering of the Tennant possessions at the hand of Sheldon had long irked Colin. Further, without the active support of the Lovells, he could see no future in owning Ortinola and thus he had become thoroughly disenchanted with Trinidad. By chance he was in Alstons' office in Port of Spain when he ran into one of their Directors, John Bayne, whom Colin had known well when he was working there in 1953. His sister Jean was married to the Chairman, Colonel Roy Alston. Although the pair hailed from Union Island, they had known a family named Hazell from the parent island of St Vincent all their lives. It was John who told Colin about a wonderful small island in the Grenadines which belonged to his friends, the three Hazell sisters, that was for sale. The island was called Mustique.

# Chapter 7

# THE OLD GREAT HOUSE

The idea of owning an island in the Caribbean instantly appealed to the adventurous side of Colin, and the next morning he was at Piarco Airport, where he had chartered a Grumman Goose, a single-engined seaplane, there being no airport at St Vincent at that time. On commercial flights the seaplanes would take off on a runway and land on the sea. Often the captain would forget to remind the passengers where they were landing and great consternation followed when the plane splashed down onto the water!

Fully prepared, the Goose touched down in the sea at Villa, beside Young Island, where Colin was met by Fred Hazell, known as Mr Fred when he was the manager of Mustique. He was introduced to Elmer Maingot, the youngest of the three Hazell sisters, and her husband, Ever.

After a chequered history of European occupation from the early 1750s onwards, when the fortunes of successive owners swung from great wealth to total bankruptcy, Mustique came into the hands of the Hazells, a Creole family from St Vincent in the 1860s. They kept it solely for their own enjoyment and stayed for months during the holidays. They raised and raced horses, shot Ramier pigeons, and farmed in a desultory way in partnership with the local population. But after three generations the island was no longer a pleasure, but an expensive burden. Matters finally came to a head in early 1955. Ever Maingot had a stroke at the same time as the islanders rebelled over the metier system of labour (share-cropping), bringing island politics to a head. The sisters decided to sell up and headed for New York where they registered Mustique with Previews Inc., real estate brokers of grand and unusual properties. The island went on the market for £60,000, the sisters paying the hefty 2 per cent registration fee in advance. For the three years Previews had Mustique on their books they received just three derisory offers of £12,000, £19,000 and £31,000, all of which they refused.

For Colin's viewing of Mustique, Fred Hazell had chartered a local auxiliary schooner, *The Transport*, from Captain Tannis of Bequia. Colin, never a good sailor, was at least braver than Elmer, who screamed the name of the captain, McRee, every time a wave hit the boat. They sailed round the island where Colin admired the succession of sandy beaches, but he never landed. He had made up his mind to buy Mustique by the time he returned to St Vincent, where he put up at the Sugar Mill Inn. He sent a cable to his father, who was on holiday in New Zealand, for permission to buy. The purchase was immediately sanctioned by Christopher on the sole proviso 'so long as there was water'. As all the well-water in the Grenadines is brackish, and rainwater caught from the roofs the only other source, Colin decided to ignore the caveat. That day Colin offered the three sisters £45,000 (BWI$216,000) cash for the island, the buildings, machinery, such as it was, and the contents of the house, which worked out at £15,000 apiece. It was Fred Hazell who advised his cousins to accept the offer, and the contracts were drawn up. The deal signed, Colin returned to Trinidad to dispose of Ortinola.

True to his word, Bhadase came to see Colin in Lovell's bungalow (called The Glen) where they agreed a price of BWI$210,000 for Ortinola. The deal was 25 per cent down in cash, and the balance over four years at 6 per cent interest which was paid, not quite on time, but in full. Thus within a week Mustique was bought for BWI$216,000 and Ortinola disposed of for BWI$210,000. Most of the value at Ortinola was Eddy's mahogany plantations: perhaps he was not such a bad businessman after all.

Colin returned to Mustique full of trepidation as to what he had bought. He landed at Walkers, the large bay on the leeward side. From the beach the party made their way up to the Great House, a commodious wooden building on a stone base. Hanging in the wide veranda were two sides of a sheep that had been killed that morning for lunch. In the afternoon, Neville Joseph walked Colin around the island. It was very run down. There were no proper roads: the fencing and stockades had long since perished, and only about 11 acres (out of a total of 1,385) were under cultivation. There were herds of feral cattle and goats rampaging around the island, damaging what little crops and provision grounds there were. Colin spent an uncomfortable night in the Great House and, as the new owner of Mustique, he wondered if he had done the right thing.

Once back in London, the enormity of Colin's purchase dawned on him. When Anne first went there the following year she told him he was totally, and utterly, mad and that he could never make it work, to which he replied: 'You mark my words, I will make Mustique into a household name.' But he cannot have said it with much conviction. Colin had realised that if Ortinola in the relatively advanced Trinidad proved difficult to manage from a distance, then Mustique, a backwater cut off from a then backward St Vincent would be infinitely harder. Letters took weeks to arrive, if at all. He had no practical knowledge of tropical agriculture, particularly on Mustique, where the sowing and reaping of crops were governed by the phases of the moon.

Then, completely out of the blue, a letter arrived from the West India Committee with an application from a young man who was looking for a position, preferably an island, in the Caribbean. He had been farming in Uganda and thus had experience in tropical agriculture. It all seemed too good to be true, as indeed it turned out to be. John Kiddle arrived for his interview armed with a reference from his vicar and a tale of how he had lost all his money through the vagaries of an unreliable partner in Africa. He appeared capable and eager and Colin engaged him as manager of Mustique at a salary of £1,500 a year. Armed with letters of introduction for the Lovells and the Directors of Alstons, Kiddle set sail for Trinidad with a list of instructions, including one to pick out any machinery or pieces of furniture from Ortinola that might be useful in Mustique.

It was Colin's idea to improve relations between the new owner of Mustique, Tennants Estates (1928) Ltd., and the islanders. Kiddle was instructed to employ everyone who wished to work for the current agricultural wage. There were, in fact, only about fifty able-bodied men and women, the rest being either very old or of school age. When Colin met the villagers he asked each what their particular skill was. Some were good with stock, some were fishermen, but most were field workers. When he asked Hilly Trimmingham what she did, she replied 'I favour the hoe!' Those who were too old were given pensions, while those who wished to leave were encouraged to go with the gift of BWI$1,000. Some left to live in Bequia, the neighbouring island; others went further afield to Toronto, and some even to London.

Under the metier system, the Hazells had provided the seed, fertiliser and the land, while the islanders supplied the labour. The revenue from the crop was then divided between them (two-thirds and one-third), only the islanders' share was paid out in the form of a credit at the Hazells' store on the island, or in Kingstown, the capital of St Vincent. The Hazells also stopped the islanders from fishing, except with their permission, so that they took half the value of the catch. The matriarchs of the village, finding themselves with actual cash for the first time in their long lives from Colin's pensions, put their savings together and chartered a schooner to take them to Kingstown. There they complained to the Minister for Home Affairs that 'Mr Tennants' was a thief for not giving them enough money on which to live.

In the beginning, Kiddle's sporadic reports showed that he had a fair grasp of the daunting task ahead of him and, to his credit, he progressed well. He imported often as many as a hundred workmen at a time to clear the land, repair the rundown buildings and control the erosion of the roads. They were employed weekly from St Vincent, and billeted on the top floor of the partially restored cotton house. He laid out a 900 ft by 50 ft grass airstrip (at right angles to its present position) and constructed a 48-ft jetty. Under him, the land for cultivation was increased to 100 acres, planting 75 acres of Sea Island Cotton and the rest in ground nuts and black-eyed peas. He established a nursery to propagate pangola grass to restore the pastures, and planted 2,000 coconuts, bought from Orange Hill, the estate to the north of St Vincent, around L'Ancecoy Beach. Strong, high, barbed-wire fences criss-crossed the island to contain the wild cattle and so protect the cultivations and new pastures. Some of the wild cattle were killed by driving them into the sea, where they were kept thrashing in the ocean until exhausted, then hauled out and slaughtered on the beach. In these respects, Kiddle achieved a great amount in a comparatively short time. But all this essential work naturally cost a great deal of money, and he spent the Tennant money freely.

Colin sent out his accountant, Ronny Ford, to try to instil some order into Kiddle's accounting system, to prepare budgets, and to rein in his extravagances. It was to no avail. Kiddle continued to live in medieval princely style, attended by eight 'oafish boys'. He entertained in princely fashion too. His extravagances were fearful, even running to a horse caparisoned with expensive saddlery and saddlecloth. He paid £2,000 for a boat to be built that turned out to be unseaworthy. In two years Kiddle had managed to spend £50,000 – £5,000 more than the whole island cost in the first place.

Colin was later to deride Kiddle's formidable contribution to the restoration of Mustique, perhaps with good reason, but at the time he was delighted with his efforts and the progress of Mustique. He wrote to him after his first visit:

> Mustique is a long way from London which, of course, I realised at the time we decided to appoint you as Manager, after only a brief acquaintanceship. I am glad that we know each other better now because, as you can imagine, during the first few months of your being on Mustique we felt starved of information and considerably disturbed at the rate of expenditure. In fact, I was very much in two minds whether the arrangement was going to work and consequently whether we should make a change when the break in your contract occurs at the end of the first eighteen month period, which would be this autumn.
>
> However, I am now re-assured that you have achieved a great deal during the period to date and are proving yourself more responsible than we first thought. I know it takes a bit of time to settle down in new surroundings and that until you know your way around you may incur expenses which you gradually learn to avoid.*xxxi*

Although Kiddle was instructed to make Mustique viable agriculturally, it had always been Colin's intention that the island should be developed once the time was right, and that the acute water situation had been resolved. As he put it 'without an adequate supply of water every penny that we put in [to Mustique] is at risk'. He had no doubt that he could attract enough of his rich friends to make the whole project viable. Colin had also been to see the Administrator of St Vincent to outline his visionary, long-term plans for Mustique, and had sown the seeds for acquiring a series of Government-held islands throughout the Grenadines for Tennant Estates to develop in a similar fashion. There was even a thought of buying the small island of Mayreau from the Eustace family when it came on the market. Kiddle thought it could be had for BWI$400,000–500,000, (then around £95,000) but nothing came of the plan.

Back in London, Colin saw less and less of Princess Margaret after she took up with the photographer Anthony Armstrong-Jones. Although they had been introduced by Colin's friend, Lady Elizabeth Cavendish, and one of Princess Margaret's Ladies-in-Waiting, her former inner circle of intimates rarely overlapped with Tony's more raffish and Bohemian set.

When the couple finally became engaged in 1960, it is an oft-told story that Colin asked Princess Margaret if she would like 'something in a small box from Aspreys, or a piece of Mustique as a wedding present'. He did, however, make the offer to both of them, but Tony took it to be to her alone. Fifty years later, when drawn on the subject, Lord Snowdon (as Anthony Armstrong-Jones became) commented: 'Odd, don't you think?'[xxxii] Colin had chosen for her Gellizeau Point, a 10-acre promontory on the south end of Mustique. It was very private and about 3 miles from the island hub around the Great House. For Princess Margaret the gift was something of a speculation. Whereas she could enjoy or sell (as she frequently did) little somethings in a boxes from Aspreys or other jewellers, a plot of land, inhabited by fierce wild cattle, somewhere in the boondocks on a remote, inaccessible, mosquito-ridden island had to be a total gamble. As Colin said: 'The development of Mustique was light years away. It was not exactly a pig in a poke, but it was a piece of land.' But choose it she did, and included an inspection of her wedding present on her honeymoon in the Royal Yacht *Britannia*.

From the start, Princess Margaret's and Tony's honeymoon was fraught with disaster. The dockyard had stitched the *Inglefield clip* to the wrong end of the Union Flag so it was hoisted upside-down, an internationally recognised distress signal. As there was no wind the error went unnoticed for an hour and a half. The crew of *Britannia* were disaffected as they were due to go on leave after a three-month cruise to the West Indies earlier that year with the Princess Royal (Princess Mary), whose presence there was to encourage the Federation of the West Indies. Instead of a lengthy shore leave, the crew were kept on board in readiness to take the newly married couple back to the Caribbean. So exasperated were they that not one coughed up for a wedding present.

After the wedding *Britannia* slipped down the Thames (The Queen thought her 'a most impressive and efficient sight') with 'crowds hanging out of windows, hooters and sirens bellowing forth, everywhere bright colours and people waving enthusiastically'.[xxxiii] The happy couple stayed on deck, returning the waves of the crowd before retiring. They were not seen by officers or crew for the next five days.

The only excitement at sea was the refuelling in mid-Atlantic from the Royal Fleet Auxiliary tanker that followed *Britannia* for the whole of the honeymoon voyage. Her destination remained a secret from the Press for the whole of the eleven-day crossing but the moment she dropped anchor at Mount Irvine Bay in Tobago, Trinidad radio announced her presence. The Governor himself took charge of the security, even impounding small aircraft and confiscating pilots' licences and rolls of film. After a brief spell in Trinidad, the Royal Yacht headed north to a 'destination unknown', in fact to the Tobago Cays. The next morning a party went ashore on Le Rameau, an idyllic deserted island, only to find that four scruffy, drunken French fishermen from Martinique had arrived and were already encamped. They could not understand the Commander's schoolboy French, but another beach was found and the Martiniquais left after twenty gallons of fuel changed hands. The next day the picnic for Princess Margaret and Tony was set up on the newly named 'Twenty Gallon Beach'. Princess Margaret and Tony took off all their clothes and swam across a narrow sound to another deserted atoll. When it was time to return before the Royal Barge came to pick them up, they saw a shoal of barracuda in the clear water between them and their clothes. The boat's officer saw their dilemma and returned after it was safe for them to enter the water!

After two days in the Cays, the Royal Yacht moved on to Mustique where Colin and Anne were there to greet her as she dropped anchor in Walker's Bay which, in honour of her first visit, was renamed 'Britannia Bay'. Princess Margaret, looking tanned and happy, stepped onto the brand new jetty: Tony, rather less happy, followed three paces behind. Kiddle had fitted out the tractor and trailer with wooden seats and the party removed to the Great House. At midday they mounted the tractor again and slowly made their way south to Gellizeau Point. As Princess Margaret recalled: 'The Island looked like Kenya. Burnt to a frazzle. We drove down a path, the only road, and sat in the brush whacking mosquitoes.' Hugh Peers, then a Flag Lieutenantin in *Britannia*, did not think much of the island either. 'Why we stayed there for four days was hard to justify. Mustique seemed shaggy and nothing like the Tobago Cays with its beautiful beaches.'

Kiddle had had an area cleared (the actual site of a former house) and built a little bamboo hut, with coconut fronds for the roof, furnished it with tables, chairs and a supply of warm lemonade. Notwithstanding the mosquitoes, for Princess Margaret it was a thrilling moment, standing on the site of the only house and land that she was ever to actually own. Princess Margaret invited Colin and Anne back to the Royal Yacht for dinner and a very welcome bath denied them for the past two weeks. As Princess Margaret recalled: 'They were in tough shape'. It was the last time that Colin was to see the Great House.

That Christmas of 1960 was spent at Holkham. The Duke of Edinburgh was amongst a number of guests who had been asked to shoot on Christmas Eve. It had been an enjoyable day for all except Colin. Since the days of the Prince Regent there has been a tradition at Holkham whereby the peg positions were not drawn by chance as with other shoots, but the guns were placed by rank. Thus, every drive, members of the Royal Family were placed in the middle of the line where they could expect the best shooting. Their Equerries were placed next to them, then dukes, marquesses, earls and so on down the social order. Sons-in-law were the lowest of the low, and as such were relegated to walk with the beaters, who then were still wearing the Holkham uniform of smocks and bowler hats. Invariably after shooting days when Colin was about to retire to bed, Lord Leicester would draw him aside to say, 'I'm afraid you were a bit out of it today!' However, that Christmas Eve, they were all in the smoking room discussing the arrangements for the following January when Colin was taking Anne, Lady Leicester and Sarah, the youngest Coke daughter, out to Mustique, when the butler sidled into the room with a telegram for Colin. It was from Fred Hazell, his St Vincent agent. It read simply: GREAT HOUSE BURNED TO THE GROUND. Later Colin learned that Kiddle had been working on the estate accounts, using the enormous mahogany table in the dining room of the Great House when the Tilley lamp blew over. The house, constructed of wood in the eighteenth century, was dry as tinder and highly flammable, and was soon ablaze. It took just twenty minutes to reduce it to a pile of ashes. Kiddle himself only escaped death by leaping through the dining room window.

Colin believed that Kiddle had burned the house down deliberately. Some years later Colin was to write that Kiddle, 'seeing that the writing was on the wall for him, [he was] determined, like Nero, to go out in style' by setting fire to the house. This is certainly at odds with the letter he wrote to Kiddle six months earlier, in which he extolled his virtues after Princess Margaret's visit, confirming that his contract was extended for a further eighteen months. The house insurance had only just been increased from £1,000 to £2,000, 'but this was poor compensation for Kiddle's act of destruction'.

The evidence is certainly stacked against Kiddle. Being Christmas, he had drawn the usual fortnight's wages as well as the extra fortnight's pay which the workers received in lieu of their annual holiday. To these sums were added the takings from the autumn crops of peas and corn and the shop receipts and the petty cash of US$300. All this money supposedly went up in flames. Kiddle arrived in St Vincent in his underclothes saying that he had lost everything in the fire, including of course the money. Later Colin heard that he had a packed suitcase hidden in a field and when he cashed the $200 travelling allowance he took the money in two US$100 bills – hardly the action of a destitute man. At the inquiry a verdict of 'arson by person or persons unknown' was returned, but never 'a word of truth was vouchsafed by his catamites'. An injunction was placed against Kiddle leaving St Vincent as he owed the merchants BWI$3,000. Colin paid them off at 10s. in the pound and Kiddle sailed away to a job with the Forestry Department in Ghana, which did not work out either. What he did do to the good was to find a house at Friendship Bay in Bequia, the island between Mustique and St Vincent, for the former Prime Minister, Sir Anthony Eden, who was married to Colin's great friend, Clarissa Churchill.

Notwithstanding the loss of the Great House, Colin still took Anne, her sister Sarah, and Lady Leicester out to the West Indies. He chartered a ropey old yacht and cruised through the Grenadines. 'Everything at Mustique seemed hopeless. Without the house there was nowhere to sit down, no shade on the beaches and the mosquitoes were omnivorous'. The island had to rely on frequent loans from C. Tennant, Sons & Co. just to keep going and Colin began to think that his venture was, after all, utter folly.

Back home in the summer of 1960, he received a telephone call from John Tysen, the senior partner of Previews, who had originally listed Mustique on their books for the Hazell sisters, who was passing through London. They met and, unparalleled salesman that he was, Tysen persuaded Colin to list Mustique again with Previews. He was confident that he could obtain at least US$1.5 million, which to Colin seemed a terrific sum. The contracts were signed and a cheque for $28,000 for the 2 per cent listing fee handed over. Colin insisted that Tysen actually went to Mustique so that, having seen the island, he would be enthused to find a buyer. Tysen took the money but did not exactly run to Mustique for another eighteen months, and it was another six months after that before a photographer and writer went down to prepare the brochure. The result was splendid: 'Previews presents a Secret Island.' In spite of the great labour, 'produced after a gargantuan period of gestation', no client was forthcoming. Every time he went through New York Colin pestered John Tysen, even suggesting that he form a syndicate to develop Mustique, but still there was not a single spark of interest.

Colin then took the view that he might as well enjoy Mustique while waiting for it to be sold, but he could not enjoy it without a house. On a fleeting visit to St. Vincent he found Percy Simmons, a builder from Kingstown. Percy was unwilling to make the crossing in the chartered cabin cruiser on the Sabbath, but was finally persuaded. Colin then marked out the house he wanted on the site of Fort Liverpool, a hillock overlooking the village and the cotton house, with wonderful views north to Bequia and St Vincent beyond. Colin left the next afternoon and, when he returned four months later on New Year's Eve, there was the house complete. It was an inexplicable miracle, for either everything in the West Indies takes forever to be completed, or it is done in a trice. The house was a triumph and became a second home to Colin, his family and his guests. More importantly, the house changed Colin's perception of Mustique from an expensive, loss-making, white elephant to a place to which he had become passionately attached, with great potential. Gone was the idea of selling Mustique and he started planning for the future. As so often happened in Colin's life, the timing was exactly right for this change of direction.

*Chapter 8*

# OLD PARK FARM

Christopher Glenconner had always planned to retire from C. Tennant, Sons & Co. when he was 65 and had hoped to pass the reins over to Colin. But over the years he became increasingly worried that Colin was not up to the task. Even at the age of 36, married with two young boys, Colin did nothing to dispel his reputation as a socialite. There was much 'gadding' amongst the couple's gilded set of friends. They were constant invitees to the grandest house parties in the land: Colin once boasted that in one year he had stayed in the three longest houses in the country – Wentworth Woodhouse with the Fitzwilliams, Petworth with the Egremonts and Haddon Hall with Lord and Lady John Manners. They were frequent guests at Blenheim, the home of (Bert) Duke of Marlborough, and once every year at Cliveden, the home of Lord Astor in Buckinghamshire (when Harold Macmillan heard that the house was to be turned into a hotel, he responded gloomily: 'but it always was!'). However, they just missed the famous weekend at Cliveden when Stephen Ward and Christine Keeler were staying at Spring Cottage on the estate that triggered the infamous Profumo scandal.

Colin and Anne were always on the move. There were weekends in Ireland with Sir Alfred and Lady Beit at Russborough, home to one of the greatest art collections in private hands, and of course holidays at Holkham and Glen. They were among the first guests to explore the Aga Khan's new resort on Sardinia, the Costa Smeralda, with their lifelong friends, Peter and Claire Ward. The Sardinian holiday was an invaluable experience for Colin to see how one man had transformed a desolate, barren outcrop, albeit with beautiful beaches, into a playground for the rich and famous. In London there were balls galore. They went to Paris for the coming out dance for Joy de Rouvre, the daughter of Colin's friend Brenda Balfour: closer to home they attended a ball at Windsor Castle for Princess Alexandra, then Luton Hoo for the magnificent dance given by Lady Zia Werner.

But life for Colin was very different at the offices of C. Tennant, Sons & Co. His step-mother Elizabeth, Lady Glenconner's view that he 'was never there' rang all too true. Although Christopher did not doubt Colin's ability as a man of business, he certainly questioned his dedication to the family firm. Colin was eventually made Deputy Chairman but the coveted post of Managing Director went to his cousin, Julian Tennant. Colin always maintained that he was an integral part of the firm and he was in the process of reorganising it to bring it up to date with modern practices. But in 1963, when Christopher was 64 years old, he was approached by the global South African mining finance house, (Consolidated) Gold Fields, who had decided that it 'needed an efficient and well-established marketing organisation in Britain and Europe. It therefore took the necessary steps to acquire (for 427,447 ordinary Gold Fields shares and £288,000 in cash) a controlling interest in C. Tennant, Sons and Company, a firm that was well-established in the metal marketing and industrial chemical business.'[xxxiv]

What they eventually bought were three companies, Tennant Trading (a major selling organisation for producers of ferro-alloys), Tennant Guaranty (a highly specialised export finance service) and Tennant Securities (that held a portfolio of investments in mining, mineral processing and industrial companies). For Colin, the sale was a bitter blow. He had long felt that he had been abandoned by his father and felt desperately let down. While Christopher was invited to join the main board of Gold Fields, there was no place there for Colin, or for him to remain with Tennants. Soon after the takeover he suffered a nervous collapse whilst driving to Scotland. He described the sensation as if he were 'dissolving into gold dust'; no doubt that mined by Consolidated Gold Fields. A car was sent to collect him from the motorway and once back in London he began a course of treatment.

Notwithstanding the mental trauma of the loss of C. Tennant, Sons & Co., Colin emerged a very rich man indeed, with well over £1.25 million in cash (at a time when the weekly agricultural wage was £9 10s.). Tennant's Estates (1928) Ltd held shares in the parent company and, with the takeover there was enough money from Gold Fields to pay off the Mustique loans. Colin then proceeded to acquire the remaining shares in

Tennants Estates by buying out his uncles David and Stephen, and receiving his father's holding as a gift. So, with a great deal of money, no employment and all the time in the world at his disposal, Colin turned his attention to Mustique.

When Christopher retired in 1963 he moved to Palaiokastritsa, a magical village to the north-west corner of Corfu where he built a house, and handed over Glen, complete with furniture, pictures and library, to Colin. There were also 10,000 acres, including Black House Farm and a useful grouse moor.

When Charles Tennant took his family away from the foul air and filth he had created in Glasgow to the sylvan valleys of Peeblesshire, he did more than just improve their health as, by the building and furnishing of Glen, he established the Tennant family in the upper echelons of society. In 1853, at the age of 30, he bought the estate, with a modest house nestling in the centre of 3,500 acres of rolling hills and valleys close to the town of Innerleithen – by chance his father had considered buying the same property, but was outbid by his son.

Colin once attended an exhibition at the National Gallery of Scotland, where he found a smaller exhibition dedicated to the architect David Bryce. There he met his friend, the Director of the Gallery, Sir Timothy Clifford, whom he found 'terribly nice, very voluble, frightfully, frightfully clever, but endlessly boring'. The one thing that Tim is definitely not is boring, and the comment says more about Colin than him. Although Colin was clever enough to hold his own in any conversation, he knew how flimsy his disguise was when he encountered academics and academia. But on the wall in the gallery he noticed what he thought was a little watercolour of Glen. It turned out, however, to be an earlier Bryce commission. It would appear that Charles Tennant, on seeing the watercolour or the plans of the house, had said to Bryce: 'I'll have one of those!' So 'one of those' was built for Charles' lasting satisfaction in that it fully expressed his solidarity, wealth and, above all, his whimsical bent. It was right up to the mark and the height of fashion with 'Scots Baronial on the outside and innovative hospitality space on the inside'.[xxxv] Lord Rosebery described Glen to Gladstone as 'the most perfect of all modern houses, architecturally speaking'.

Life at Glen under The Bart was sumptuous with '105 indoor and outdoor staff'.[xxxvi] His wife's great niece, Sophie Bühler, has left a contemporary account of Glen:

It was not a county house it was a Schloss. A fine grey stone castle, pepper pot turrets, high pitched roofs like a French châteaux. All was spick and span, superbly groomed and appointed. The gravel was meticulously combed as the children's curls, the lawns as smoothly ironed as their nightgowns. Only the hills were rugged and unkempt. Everything else was new.[xxxvii]

Bryce returned twenty years later to add a tower to the house:

A disastrous addition which destroyed the otherwise comfortable domestic scale of the original. Who knows what instruction he received from Charles Tennant or, indeed, whether an elderly Bryce was even much involved in the design/execution. What they got was a new, much bigger sitting room, two more comfortable guests rooms (Valley & Honeysuckle) and a very awkward block of stone inserted into the rather traditional open courtyard of the original 'L' plan.[xxxviii]

Along with the alterations to the house came new farm buildings, a kitchen garden, estate cottages and a school.

In 1905, during Eddy Tennant's tenure, there was a serious fire at Glen. The exact cause of the fire was unknown, either a wood beam against a chimney in one of the attics catching fire or an early victim of electrification. Whatever the reason, the slow progress of the flames gave the household two hours to remove the considerable contents to the stables. Robert Lorimer was brought in to restore the house, and to make certain alterations and improvements to the interior. Lorimer's craft additions brought a lightness to the house, not that Eddy really noticed. In his typically boring and laconic fashion, his only reference to the work was a note in his diary that the family had moved back from Kirk House after a two-year absence.

When Christopher inherited the house and estate in 1922, at the age of 22, the Scottish Baronial style, in particular the interiors, was under siege and fast going out of fashion. At the height of the slump in 1932, Christopher put Glen on the market. A brochure was produced but, thankfully for Colin and the rest of the family, no offers were forthcoming. Colin maintained that his father was ashamed of his 'old-fashioned' house and vowed to remodel it. Christopher commissioned an architect 'to make the exterior look more Georgian, or perhaps just less Victorian',[xxxix] but these drastic plans were never carried out. He did, however, attack the interior, consulting Elizabeth's friend, the famous interior decorator, Syrie Maugham for advice. The fine Edwardian moulded ceilings were covered over (fortunately with a suspended ceiling leaving the plasterwork intact); fireplaces were ripped out and replaced with Regency chimney pieces. Everything had to be light and bright, so the hall panelling was ripped out and painted white, as it is enjoyed today, with the light green carpet.

When Colin took over Glen, Scottish Baronial was back in fashion and much to his High Victorian taste, so he set to, removing all his father's alterations and updating the house. While Anne was responsible for the bedrooms, Colin tackled the reception rooms. He began by restoring the moulded plaster ceilings and cornices to their original glory. The Edwardian fireplaces reappeared, old bathrooms were reinstated and a new, though inadequate, oil-fired central heating system was installed. The final touch was the specially woven Tennant tartan carpet in the drawing room, and once again Glen became supremely comfortable, warm to a limited degree, and very elegant. Through Colin, Glen had returned to its original concept, a grand house full of lovely things, made for entertaining on the grand scale as in The Bart's day when, according to his niece Sophie Bühler, 'Money seemed to flow in and out of Glen as easily as the brown burns flowed down the hillside. Zellie [Sophie] had never dreamed of any place where pounds, shillings and pence … did not prove an insuperable object to any projected pleasure scheme'.[xl] She could have equally well have been writing of Colin a hundred years later, except that with him the money was flowing, like the brown burns, downhill with no feeder at the top.

Colin had many recurring themes running through his life, one of which was the Royal Families of Uganda. The association began in 1953 when King Freddie, the *Kabaka* of Buganda, was deposed and came to London. He knew England well, having been to Magdalene College Cambridge (when he ordered a Rolls Royce with the switches and steering wheel turned out of the ivory of an elephant he had shot). From the Officer Training Corps he was commissioned into the Grenadier Guards as an honorary captain. He began his exile staying in Claridges Hotel, then decamped to a flat in Eaton Square. Exiled African potentates, such as King Freddie and Sir Seretse Khama of Bechuanaland Protectorate, the present-day Botswana, were ignored by all but the Victoria League, and there only to shake the white-gloved hand of the President, the Duchess of Roxburgh.

Jeannie Campbell and Colin thought that they deserved better and organised a King's Club whereby they would be entertained. In fact they only managed one dinner given by Ingrid Wyndham, where the guests all fell in love with the hostess, but it did mean that Colin became friends with the *Kabaka*. Oliver Messel, Tony Armstrong-Jones' uncle, painted a fine portrait of King Freddie shortly before he was restored to power in 1955.

At about that time, Colin became involved with Ludovic Kennedy, Tony Essex and Malcolm Muggeridge who, disaffected with the BBC, had broken away from the Corporation. They were joined by rich backers, including Colin, Viscount (Harry) Hambledon and Tom Egerton to form a company called Television Reporters International. Although slightly older, Ludo Kennedy was an old friend of Colin's, who found Ludo 'an outstandingly attractive person. [He had heard that] people used to sit and get into throes of orgasm watching him on television in the early days. He was really the first reporting star'. At an early meeting, when they were throwing around ideas for programmes, Muggeridge came up with the suggestion 'I think that we should make a documentary on the history of fucking, from the earliest days right down to the present times'! The idea was not adopted but they did make several films in Africa for Lew Grade's Associated Television. The one made in Uganda with Colin's introduction was, however, never shown.

One of the first guests to come to Old Park Farm was the beautiful Princess Elizabeth of Toro, with 'the longest neck, supporting an exquisite dead-pan ebony sculpture'. She was the daughter of King George of Toro, one of the four kingdoms to the west of Uganda. She had come to England to attend Sherborne School for Girls, where she was the only black pupil. After only a year she went up to Girton College, Cambridge, to read law. When she came to visit she was a pupil in the barristers' chambers of Dame Joan Vickers. Princess Elizabeth invited Colin and Anne to attend the Independence celebrations in Uganda. Anne was unwell, so Colin went on ahead and stayed with Princess Elizabeth's father, King George, in his residence in Kampala, a modern bungalow on the outskirts of the city. The next day there was a grand lunch at Government House in Entebbe for the Duke and Duchess of Kent given by the Governor General, Sir Walter Coutts (who had formerly been Administrator to St Vincent and the Grenadines) to which King George had been invited. Naturally Colin had no invitation and certainly did not expect to go, but Princess Elizabeth had a plan up the sleeve of her pretty pink Dior dress. As a large open Buick hove into view, she asked Colin if he was ready to leave. King George then manoeuvred his enormous bulk into the back seat and when he was comfortably ensconced she told Colin to climb in beside him. Colin demurred asking:

'What about the Queen?'

'She is tired', said Princess Elizabeth.

'Or Princess Ruth'?

'She is not ready.'

So the Princess pushed Colin into the seat beside her father. When they arrived at Government House, the King, leaning heavily on Colin's shoulder, was greeted by Lady Coutts, 'a rather bossy looking lady'. They swept past Sir Walter into the drawing room, where they were approached by an ADC bearing a large leather folder with the seating cards for lunch. None, of course, was for Colin.

'So who are you?' the ADC inquired officiously.

Recklessly, Colin answered: 'I suppose I am the Queen of Toro' and swept past the livid man deeper into the drawing room, still bearing the King of Toro on his shoulder. He sought refuge by the French windows with the Bishop of Kampala and the Aga Khan, whom he knew slightly from his days in Sardinia. The Duke and Duchess of Kent were marking time on the mezzanine landing upstairs waiting to come down to lunch, when the ADC came up to Colin and informed him that Lady Coutts was in tears as he had ruined her day, while His Excellency demanded that he leave at once – through the back door. So he hurried out through the kitchen and away in the Buick back to the King's bungalow.

Soon afterwards, Anne recovered and joined Colin, who by that time had decamped to the magnificent straw palace of his old friend King Freddie, recently sworn in as the first President of Uganda after Independence. Anne was given her own Lady-in-Waiting, a young woman from the Monkey Tribe. King Freddie told Colin that now he was President 'he had to walk the tightrope of affairs', which is something that he never even considered as king.

From the straw palace, Colin and Anne were driven to King George's palace at Fort Portal, which turned out to be a former mission house, a wide two-storey wooden building, with a long veranda, set on a mound. There King George lived with his very extensive, and extended, family. Colin found the king 'a magnificent, noble person and an affable, commanding autocrat', whose instinctive rule, according to Oliver

Lyttleton, the former Secretary of State for the Colonies, was ably supported by Messers Haig & Haig (whisky).

Every morning Colin would be invited to wallow with the King in the royal bathroom, part of which, an area of about 20 ft by 15 ft, had been blocked off, tiled and filled to a depth of some two feet with water, where they stayed talking until it was time for breakfast. This, like every other meal, consisted of various parts of a goat, prepared in a variety of ways, but always accompanied by a thin gruel of goat that had been masticated to digestibility by the kitchen staff. Custom dictated that everyone, including Princess Elizabeth, sink to their hands and knees when the King entered the room. This was acceptable for her sisters, who were universally dressed in Horrock's printed dresses, but this constant genuflexion laddered Elizabeth's nylon stockings every time she saw her father.

Ever courteous, the King asked his guests what they would like to do. He suggested a tour of his kingdom, starting with a visit to the Mountains of the Moon. Colin's heart leapt at the picture of gorillas and giant spurges in the swirling mist. The King then summoned the entire Cabinet, who came in looking like the seven dwarfs as they entered on their hands and knees. The Prime Minister reminded His Highness that a visit to the Mountains of the Moon was not possible as the pygmies were in revolt. His Highness then suggested some magnificent lakes, starting with Lake George. The Minister of the Interior reminded the King that it was the rainy season and they were therefore inaccessible. So for three days Colin and Anne took long drives through very flat country.

Somewhat ashamed of his actions at Government House Colin had sought the advice of the Duke of Devonshire, whom he knew through his sister, Lady Elizabeth Cavendish. He was there as Under Secretary of State, representing the Government, but certainly did not wish to become involved in the affair and suggested that Colin wrote a letter apologising to Lady Coutts for upsetting her great day. The first-class grovelling letter was duly written. Colin and Anne then returned home, then went on to Glen, where there was a letter from Sir Walter Coutts' ADC with the unlikely name of E. Major. It read: 'Dear Mr Tennant, His Excellency does not accept your apology and under the circumstances he is pleased that you left by the back door.'

It turned out that the whole episode was a ploy of Princess Elizabeth. Her father had renovated his palace to entertain the Duke and Duchess of Kent, but Toro was not on their official tour of Uganda, which upset him greatly. She thought, somewhat naïvely, that if Colin were to talk to the Duke he would persuade him to make a detour to her kingdom. Princess Elizabeth went on to have a remarkable career. While she was practising as a barrister in London, Princess Margaret asked her to model at one of her charity fashion shows. This started her very successful international modelling career. She was intensely political, and became Minister of Foreign Affairs to Idi Amin, the dictator of Uganda. Years later when Colin was watching *Sheena, Queen of the Jungle* on a DVD in St Lucia, he suddenly recognised her playing a 'mystical witch woman'. She has been Uganda's Ambassador to the United States, the Vatican and Germany, followed by her appointment as Uganda's High Commissioner to Nigeria.

As far as King Freddie was concerned his tenure as President was short-lived. In 1966 his Prime Minister, Milton Obote, seized control and attacked the straw palace. When Colin said that it must have been nothing short of a miracle to have escaped the burning compound, with rebel soldiers shooting anyone who moved, he replied calmly, 'Oh no, I simply climbed the wall and hailed a taxi!' King Freddie, with two attendants, travelled incognito through Uganda for six weeks. Colin and Edward Montagu went to see Fred Lee, the Secretary of State for the Colonies, for help in rescuing King Freddie, but the Labour Government was nervous of interfering in Africa in the wake of Rhodesia and UDI. King Freddie, however, managed to cross into Burundi, a Belgian mandate, where Colin chartered a plane from SABENA to bring him back to London. Colin went to meet him at Heathrow Airport amidst great Press interest, and paid for him to stay at the Ritz Hotel.

One evening, when Colin and Anne were just about to leave for dinner, King Freddie telephoned and said that he needed to see him urgently. He seemed so distraught that Colin said he would wait. When he arrived by taxi King Freddie told Colin that he was going to marry. Colin, of course, knew of King Freddie's complicated marital arrangements. Anne had been at school with Elizabeth, the *Nabagereka* (the official wife), who had been imprisoned so that he could live with her sister, Sarah. Being Church of England he had even been to see Geoffrey Fisher, the Archbishop of Canterbury, for permission to marry his wife's sister, but he was refused.

Colin asked him: 'What about the *Nabagereka*?'

'I cannot rely on her', said King Freddie.

'What about Lady Sarah?'

'She's not suitable. I was thinking of someone more suitable.'

'Who?' inquired Colin.

'Your sister Catherine!'

'For once the wind failed' said Colin, recalling the family motto: 'Deus dabit vela' ('God will fill the sails'). King Freddie and Catherine, then just 21 years of age, had met two days before at a lunch at the Ritz, where he had fallen for her charms, her ample bosom and hour-glass waist. (Eric Gairy, the Prime Minister of Grenada, also fell for these charms a decade later. Being rather short-sighted, she tended to peer close into people's faces, which was endearing and perhaps inviting but, more often than not, wrongly interpreted.)

When Colin could no longer afford to keep King Freddie in the Ritz, he sank gradually lower and lower until he was living in a council flat in the East End of London, a far contrast to the autocratic life that he had led as ruler of a nation. Colin saw less and less of him. He drank heavily and one day a member of his entourage gave him a bottle of red wine that had been poisoned. He died soon after. Now that he was dead the Government could recognise him. As an honorary Colonel in the Grenadier Guards he was given a memorial service in the Guards Chapel. His son, Ronald, by Sarah, is the present *Kabaka* of Buganda.

Never one to miss an opportunity where Mustique was concerned, the moment it was announced that The Queen would be going to the West Indies, Colin wrote to The Duke of Edinburgh suggesting that they might like to visit the island during their Caribbean tour. The Duke's Private Secretary, Sir Edward Ford, replied (two months later) that he had put the idea to The Queen who suggested that HMY *Britannia* 'might lie off Moustique [*sic*] on 2nd February when perhaps they could go ashore and have a picnic'.[xli] In fact *Britannia* returned to Britannia Bay on 25 March 1964 and the party came ashore in the Royal Barge. Colin had arranged that the villagers should be the first to greet The Queen and her party. As she stepped ashore she was met by a strange sight. There were the elders sitting, appropriately, on Windsor bentwood chairs, dressed in the apparel that had once belonged to an aged cousin of Colin's, and her husband, who had both recently died. Colin had sent out trunks and trunks of their clothes, sight unseen, to Mustique. It turned out that the entire wardrobes were Edwardian. So there the villagers were seated, completely silent, with the men wearing top hats, morning coats with waistcoats, cravats, stripped trousers, spats, but no shoes. The women were similarly attired in long dresses, ostrich-feathered hats, and dainty parasols. The Queen thought that she had stumbled across some sanctuary of very grand, but impoverished, members of the black aristocracy. They did not rise.

The new manager, Simpson Hamilton, (who had formerly been the tractor driver in Kiddle's time) drove the royal party around the island, ending up at Colin's new house. They then staggered down onto the beach for a barbecue. Lady Jean Rankin, Lady of the Bedchamber, wrote to Colin that The Queen 'was so enchanted by the island that our departure has been postponed and we are having another day here. Your people did magnificently, appearing with the transport and every form of comfort, such as mattresses at Macaroni.' At Macaroni, the most beautiful bay on the windward coast, The Queen, who normally dislikes swimming in the sea, was so moved by the beauty of the place that she jumped into the surf, while The Duke of Edinburgh swam the whole length of the bay. Patrick Plunket, Deputy Master of the Royal Household, painted a vivid picture of them all when he reported that, after the exertions of their swim and picnic lunch, they lay down on their backs on the mattresses where 'they looked as if they'd been gassed like something out of the First World War'.

As *Britannia* steamed out of 'her' bay, The Queen sent a telegram to Colin which read:

'We have just spent two happy days in your beautiful island, and send you and Anne a thousand thanks for an unforgettable experience = Elizabeth R +.'

In 1972, John Lindsay, when Mayor of New York, visited Mustique and was driven round the island by Colin. When they reached Macaroni Bay, Colin recounted the story of The Queen swimming in the sea, whereupon the author, sitting in the back of the jeep, added: 'And we haven't changed the water since'!

# Chapter 9

# 35 TITE STREET

'What do I have to do for you to produce my brochure on Mustique?', Colin asked of John Tysen, President of Previews Inc. in the midst of that 'gargantuan gestation period of inactivity' of 1963. 'Buy your company?' To Tysen such a remark was taken as a challenge rather than a rebuke.

'As it happens', he replied, 'I suppose I *could* let you have Previews!' and through the silver tongue of the consummate salesman Tysen, Colin unwittingly found himself the owner of 85 per cent of the prestigious real estate company. So once again Colin embarked on a new venture, at exactly the right time.

Previews was the brainchild of Douglas L. Ellimam who came up with the idea of simplifying the task of selling property by showing clients films rather than dragging them around each house. He was joined by a few friends who then set up the 'See-it-First Bureau', which changed its name to Previews Inc. in 1933. After seven years of trading, Previews had lost $250,000, but the firm was saved from bankruptcy when they were joined by John Tysen, who suggested that they should charge their clients a registration fee of 1 per cent of the asking price, as opposed to a flat fee of $50. From that moment on, Tysen (and Previews) never looked back as he rose to become President of the grandest real estate brokers in the world, and the most respected realtor in the United States.

Tall and urbane, John Colquhoun Tysen was exactly the kind of man that Colin admired. An American by birth, he was a native of Paris, but English by adoption, being educated at the Roman Catholic public school, Downside, and Cambridge University. With his patrician features and immaculate, Savile Row suit set on a spare frame, he breezed through life with ease. While his aristocratic, cosmopolitan air was enjoyed by most, his charm disarmed all. He was rarely seen without a clove carnation in his buttonhole. John Tysen was a real 'people person' with the knack of being able to sell anything to anybody: as his widow Connie said, 'he could sell the ears off a brass monkey: with John, you didn't even know that you had bought.'

Although he virtually owned Previews Inc. in its entirety, Colin had little or nothing to do with its operation, which remained in the hands of John Tysen, with Ronny Ford – 'a difficult man' – to look after his interests. Bill Craig, a Vice President of Previews, remembers Colin arriving straight from the airport at the offices in New York City in the depths of savage winter, invariably wearing his Caribbean clothes of tell-tale fedora, striped cotton suit, no socks and patent leather shoes. He never carried money and the office boy was sent down to pay off the taxi.

The arrangement whereby Colin owned Previews Inc., with its fourteen offices and large sales staff, was short-lived, as it was soon overtaken by events in the Bahamas. Previews had an office in Nassau, where they had sold a part of Tamarind, a desirable tract of land on Grand Bahama, to a development company owned by Sir Francis Peek. (Sir Francis Peek had been ADC to the Governor of the Bahamas, Sir Charles Dundas, before the Second World War. Dundas handed over to the Duke of Windsor, having succeeded Sir Clifford Bede, father of Colin's first great love, Pandora.) Colin became excited by this operation as he could see that it was far closer to his aims of marketing Mustique, his ultimate goal, than the sale of grand houses throughout the world. He therefore formed a subsidiary, Previews International, with offices in Nassau and London. To Tysen's disappointment, he later sold Previews Inc. on to a consortium from Connecticut, hiving off Previews International for himself. Wearing his Previews International hat, Colin then went to the Grand Bahama Development Company and secured the exclusive agency to market all their properties in England, in particular two of their new developments, Leicester County, 2,167 acres of virgin land 14 miles out of Freeport on a dead straight road, and Buckingham County, roughly half the size, a mile further on. At that time, as indeed today, there was little beyond a few roads dividing up the scrub-covered land into lots of varying sizes. For Colin, this was a challenge he relished. Again, his father insisted that he have the services of his accountant, Ronny Ford to 'look over his shoulder' and that he should take on Bill Hurlock, an American real estate expert, to advise him. It was Hurlock who hired the salesmen, mostly drawn from the upper echelons of English society, not least the likes of Nevill Turner, who was to be associated with Colin, on and off, for the next thirty years.

Nevill was typical of the salesmen employed. He had served in the Welsh Guards and, after Cambridge, went to work for Texaco as an industrial chemist in Trinidad. When living in his home county of Kent and working for ICI (which he hated), one winter's afternoon in 1964 Nevill helped an attractive woman whose red sports car had come off the road in the snow. She was the wife of Bill Hurlock, the Previews realtor, who immediately asked Nevill and his wife for a drink to thank him for his gallantry. Hurlock suggested to Nevill that he would make the most excellent real estate salesman for their new project in the Bahamas. Nevill demurred at the change of career but, as an answer was needed that night, they agreed that if his porch light was on, then he would take up his offer. Nevill decided against the proposal, but inadvertently left the light burning outside. The subsequent meeting with Hurlock was to change his life. Nevill signed on with Previews International the next morning at their offices in Grafton Street in London, and joined the team.

Viscount (Simon) Erleigh, the present Marquess of Reading, was another salesman who joined slightly later in 1965. An Etonian, he had been recruited by John Tysen having left the Queen's Dragoon Guards, followed by a short spell in the City – then a dismal place to work within the confines of the Labour Government. Simon leapt at the chance of something more exciting. He recalled:

> Colin wandered into the office on most days. He acted as a kind of non-executive chairman. But Bill Hurlock, the top-class thrusting American Managing Director, simply could not get to grips with Colin, his mystique, or his body language. Unlike his grip on his sales team which was masterly, he was definitely on the back foot when it came to Colin. And Colin played on this unease. It can only have been irksome for Bill to see how well the others got on with Colin, while he simply could not work him out.[xlii]

Colin was not there to sell, but to enable the sales to happen. Soon after, an advertisement was placed by Previews in *The Times* offering land for sale in Leicester County, Grand Bahama. On the face of it, it appeared an immensely attractive proposition – £710 for a ¾-acre lot that, if desired, could be purchased over a period of five years. Previews promised 'a sound economic base for development' and 'proximity to high-spending tourists', with the 'natural endowment of sun, sand, sea and fresh water' all in a tax-free Freeport. The response to the single advertisement was phenomenal and the sales team criss-crossed Britain signing up clients for land, sight unseen. Such was the demand from the advertisement, and the subsequent mail shot, that Previews chartered a jumbo jet to take prospective clients out to Freeport for a 'free' holiday. These 'punters' were then taken to Leicester County to see the land and several other well-developed parts of the island to show what the virgin land could become, then the salesmen moved in to close the deals. Others went for the better beachfront property at Tamarind.

There were two such sales trips in the mid-1960s, but Colin did not go with either of them.

Although the new developments at Leicester and Buckingham Counties never took off, and the ethics of the sales were certainly questionable, the commission at 28 per cent was substantial. For Colin, the dividend was twofold, for not only did he have Previews International, a ready-made sales agency set up to market Mustique and other developments when the time came, but he also made a great deal of money on commission with which to fund the island until the time was right to launch the sale of land. But as so often in his life, while Colin loved setting up projects and making them work, after they were established, he lost total interest, not caring what subsequently happened to them. Keeping the name Previews International, Colin sold the UK selling rights for the Grand Bahama Development Company to three individuals rather more suited to the Leicester County-type operation. With the commission and the sale of the rights, Colin walked away from the Bahamas with well over £1 million to put into the development of Mustique.

Throughout his life Colin wore controversy round his neck like a talisman. He fed on it daily and relished the effect it had on others. The greater the shock he created, the more he enjoyed it. That is not to say he was consciously perverse, but he merely liked causing a stir. It was only the degree that altered in his desire to be noticed. At one end of the scale it was something quite trivial, like changing into his dinner jacket on the steps of the Tate Gallery in front of the guests arriving to a black tie dinner given by *Hello!* Magazine. Another favourite antic was to change in the aisle of a plane where the hapless passengers not only had to witness a near-naked

Colin but also had to hold various items of his discarded clothing as he dressed for a colder clime. Right at the other end of the scale his shock tactics were major, like the building of his London residence. For this he chose a large house near the Thames Embankment in Chelsea.

The house was important and carried a Grade II listing in the register of Buildings of Architectural and Historic Interest for, in 1877, James McNeil Whistler, 'the most daring painter in England', joined forces with E. W. Godwin, 'the most daring architect'[xliii] to build a house on two plots on the east side of what was to become Tite Street. Whistler encouraged other young men with artistic aspirations to follow and to use Godwin as architect for both house and studio. The migration began with Archibald Stuart-Wortley, a pupil of Millais, who painted 'chocolate box portraits of women', and Carlo Pelligrini, better known by his pseudonym 'Ape', under which he drew cartoons of the great and the good for *Vanity Fair*. They were followed by Frank Miles, who brought his friend, Oscar Wilde, to build houses and studios. In time, Sickert and John Singer Sargent were to live in the street at various times.

Godwin's plans for what was to be known as The White House were submitted to the Metropolitan Board of Works, who disliked the radical design, declaring it a 'dead house'. They objected to the plainness of the front, the lack of ornamentation, and found the 'large roof of green slate broken by a single window'[xliv] objectionable. A compromise was reached whereby the roof was foreshortened with carved panels. No sooner had Whistler moved into his new house than he left, having been bankrupted by his libel action with Ruskin. The house was sold to the art critic, Harry Quilter, who ruined Godwin's design by building up the front wall to create another storey whereby the 'roof by which Whistler and Godwin set such store was quite hidden'. As Mark Girouard pointed out, at that time 'Tite Street was more than it could stomach. Artistically, it made Whistler a bankrupt; architecturally, it emasculated Godwin's designs; morally it sent Miles to a lunatic asylum and Wilde to prison.'

When Colin bought the house for £48,000 in 1963 it was uninhabitable and very run down. It had been his intention to resurrect the house to the original Godwin design, but it had been built with no foundations and was gradually sinking into the Thames mud. Colin regretfully decided that it could not be economically saved and that it should be pulled down and a new house built in its place. Two years passed while planning permission was sought, first to demolish the much-altered listed building, and then to have the radical plans of the architect, Frank Hodge, approved. The outcry by a large and vociferous lobby of conservationists that the demolition of Whistler's house was an act of vandalism, and much more, was dismissed simply by Colin with: 'it was tumbling down and no longer of any architectural interest'. Planning permission was finally granted through a loophole in the planning law and the old house was demolished. The artist Julian Barrow, a long-term resident of the street, recalls a 'demolition party' for charity given by the Tennants to which the guests brought hammers and jemmies to begin its demise. Guests could paint murals wherever they liked, or do as much damage as they wished (so long as they did not set fire to the house), for which they were charged 1 guinea a head, which went to Anne's favourite charity. Over the next three years, a new and gleaming ultra-modern house rose in its place. The dazzling white Portland stone accentuated the clean lines of the building that contained elements of the old, such as the shape and proportions of the fenestration and the double-height triangular bay window.

Like the original, the new house (which cost £35,000 to build) was radical in its design and far ahead of its time. Strangely, both attracted similar reactions. The report of the original White House, whose 'fame and historic interest rests not just on the high quality of the original design, but on the sensation it created. First for its novelty and secondly for its controversy that arose for its alteration so soon after its building',[xlv] could equally have applied to Colin's house, which lasted just twenty years before it, too, was remodelled into a pastiche Queen Anne town house. While Peter Coats, the famous gardening writer, praised it as the best 'private house to be built in London since the War', others were horrified by the structure. Tom Roland of the *Financial Times*, wrote that it was a sad day for Chelsea when the house was built, dismissing it as 'a stark white elephant ... a mid-European monstrosity deserving a place alongside the ugliest office blocks of the Sixties'. The man is entitled to his opinions, but 35 Tite Street was as original as it was innovative as it was extraordinary.

There were many unique details, both inside and out. Colin 'wanted to use contemporary materials, like plastic [for the contemporary mouldings throughout the house], and the champagne Portland stone that was set upright, rather than horizontally, like Peter Jones'. It was a masterpiece. The blue of the cobbles in the area, brought from Brittany, matched the colour of the front door. The sub-marine atmosphere of the octagonal hall was conjured by the art and audacity of the French architect, André Mauny, who was also responsible for the interior of the rest of the house. He created (in the hall) a marble black and white patinated floor that was inspired by pebbles on a beach; the form of the cantilevered staircase came from the inside of a nautilus shell, while the banisters, in the Giacometti style, had the look of seaweed floating upwards. They were made at the Chelsea Forge, the work of the French architect, Chavigne. Even the door furniture was cast in silver in the shape of conical turret shells. Light filtered through the opalescent plastic windows, the work of Chapuis. The dining room was furnished around the quartet of fruity profiles of the four seasons by Achimboldo that had come from the collection of the Winter Queen, while the inspiration of the aubergine silk-covered walls was taken from Zoffany's portrait of Queen Charlotte. The drawing room was equally grand and dominated by the carpet specially woven in Portugal to the design of a scrap of French eighteenth-century embroidered silk, with the walls lined in ivory silk. The moss-green carpet strewn with daisies in Anne's bedroom came from the Aubusson factory in Paris: the tiles for her bathroom were specially made in Holland from an eighteenth-century design in the Rijksmuseum.

The whole house was grand and opulent without being remotely vulgar. Although filled with great treasures and the finest pictures, including the fifteen Lucian Freuds, Colin and Anne had created a home rather than a show house. Their life was rich and glamorous, with a live-in Spanish couple in a self-contained flat at the top of the house to look after them, and a nanny to care for Charlie and Henry in the nursery. There the two boys were joined by another son, Christopher (Anne so hoped for a girl) in April 1968. Another vital addition to the Tennant household at that time was Barbara Barnes, the daughter of a forester at Holkham, who came as nanny to Christopher and was to stay for fourteen years. She had all the attributes of an old-fashioned nanny, combined with compassion and wonderful common sense. Her charges were never idle or bored. Colin always admitted that had she looked after Charles and Henry they would never have gone off the rails.

*Chapter 10*

G

# BOND STREET

An integral part of Colin's aesthetic eye was his personal appearance. He would take an hour each morning preparing his toilet and dressing from a large and extensive wardrobe. Since boyhood, he had always enjoyed clothes, and loved dressing up. Once again his dress was unconventional, not necessarily designed to shock, but at least to be noticed. Tall and lean, he had a model figure, so much so that whatever he wore invariably looked good on him. He also had the *chutzpa* to wear the outrageous. Those conventional clothes that he did own were well made by Savile Row tailors, much in the dictum of Beau Brummell, who declared that 'the well-dressed man was one whose clothes were so perfect that they were not noticed'. But he preferred the more modern tailors, the likes of Tommy Nutter, Mr Fish, and especially Blades, his favourite of all. 'Very tall and very skinny, he [Rupert Lycett Green, the creative partner of Blades] was married to John Betjeman's daughter [Candida] and was charming, quick with a quote and well equipped with enemies.'[xlvi] He and Colin could have been made for each other: the one a rich, ready and receptive client, the other, with his whimsical and inventive style, ready to feed his client's foibles with expert Savile Row tailoring.

Between them, they came up with the most original creations. There was a suit with no pockets 'that caused outrage for weeks', or a shooting suit complete with breeches, waistcoat and Norfolk jacket made up of a patchwork of different tartans – Colin called it the 'gathering of the clans'. There were velvet numbers, mostly for the evenings, including knickerbockers in five different colours. Michael Maxwell-Stuart, a near Scottish neighbour from Traquair, recalls dining one evening at Glen when

Colin rushed up and down stairs manically changing his breeches from one colour to the next. Being nearly bald from a comparatively early age, he invariably wore a hat of some description – having been in the Brigade of Guards he extended their tradition of wearing caps in the Mess by wearing his hat indoors. Herbert Johnson, his favourite hatter, came up with a succession of brightly coloured fedoras. When the author first met Colin in Previews International's offices in Buckingham Gate his jaw literally dropped in amazement. Colin was wearing a purple fedora and matching purple shooting stockings, an oatmeal tweed jacket and breeches, and fringe-tongue brogue shoes that snapped like crocodiles when he walked. Less successful, although greatly to his liking, was his craze for vinyl in which he had several in different colours, complete with jaunty sailor caps. They were extremely hot to wear and Colin fainted several times when wearing them.

A lifelong friend of Colin's was Reinaldo Herrera, a Venezuelan whom Colin had first met in the middle 1950s in Venice, but their paths diverged for a decade until they came together through Princess Margaret and Oliver Messel. Reinaldo was always a great admirer of Colin. As he recalls:

> He had this amazing quality of doing the unexpected. He was never obvious. He once came to stay with us in New York – we had a small house on 54th Street between Madison and Park that was tall and narrow and he slept way upstairs at the very top in one of the children's rooms. He arrived in the middle of winter with a big, empty-looking bag, filled with nothing but a few handkerchiefs, some rope-soled espadrilles, a spare shirt, a pair of green linen trousers and no jacket, as well as the usual large Panama hat. I said 'Can I lend you anything?' 'No', said Colin, 'I will be all right, but I do need to go out and buy a new dinner jacket, so I will also find a coat.' A little later the maid came to Carolina [his wife] in a dreadful state. 'Madam, Mr Tennant has left wearing Miss Patricia's green linen jacket.' Carolina replied 'That's not possible. She's tiny and only 14. That little linen summer jacket couldn't possibly fit him.' So out he went to have lunch with Drue Heinz wearing this child's tight-fitting green linen jacket, espadrilles, and large straw hat! He was frightfully delighted with that. It was typical of Colin.

That evening he showed us the most appalling dinner jacket he had bought from the designer Ted Lapidus that you have ever seen in your life – it would have embarrassed a travelling salesman. It had satin lapels and two satin stripes down each side on the front. Colin asked me what I thought about it and I replied 'I hope that I never think about it again!' Then we went to a dinner given for Princess Margaret and we were all sitting at a table with Elizabeth Taylor who was a great friend of us all. Looking at Colin's ghastly creation she kept saying 'Very strange', and for her to say something was strange – it was very strange indeed!

Added to the many mistakes was the phase of disposable paper knickers, of which Colin was inordinately proud, showing them off to all and sundry. He even swam in the sea in them with the predictable result. Often he would lose a bet on purpose. 'I'll eat my knickers' he would cry, then proceed to consume the mouthfuls of paper pulled from beneath his trousers.

From the moment he bought Mustique, Colin recognised the admirable qualities of Sea Island Cotton, which is so fine, with the feel, and sheen, of silk. In an effort to bolster cotton production in the Grenadines (their only export), Colin went to Judith Heart, the Labour Minister for Overseas Trade and Development, who gave him an introduction to Viyella, the shirt-maker. Sir James Mitchell, the MP for the Grenadines and Minister of Agriculture, came over to London for the meeting, but their entire cotton production was too small for Viyella to take. Colin stepped up the cotton production on Mustique, where Sir James remembers the Cotton House filled to the rafters with lint before being shipped to Kingstown to the Government ginnery. From there it went to Bury in Lancashire to be woven into cloth. Colin was his own best customer. Besides the Sea Island Cotton sheets and pillowcases, he had bolts woven in bright stripes that he sent to Turnbull and Asser to be made up into pyjama-type suits and shirts, which were to become his 'signature' clothes in the West Indies. There were seventeen of them in different colour ways – when a visitor admired one version, complete with matching tie and hatband, Colin replied 'I'm so pleased you like it – I grew it myself!' Once, when going to greet Princess Margaret at the airport on Mustique, he was seen standing up in the back of a Mini-Moke like Hitler reviewing his troops as he did not wish to crease his immaculately pressed suit by sitting down. Sadly the St Vincent ginnery burned down and in the flames went the whole of their cotton industry.

After Colin's love affair with India and self-imposed exile to St Lucia, for the last three decades of his life he adopted long white flowing kurtas and white tight-legged pyjamas with a drawstring, topped by a stylish straw hat that was specially woven for him in Martinique. These became his new signature clothes, for which he became known by tourists and residents alike. His 'best' kurtas had his stylised logo of a baron's coronet surmounting a 'G' in a circle in red – he always hoped that he could brand his name and the logo and that they would be taken up by a major clothing manufacturer on licence, but nothing ever came of the venture.

Living permanently in the West Indies, his wardrobe became seriously depleted. On his many trips home he would resort to the jump-suit given to Upper Class passengers on Virgin Atlantic and a battery-operated hot jerkin against the cold. But his love of the sartorial never left him – in the last decade of his life, when seriously short of money, he bought two unsuitable leather jackets in Venice for 4,000 euros each, which he never wore.

Another exceptional facet of Colin's was his gift for discovery. He was totally brilliant at spotting potential, whether in people, a deserted island, a photographer, or a work of art. His unerring eye for discovering *objets* and artists before they became fashionable, and therefore expensive, kept him afloat financially throughout his life, although of course there were mistakes. Had he not been born to great riches he could have easily made a very decent living as a dealer simply by backing his hunches and his eye. But his temperament was wrong for a professional dealer. He enjoyed the 'thrill of the chase' and acquiring the piece, but once he had it, like a small child with a new toy, he soon tired of it and was indifferent as to its sale, or the price realised.

At the lower end of the scale, he put together collections, for example, of Wemyss Ware, mostly pottery pigs, plates, bowls and vases made in Fife and decorated with roses, clover leaves, thistles and the like. Nothing cost more than a few tens of pounds, but after it was known that The Queen Mother was also a collector, the prices rocketed to hundreds, sometimes thousands. At the other end of the scale, and long before their time, he bought Chinese ceramics, but sold out well before that market really took off.

Spending money was almost like a disease for Colin. He was akin to a child in a sweet shop. If he saw something he liked he simply had to have it, whatever the cost. If there was money in the bank, it was there for spending. Nor would he be put off from buying if the coffers were empty. He lived by the maxim that 'you never regret an extravagance'. He could recognise quality when he saw it, like the wonderful Russian carpet he bought from S. Francis Ltd., the renowned antiques dealer in London's Jermyn Street. One glance assured him that he simply 'had to have it'. It was priced at £220,000. Colin was in funds but could only afford £180,000 which was accepted by Mr Francis. It was very large and had belonged to the 10th Duke of Hamilton which, somehow, Colin discovered. Rushing to his copy of Burke's *Peerage*, Colin found that the Duke had been the British Ambassador to Russia in 1806 where he had either had it made or it was a gift from the Czar. The carpet even went to the 'Lord's Room' at the Jalousie Hotel in St Lucia, but was repatriated and sold back to S. Francis for £200,000. As Mr Francis said 'It is rare to make a profit out of a carpet dealer'. He greatly admired Colin as a man and a client.

Painters like Lucian Freud certainly owed Colin a great debt for his patronage, as did the galleries and salerooms. With time on his hands and money in his pocket, he was a regular buyer of paintings. An early venture was with his cousin, Francis Wyndham, when they sought to corner the market of John Atkinson Grimshaw, whose works Colin had hung in his room at Eton. They placed a small advertisement on the front page of *The Times* asking for information on the artist and received dozens of replies, amongst them one from a vicar in Leeds who, Colin explained

> wrote to say that he had a typical autumn scene by Atkinson Grimshaw which I ultimately bought for £5. It was a smallish picture, rectangular 12 inches by 8 inches. I ended up with thirty paintings for which I never paid more than £30 for any single one. When I married I sold the lot of them for a few hundred pounds. They are now worth upwards of £200,000 each.

Other notable purchases followed. In 1971 he paid just £10,000 for the *Death of the Wild Bull, a Scene in Chillingham Park with Lord Ossulston* in a private sale from Ossulston's direct descendent, Lord Tankerville. One morning in early January, after a fresh fall of snow, he was walking along the street trying to find a taxi to take him to his office. When he reached Smith Street he came across an acquaintance, the art dealer, Peter Johnson, who was clearing the snow off his Austin Healey. Colin asked for a lift. 'Only if you come and see a picture I have upstairs. It has been crated up since 1937 in Northumberland',[xlvii] was Peter's reply. It was a fine oil painting by Sir Edward Landseer of an enormous white bull of the Chillingham herd, thought to be the last of the indigenous wild cattle that had originally roamed the Caledonian forests of Britain. Colin bought it instantly. Like many of his clever purchases, it was sold for a large profit at £132,000 when money was tight in the 1990s. It later changed hands again for over £1.25 million.

Inevitably, with so much buying, some deals went awry. Colin bought a watercolour, *The Horse Chestnut*, by 'Samuel Palmer' from the Leger Gallery. When he saw one similar at the Ashmolean Museum in Oxford but 'nicer' than his, he immediately sold his version at Sotheby's, where it made £15,000. The purchaser discovered it to be a forgery. The trail led straight back to the arch-forger Tom Keating through his erstwhile girlfriend, Jane Kelly. Both had gone to ground, leaving Sotheby's 'holding the baby'.

Colin never minded passing on his treasures. As he explained: 'I am by nature a patron-cum-dealer. The Tennant in me is always ready to do a deal. Patrons never do, they just store things endlessly in the attics. I am not sentimental in selling anything, because I have experienced it and personally had my fill of it so cannot experience any more.' He was particularly scornful of collectors. Once, at a dinner in New York and bored by his fellow guests bragging about their own collections, he was asked what he collected. 'Dust', replied Colin. 'I have the finest collection of dust from the fourteenth to the nineteenth centuries!' His fellow diners believed him.

Colin admitted that he never wanted to see another Old Master. 'We share a longing to get away from European civilisation', he admitted. 'I have seen as many Old Masters as I need to. Most of the pictures that I have owned and sold are etched in my memory. I can see Constable's *Whitehall Stairs*, now hanging in the Tate, just by closing my eyes.' The greater part of The Bart's collection was sold by Colin's father soon after he inherited in the 1920s, but Colin consigned almost as much to the sale rooms on the excuse that, through a loophole in the law, death duties would be paid on the 1922 values as opposed to the sale value sixty years on.

There was a period in Colin's later life when he said that he had never made a mistake. But during the months of inactivity in St Lucia he had plenty of time to reflect on, and regret, his past actions. As explained earlier, when the estates in Trinidad were sold the oil rights were retained. When oil was finally discovered Colin received around £20,000 a year in royalties, tax free, so long as it was not repatriated to him in England. The money was quickly hoovered up by Mustique and, in 1967, it was still a negligible amount in Colin's book. Having engineered the royalties to be counted as capital in Trinidad, and therefore free of tax, all was well until Trinidad imposed a 60 per cent capital gains tax. Colin, not really needing the money and peeved at the change in the law, sold the leases in 1973. Had he kept them he would have been receiving an income of £1.5 million a year at the time of his death in 2010.

*Chapter 11*

# FORT LIVERPOOL

Throughout the late 1960s Colin's life was consumed by Mustique. It provided a rudder in an otherwise hedonistic life. He visited the island more and more and, with Cardinal Simon to cook and May Lewis to keep house, he was able to entertain. To one memorable house party in the early 1960s he invited Michael Astor (who had married the exquisite Pandora Clifford), Anne's closest friend Margaret Vyner and her husband Henry, and his cousin, Ingrid Guinness née Wyndham. Ingrid, who had fallen for Paul Channon, the Member of Parliament for Southend, spent an agonising fortnight wondering if he was trying to contact her, there being no form of communication between Mustique and the outside world. The distance apparently concentrated Paul's mind as he proposed to her at Heathrow on her return. Mustique became a regular feature, too, for a three-month summer holiday for the whole family. Just as Colin's friends came from the village when he was a boy at Glen, so Charlie and Henry's friends were drawn from their contemporaries in Endeavour Village.

In the summer of 1967 Patrick Lichfield (the Earl of Lichfield) was sent out by Jocelyn Stevens, the owner and editor of *Queen*, to photograph Colin, Anne and the island. In the flummery article that accompanied the photographs Colin, for the first time, was able to tell the readers of the society magazine of his visions for the development of Mustique. Soon afterwards, Patrick's great friend from Harrow, the Hon. Brian Alexander, came into Colin's life. Brian, the younger son of Field Marshal Earl Alexander of Tunis, was working in the hotels division of the Rank Organisation, having left the Irish Guards after a short service commission. He met Colin and Anne staying in the same house party given by Patrick

Plunket at his home in Kent. Later, in his speech at the dinner to mark Colin's eightieth birthday, Brian recalled the meeting (and his amazement at Colin's white vinyl suit and sailor cap), and how the meeting had changed his life. Colin had recently set up the offices of Previews International in Buckingham Gate with a secretary, Ruth Thompson, and an accountant, both of whom had worked for him before at C. Tennant, Sons & Co. Colin was ruthless when dealing with his staff. One day he came back from lunch and asked her to book him a first class rail ticket.

'Where to Mr Tennant?' she inquired.

Colin exploded 'Don't be so impertinent. How dare you pry into my private life', he shouted.

Ever foresighted, Colin asked Brian to join the team, and he accepted at once. One of Colin's many talents was to surround himself with people on whom he could rely implicitly. He engendered great loyalty and made working for him so entertaining that the downsides, like the frequent short-lived explosions, just became an irritating part of the job. At that time Previews International was still a real estate sales company, marketing odd pieces of land in the Tamarind development in the Bahamas, but not long after Brian joined, the sales side was dropped while he and Colin concentrated on setting up Mustique.

The first task was the formation of the Mustique Company. Colin had approached his old friend from Eton and Oxford, Hugo Money-Coutts, and invited him to become his partner and to invest in Mustique. Hugo was the heir to the ancient barony of Latymer, to which he succeeded as the 8th Baron in 1987. Tall, urbane, with patrician looks, he was a real Renaissance man with encyclopaedic knowledge about practically everything, particularly the sciences. He had an acute financial brain and, had he stayed in the City, would undoubtedly have headed up some great fiscal institution. His sporting prowess was legion: as an amateur he was first to cross the finishing line in the Monte Carlo Rally and sixth overall after the special stages; he represented Britain in the Cresta Run, coming second, and drove a Rover saloon car from Cape Town to Cairo in the early 1950s. As a gardener he combined knowledge with his mountaineering skills, once adding to his specimen collection of daphnes by climbing a mountain in Switzerland to gather some seeds from the summit.

Yet again Colin's timing was right, as Hugo's life had altered dramatically. Some years earlier, Hugo, a married man with three small children, had fallen in love with his wife's cousin, Jinty Calvert, and she with him, while still at school. They secretly planned to run away together sometime in the future. Hugo commissioned a boatyard in Fife to build him a ketch, the *Heliousa*, the design being based on a sturdy fishing boat, in readiness for their flight. When the time came a few years later, Jinty left her studies at the Courtauld Institute (she was a protégée of Anthony Blunt), abandoned her modelling career, and sailed off into the sunset with Hugo. Hugo had left a note for his wife, propped up against the electric toaster, telling her that he was leaving her and their children. That same morning, his secretary at Robert Fleming, the merchant bank where he had been instrumental in setting up the first unit trust, Save and Prosper, delivered to his Chairman his letter of resignation that she had found propped up on her typewriter. The storms the couple encountered in the oceans on their way to Australia were nothing compared to the ones they left raging at home.

On the birth of their son, Henry, they returned to Mallorca where Hugo set up a successful nursery garden. There, Colin tracked him down and invited him to join him in Mustique. He was an admirable choice. Complete opposites, Colin and Hugo initially worked well together, for while Hugo was a xenophobe and relished the idea of living on a desert island (less so Jinty, by then his wife), Colin was extrovert and lived to entertain. On the formation of the Mustique Company Hugo had 10 per cent of the shares along with Colin's house on Fort Liverpool surrounded by 4 acres. The other investor was Gerald Ward. However, when Hugo and Jinty Money-Coutts moved into the house, not unnaturally the villagers thought that their name was Mr and Mrs 'Manicou', like the small indigenous possum (*Didelphimorphia*) they knew so well on the island.

With the 'Manicous' in residence, and Colin and Brian in London, the development of Mustique finally moved forward. They began with the Mustique Ordinance, the agreement with the Government of St Vincent. From his time in the Bahamas, Colin was familiar with the Hawksbill Creek Agreement, whereby the Grand Bahama Port Authority (GBPA) was granted a generous tax-free holiday in return for an annual sum. Colin charged David Wilson, a solicitor who had worked for Wallace Groves, the founder of the GBPA, to draft something similar between Mustique and the Government of St Vincent. This was then presented to James Mitchell, the Member of Parliament for the Grenadines and Minister of Trade, Agriculture and Tourism. Eventually agreement was reached and the Mustique Ordinance was given assent by the Legislative Council in April

1969. In return for a mere BWI$50,000 (roughly £10,000) per annum Mustique was given virtual autonomy whereby they were free of all taxes, including import duty, on all income for twenty years. In return, Mustique was expected to provide an 'adequate medical dispensary and primary educational facilities' along with accommodation for all migrant workers from St Vincent.

From the very outset, Colin had known how he wanted to kick off the development in Mustique, and in the ten years before the formation of the Mustique Company, he worked slowly and steadily towards his goal. It was clear that the village needed to be moved from Endeavour Point as it occupied the best site on the island. As the houses were in a dreadful state and virtually uninhabitable, Colin's task was made easier. He chose another place, above Walkers Bay, with equally commanding views of Bequia and St Vincent, where he built ten three-bedroom houses to his own design, one for each remaining family, and two bunk houses for the bachelors. There was a new school, and also new houses for Doreen Simon, the schoolmistress, Simpson Hamilton, the overseer, and one for his assistant, Cleeve Thomas. To clear the land on Endeavour Point he grew a crop of Sea Island Cotton before having it surveyed and divided into lots. The vast cotton house was designated to become a hotel and the focal point of the first phase.

But clearly, a comprehensive development plan was required for the whole island: not only was it required by the St Vincent Government under the Mustique Ordinance, it was also, naturally, essential for Colin to know where he were going. For this he needed outside help. Colin had formerly owned Petite de Maddalena, a small island off Sardinia. He had been impressed by the architecture of the Costa Smerelda, and in particular the Hotel Romanzzino in Porto Cervo, and he tracked down the architect – the 'famed Italian Michele Busiri Vici, considered the father of Mediterranean architecture'. Michele, who was also responsible for much of the overall planning of the development and of many of the villas, was invited to advise on Mustique.

Colin turned up at the Busuri Vici offices in Rome armed with maps, surveys and photographs of Mustique. From these Michele and his son, Giancarlo, worked out an overall development plan, and came up with the designs for some sample three- and four-bedroom villas, the airport complex and the Cotton House Hotel. The designs were sympathetic to the island, Michele having made a comprehensive study of Caribbean architecture. Michele and his assistant then flew first class to Barbados and stayed at the Sandy Lane Hotel for a few days to recover, before flying on to Mustique. Later his son, Giancarlo, and Leopoldo Mastrella went back for another visit, where they stayed in Colin's house and, according to Giancarlo, they drank crisp white wines from the Rhône. Their report and designs were comprehensive, but for some reason Colin chose to dismiss them out of hand, even though they were working to his brief. The Busuri Vicis were paid off, eventually, and vilified by Colin, who made the excuse that he could not speak Italian and, as neither Michele nor Giancarlo had mastered English properly, he could not understand them. The final straw was the first class travel.

While the strategic planning was going ahead, there was still plenty to do with the infrastructure. Hugo, intensely practical, understood what needed to be done and how best to achieve it. He addressed the most pressing problem of water by installing a 10,000-gallon black blancmange of a rubber water bag that was fed from a newly constructed dam. A plumber from St Vincent, known as 'Pipeman', was employed to mastermind the scheme. When the rains came the new dam filled up, but Pipeman had plumbed the filter in the wrong way round and filled the bag with heavily silted water, which rendered it virtually unusable.

Desert islands, by definition, are difficult to access. Up to then the only way on or off the island was by *Whistler*, the local schooner. She had been built in Rhode Island in 1900 for a couple who planned to sail around the world but abandoned their plans once they reached the Grenadines. For years she plied the islands, their only link with the outside world. Bob Dylan, the American singer, was so impressed by her that he had a replica, *Water Pearl*, built on the beach in Bequia as his private yacht. Clearly, this erratic transport was insufficient for the major development and again Hugo addressed the problem in his dashing, inimitable style. He and Jinty flew up to Miami where he enrolled in a flying course at Opa Locka. In ten days he had clocked up forty-five hours of flying time, qualified as a private pilot, and bought a small, second-hand Cessna 172 four-seater, single-engine, high fix-winged aeroplane for US $4,000. He then island-hopped back to Mustique, a distance of 1,650 miles, mostly over water, and landed on the cricket pitch below his house. It was an extraordinary feat although terrifying for his passenger. Jinty, highly strung, never liked flying with her husband and always travelled with her foot in the open door and, on long journeys, was armed with a bottle of Gordon's gin. When Colin was forced to fly with Hugo he took a snorkel and mask, believing that he could swim further wearing them if they ditched in the water. He extended this eccentricity to commercial transatlantic flights. If it was not scary enough flying with Hugo anyway, he was not above adding to his passengers' acute fear by turning off the engine mid-flight and gliding for a mile or two.

*Chapter 12*

G

# SS ANTILLES

Essential to the operation was, of course, a competent builder. Like Kiddle, who appeared out of the blue when Colin first bought Mustique, so Arne Hasselqvist appeared, with the right credentials, in the right place, at the right time, the right man for the job. Arne had been a construction engineer, married to his childhood sweetheart, Anita, and lived in Sweden. In their late twenties with typical Nordic looks – blond, blue-eyed, and fit – they were living a self-satisfied, middle-class life with a mortgage. But they were bored. One of Arne's school friends, Bosse, was a seaman and yacht skipper who had travelled the world and occasionally sent them a postcard of some exotic place.

Eventually, the restrictions of Sweden and punitive tax were too much for the Hasselqvists, and they decided to leave their home country and start a new life, preferably somewhere warmer. They sold everything they owned, house, car, furniture and, armed with their entire wealth in cash, moved into a hotel where they threw the notes around the room laughing hysterically. From that moment on there was no turning back. They travelled along the north coast of South America and then headed north into the Caribbean. When they reached St Vincent they were advised to take the mail boat, *Whistler*, through the Grenadines. After Bequia and Canouan, they reached Union Island, where they heard that an American had just leased the tiny Palm Island from the Government. They crossed the 2-mile sound to see it. They had found what they had left Sweden for – a deserted tropical paradise. Arne bought the hilltop site in exchange for US$2,000 and the promise to design the new hotel for the owner, John Caldwell. It was a Robinson Crusoe life for a whole year – sometimes, during the hurricane season, the mosquitoes and the sand flies were so bad they had to remain in the sea for hours to avoid being eaten alive. Slowly,

Arne built up an efficient and loyal workforce to help build his house and the hotel. Soon after its completion, the new owner of the nearby Petite St Vincent arrived on a charter yacht and admired what Arne had achieved, and immediately engaged him to mastermind the design and building of a hotel and cottages on his island.

Although close to Palm Island, Arne spent much of his time working on Petite St Vincent, leaving his wife quite alone. When Anita was eight months pregnant, however, Arne went to St Vincent to arrange for her to stay with a doctor for her last month and to have the baby there. Alone on the island, with no telephone, no radio, nobody, Anita went into labour a month early. She made it to the jetty and rowed herself the 2 miles to Union Island against the current. There she was taken to the local guest house where, early the next morning, she gave birth to her daughter, Petronella. The Hasselqvists were certainly made of stern stuff.

Soon after this traumatic event, Hugo flew down to Palm Island to see Arne. The development of Petite St Vincent was coming to an end and Hugo's offer to start afresh in the emerging Mustique was too good an opportunity to pass up. So, with Anita and Petronella, Arne moved to Mustique to found The Mustique Construction Company. Colin realised that someone like Arne was essential to his operation, and financed the company, taking a 40 per cent share. Many years and fierce battles later, Arne said he was leaving after one spectacularly bad fight, and drove his family to the airstrip. Colin realised what he had done, chased after him, and gave him his shareholding to keep him on the island.

After the departure of Michele and Giancarlo Busuri Vici, Mustique still needed a development plan and their replacement came from an unusual quarter: Kensington Palace. While the marriage of Princess Margaret and Tony Snowdon survived, Colin and Anne saw little of them as they took up with a more Bohemian media set of Tony's friends. Since the day of their wedding Tony had made no pretence of liking Colin. Colin, on the other hand, was ambivalent towards him, and made a point of being pleasant to him whenever they met, which seemed to irritate Tony further. Years later, in St Lucia, reflecting on the Snowdon marriage, Colin wrote:

Tony had great charm and presence of mind and could lead any girl up the garden path ...

Meanwhile PM [Princess Margaret] in full peep-toe and headscarf, striding out across the lawn, would come across mistletoe, and later love-lies-bleeding.

Once the garden door was opened, however (by Lady Elizabeth Cavendish) and PM had stepped out into the sunlight, Anne and I were to see nothing of her and T[ony] for several years: thereupon she was led, like Alice in Wonderland, through a maze of unlikely encounters, until tumbling back into the drawing room at KP [Kensington Palace], crumpled and forlorn.

I was sorry T could not bear me, because he was perfect for PM. An occasional drop of his (agonism) Angostura into our gin fizz would have jazzed up our *Jolies Eaux* [Princess Margaret's house on Mustique].

But there was no placating Tony. As mentioned earlier, he was unhappy that he thought, unjustly, that the wedding present of the Mustique land was for Princess Margaret alone, and he accused Colin of using her to publicise the island. Colin bridled at the suggestion. 'She is just a friend', he riposted. 'I gave her a wedding present. It wasn't premeditated, that's why it is such a success. If she hadn't known or trusted me, she never would have accepted it.' Not everyone agreed with him.

After the Snowdon marriage was severely dented, Princess Margaret took up again with old friends, in particular Colin and Anne. Dining one night they were discussing the progress of Mustique and Colin relayed the Busiri Vici fiasco and how he was looking for a replacement architect. Princess Margaret asked Colin if her wedding present was for real and if it was, whether it also included a house. Colin was caught on the back foot, but graciously said that of course it did. She then invited herself to stay on Mustique in early 1969, but Anne reminded her that the only house, by now owned by Hugo Money-Coutts, was still primitive in the extreme. Electricity was provided by an intermittent generator: the water was coloured orange from the roof shingles and, although there was a single shower, there was no hot water. Undaunted Princess Margaret came, without Tony, and had a blissful time. Apart from the locals, the place was, of course, completely deserted. Life was gloriously relaxed, simple and far removed from the mounting cares at home – as indeed Mustique was to become for virtually the rest of her life. Colin was at his witty and charming best, to which she, a marvellous conversationalist when with him, responded. 'Her voice, which I never heard raised', he recalled, 'had the clear, bell-like, unhurried BBC announcement of the '30s, and everything was beautifully expressed'.

During her visit Princess Margaret inspected her land again. Wearing one of the famous striped pyjama suits against the mosquitoes and scrub, she advanced to Gellizeau, where Colin had put in stakes to mark out the land. When Colin was not looking, Princess Margaret pulled the stakes up, and hammered them in further up the promontory, giving herself more land. Colin caught her at it, and put the stakes back where they were. The charade went on: the stakes danced back and forth until eventually a compromise was reached, and her 10-acre lot was settled.

Princess Margaret had also suggested to Colin that she wanted Tony's uncle, Oliver Messel, to design her house. She had stayed with him at Maddox, his house in Barbados, and had seen the magic he had woven for himself and for other clients on the island, both with renovations and new-builds. She thought that, with Oliver involved, Tony might take more interest in the house. Colin instantly saw the brilliance of the idea of harnessing Oliver's skill, not only for Princess Margaret's house but for all subsequent houses on the island, and immediately invited himself and Anne to stay on their way back to London the following week.

Colin had, of course, known and admired Oliver's work in the theatre, where he had been at the top of his profession for three decades. After Eton and the Slade School of Fine Art, Oliver launched himself as a portrait painter before being commissioned to make the masks for a Diaghilev ballet. From there he designed sets for C.B. Cochran reviews in the 1920s and 30s, moving on to Broadway shows, films and finally the costumes and sets for the Royal Ballet at Covent Garden. In addition he had carried out some exceptional commissions for the Dorchester Hotel, where he created the Oliver Messel Suite, and also Rayne's shoe shop in Bond Street and the Bath Assembly Rooms. There seemed no end to his talent and diversity. As a man, Oliver was:

> charming, hospitable, the host of spectacular parties. He was short and immaculately dressed, with dark hair, sparkling eyes, and an elf-like smile that was a lifelong characteristic. He giggled a great deal and could cry at will – an extrovert, emotional quality that had its dark side, when he could be angry, moody, temperamental, and the author of sudden, vehement letters.[xlviii]

Colin took to Oliver and asked him to come to Mustique, where he commissioned him to turn the cotton house into a hotel and to design two 'cottages', each with four rooms. He was so excited about Oliver's ideas and sketches that he gave him the brief to design all future houses *and* to draw up a development plan for the whole island. Oliver was enchanted with the proposal and came up with such ideas as a Mediterranean fishing village at Britannia Bay and a yacht marina around the lagoon, based on the harbour at Mahon on the island of Minorca in the eighteenth century. Nothing came of these plans but, over the next decade, Oliver did design thirty houses for various Mustique clients, of which fifteen were actually built. Oliver's contribution to Mustique cannot be understated. Coupled with Colin's great vision, Hugo's practicality, and Arne's building ability, Oliver put his own unique stamp on the island that has lasted to this day.

The Cotton House was nothing less than a triumph for Colin and Oliver. From his years in the West Indies Oliver understood the need for shade and the natural flow of air through a building. To achieve this he built wide verandas and made doorways, with louvred doors, along each side. The roof was raised with a steep pitch – the whole room was spacious, in perfect proportion, and very pretty. He had the sofas and chairs made and upholstered in hand-blocked blue and white linen. Oliver had furnished the verandas with his iron tables and chairs painted in his trademark green – now available commercially and known as 'Messel' or 'Mustique Green'.

The rest of the interior of the Cotton House was taken over by Colin, who had overdosed on his favourite pastime, the buying of decorative antiques. Crates and crates arrived with furniture and embellishments – a large case of stuffed tropical birds on a stand, vast brass-bound trunks, a narwhal tusk, yards of faux leather-bound books that were actually Huntley and Palmer biscuit tins, shell mirrors, and a font made from a giant clam from Anthony Redmile. Oliver was disappointed that Colin had taken over 'his' interior, but he cannot have failed to be impressed by the result. It was once described by *Paris Match* as '*une maison anglaise, tres rafinée et bien cosie!*'

When Princess Margaret returned the following year, 1970, the Cotton House and two guest cottages were only just ready. She recalled that there was 'one, naked light bulb on the floor' as the electricity had only just been installed. 'Nothing worked. No telephone and the power went on and off at random – mostly off. We didn't care. It was a getaway, a back eddy'.[xlix]

Like the burns at Glen, the money was swiftly flowing just one way. The original investment of the other shareholders, along with the £1 million from the Bahamas, was being used up at an alarming rate, mostly going to Arne Hasselqvist and the Mustique Construction Company who, if not exactly moving mountains with his new bulldozer and 150-strong workforce, was at least constructing roads and an airstrip. As so often happened on Mustique, people just turned up. One day a yacht anchored in Britannia Bay and an American couple, Fred and Susie Harris, with their Australian friend, Rick Brammell, came ashore and were soon employed – Fred with Previews, Susie by the Mustique Company and Rick with the Mustique Construction Company, with responsibility for the roads. Nobody's life was easy then. In his speech at his party celebrating his twenty-five years in the Caribbean, Arne recalled the real pioneer days, and described the occasion when Fred was 'showing land to a couple of visitors (the first possible buyers) and was fifteen minutes late bringing the only working car on the island back to Colin. When Fred eventually turned up, Colin beat on the bonnet with his stick and yelled at the visitors to get out. They did not buy land.'[1]

But the haemorrhaging of money was temporarily staunched with the early land sales. Colin had become a close friend of Paul Channon, who had married Ingrid, and through them had met Lady Honor Svejdar, daughter of the 2nd Earl of Iveagh and Paul's mother. As Honor Guinness (they were the brewing family, as opposed to bankers: draught not overdraft) she had married 'Chips' Channon, the great social commentator. After their divorce she married a Czechoslovakian pilot, Frankie Svejdar, with whom she lived throughout the Second World War in a single room in Claridges Hotel. Having reached 60 years of age, Honor had decided that their yacht, *Clonsilla*, was too great a responsibility and expense and decided to come ashore and invest in Mustique. As Colin's original client, she was given first choice of Endeavour Point, where she naturally chose the two best plots with their own private beach which was named Honor Bay after her. Buying two plots, for £100,000, she was committed to building two houses that had to be designed by Oliver. She was followed by Michael and Lorelei Robinson, large land owners in Northamptonshire. Michael had farmed pyrethrum in Kenya, and when he sold up to come home he wanted a safe place in the sun. Many sales came from yachts, as with Serge Coutinot, who arrived on his schooner, *Thamila*, fell in love with Mustique, and bought a single lot. The financier Charles Gordon arrived on *Sea Star*, the yacht he had chartered from Nelson Rockefeller. He was married to the prima ballerina, Nadia Nerina, who was close to the balletomane Princess Margaret.

Oliver, who charged £1,000 for the design of the house and the overseeing of its construction, was delighted with the rich mix of nationalities of those initial clients – Irish, Czech, French, English and South African. But, in the early months of 1970, the realisation of their dream houses was still far in the future.

As Colin knew only too well, the presence of Princess Margaret on the island was certain to create interest. He was approached by Yorkshire Television to appear in Alan Whicker's documentary series, *The World of Whicker*. The eventual film was shown nationwide on ITV at prime time and was generally well received and reviewed. In a marvellous scene in the village, Colin and Whicker approached one of the old ladies, Tilly, who was standing by a cow. Colin graciously raising his hat asked her:

'Is that your cow, Tilly?'

'No, Mr Tennants'.

The producer told her that, although it was not her cow, she has to say 'Yes'. After three takes, during which Tilly resolutely denied ownership (it belonged to Hubert Trimmingham, whose father was one of the last slaves to be born on Mustique) they ran with her negative answer.

'Do you have any animals?' asks Colin.

'I had chickens', says Tilly, 'but they all die.'

'How did they die?'

'They died of the giddy head!'

The documentary was subsequently called *A Giddy Head in Paradise* – an apt title. In one classic scene, Alan Whicker is interviewing Colin. The rain is sheeting down and Colin's shoes are filling up with water as they stand in a muddy pool. Whicker says to him: 'We are drenched, eaten alive by mosquitoes. We have little chance of getting back to the hotel through the mud. How on earth can you call this paradise?' To which Colin simply replied 'You just wait and see'. And he was right.

On Mustique Colin was in his element, having the most wonderful time doing what he did best, planning, selling, spending money and generally organising everybody and everything. Above all, he made sure that everyone was having a perfectly lovely time. At last he had a proper role in life of his own making. Back home, the gadding continued. There were the usual jolly house parties at Glen in August and at Christmas. Tite Street was operating at full swing. Then, in November that year, Anne at last had the daughter she longed for – though not one but two. The twins were christened Amy and May (Colin said that he was pleased that they were not triplets, as the third one would have had to have been called 'Yam'). There were six godparents apiece – Princess Margaret standing sponsor for May.

A very early victim of the breathalyser (the Northamptonshire Police had caught him lying, leopard-like, on a branch above his crashed MGB) the author had exiled himself from England for a year. On his return in December 1970 he was casting around for a job as a land agent when he heard that Colin was looking for an assistant to go out to Mustique for six months. He was interviewed by Brian, who had rattled off a stream of relevant questions when Colin appeared in the doorway. They were introduced and Colin said that he was also looking for an electrician: 'Possibly Lord Finchley would do'? The author replied that he was a very bad choice, and anyway he was dead, for:

> *Lord Finchley tried to mend the Electric Light*
> *Himself. It struck him dead: And serve him right!*
> *It is the business of the wealthy man*
> *To give employment to the artisan.*

Colin immediately told Brian that the author was to be employed – clearly anyone who knew about Lord Finchley had to be acceptable. On 7 December 1971 he and Colin's first cousins, Patricia and Liz Paget, flew out to Mustique.

Two days later, Colin was woken at 3 o'clock in the morning with a call from the *Daily Mirror*. They had heard that the French liner, the S.S. *Antilles*, had gone aground off Mustique and had telephoned Hugo for verification. Ever mindful of the cost of transatlantic calls, he made them bring Colin into the telephone loop as he described the extraordinary happenings of the evening before. Flying back from St Vincent, Hugo saw the great white liner sailing up the east coast of the island and, to his horror, saw her turn in between the Pillories, three small islands about half a mile from the shore. Hugo tried to warn her off by flying low over her, wiggling his wings. He radioed Arnos Vale, the airport at St Vincent, who immediately contacted Trinidad, who contacted the *Antilles* saying that she was about to hit a reef, but by the time the message reached the radio officer, she was already fast aground. The parallels between the grounding of the *Antilles* and the *Costa Concordia* off the Tuscan island of Giglio in 2012 are numerous: both ship's captains said that they were following orders to go close to islands to give the passengers a better view, and when both ships struck they did not take the passengers off immediately. Worse still, both captains left their stricken ships, the French captain going with the rest of the officers in the only motorised lifeboat to Bequia. There he was collected by helicopter and taken to Martinique, and thence to France. (Both captains blamed faulty charts.)

Jinty and the author witnessed the whole sickening scene from North Point and, having collected Hugo, went down to Hugo's yacht *Heliousa*. Circling the stricken liner, at dusk they saw a sheet of flame shooting out of the funnel as the ship caught fire. Only after it was dark were the passengers told to abandon ship and take to the lifeboats. These were a push-me-pull-you affair, the mechanism painted solid, and had it not been for *Heliousa*, the charter yacht *Lincoln* and a cabin cruiser that happened to be in the bay at the time to tow the lifeboats and rafts into Mustique, they would all have drifted off towards Central America. The 1,000 passengers and crew came ashore and were bedded down in the Cotton House, Lovell Village and Tennant's Tenements (the collection of primitive bamboo huts occupied by the European staff), only to be woken at midnight and taken to the jetty. There they were picked up by the tenders to the Cunard liner, *Queen Elizabeth II* and taken on to Barbados. The *Antilles* burned for eight weeks.

Colin arrived the next day to assess the situation. Clearly the *Antilles* was going nowhere and would become an eyesore (which is what happened). Then followed a cat and mouse game with the French. Believing there was a fortune to be made out of scrap, Colin decided to claim the burning wreck for Mustique. *Heliousa* towed out a small fishing boat carrying Simpson Hamilton and Cleve Thomas, who then rowed to the side of the ship, on which Simpson painted a large 'M' (in Mustique green, of course). As the current carried them down, Simpson was about to paint the 'U' to the left of the 'M', when Cleve was exhorted to row frantically against the stiff current so that MUSTIQUE was finally achieved the right way round. Colin was photographed claiming the wreck. The French retaliated by dropping a man on the stern of the ship by helicopter and raising the Tricolore. Hugo went out and removed it. Colin repeated his claim, to be met with the headline in *La Monde, Qui est cette homme Colin Tennant, est-il un autre Sam Lord?* (Sam Lord was a notorious wrecker on Barbados, who used false lights to lure ships on to a reef.) In the end, the French Government won by telling the Premier of St Vincent and the Grenadines, Milton Cato (also a Director of the Mustique Company), that if Colin persisted in his claim they would not buy their bananas. It was simple blackmail but fun while it lasted. There was one sad epilogue to the tragedy. On board were a husband and wife who had been given the cruise when voted the most devoted couple in France. As the passengers were ordered into the lifeboats he panicked and not only abandoned ship but his wife as well. They divorced soon after.

That winter season of 1971 settled down into a regular pattern. Guests, mostly friends of Colin's, came to stay in the Cotton House, some paying, some free. It was all very jolly, with the air of a grand Scottish house party. The hotel was run by Billy Mitchell. Billy was from Texas and, at the tender age of 16, had married a young RAF pilot and heir to the family brewery, Mitchell and Butler. After he died she continued sailing the Caribbean with Arne's Swedish school friend, Bosse, who took her to Mustique. Coming ashore she saw 'two beautiful men in white suits standing on the jetty: Colin and Hugo'.[li] On the strength of that she immediately bought a piece of land above the port and built her house, Firefly. Billy, short and jolly with a mane of blonde curly hair, never lost her Texan drawl, or her risqué humour. When she complained about the men on the island, the author admitted that they were all frightened of her. 'What-ar-ya scared of – that I'll say yes?' It was she who employed Basil Charles as the barman at the Cotton House.

A year earlier, Colin and Hugo had found Basil unconscious in a ditch after a motor bike accident, and took him to hospital where Colin offered him a job if he recovered. Over forty years later he is still on Mustique, the owner of the Beach Bar and restaurant and two shops, along with outside interests. Basil rose to prominence by being efficient and personable. He wore a permanent smile and was ever charming. When some obese American women came into the Cotton House they asked about the peanuts on the bar. Basil told them that they were local, at which they took handfuls believing them to be 'low-cal.'!

Mustique was becoming internationally famous, and the internationally famous drifted in and sailed out. Count Theo Rossi, of the Martini Rossi family, anchored off in *Tritona*, his vast and beautiful schooner. A former marble carrier, she was converted with great taste regardless of expense and filled with works of art – there was a Dali portrait of the Contessa, half face, half moons: there was a Rubens of five lions. When the boat's architect requested he be allowed to cut off their feet so that he could fit it in the saloon, Theo told him to raise the roof and lower the floor. The financier, Charles Gordon, chartered Nelson Rockefeller's yacht, *Sea Star*, and came with friends who included Lady (Maureen) Dudley and Charles Clore. He was to name his house on Endeavour Point after the yacht. Ahmet Ertigun, the founder of Atlantic Records, flew in with his wife Mica and friends: Chris Blackwell of Island Records landed from Billy's yacht, *Nosegay*. Jocelyn Hambro, Chairman of Hambros Bank, with whom Colin had worked in his early City days, came to stay. He was driven around the island in a Mini Moke with his tin leg sticking out of the side. A notoriously bad driver, Colin drove too close to a tractor, which resulted in a cry from the back. Without turning round he asked Jocelyn which leg was damaged as he wanted to know whether to drive to the mechanic's shop or the medicine chest.

Titled folk pitched up too, such as the Marquess and Marchioness of

29. The Great House, Mustique. The island was very run down when Colin bought it in 1958, but even then he could see its vast potential. The house was burned down four years later.

30. The new owner of Mustique under a gourd tree.

31. Princess Margaret surveys her land above Gelliceaux Bay, Mustique, for the first time.

32. Tony Armstrong-Jones reading a magazine aboard the only island transport – wooden seats on a trailer behind a tractor – during part of his honeymoon on Mustique. Later they drove to Gellizeau Point to inspect their wedding present from Colin and Anne.

33. King Freddy, the Kabaka of Buganda, and later Uganda's first President. He and other deposed African rulers were befriended by Colin and Judy Montagu. He died in poverty in the East End of London.

34. Anne, Colin and Princess Elizabeth of Toro in Kampala for Uganda's Independence celebrations.

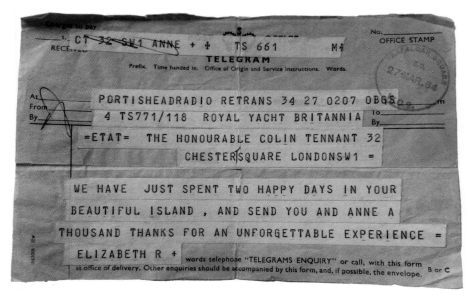

35. Telegram sent from HMY *Britannia* from The Queen thanking Colin and Anne for her visit to Mustique, 1962. The Royal party enjoyed it all so much that she stayed an extra day.

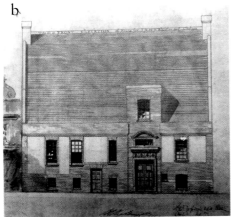

36. 35 Tite Street, (a) the most radical design for a London residence in the early1960s by the architect Frank Hodge. Colin had bought The White House, designed by E. W. Godwin for the artist James McNeil Whistler (b), which was considerably altered after he sold (c). By the time Colin bought it in 1963, it was beyond repair (d). The fantastic octagonal hall at 35 Tite Street was created by the French architect, André Mauny, with a sub-marine theme.

37. The piscatorial meets the sartorial in Colin's pursuit of the brown trout in the burns of Glen.

38. The 'gathering of the clans', Colin's patch-work tartan shooting suit. Standing by a statue of Rob Roy, he always prided himself on how best to pose for any photograph.

39. Ever the dandy, Colin poses in front of his portrait by Lucian Freud. It took months to complete and, during which time, they forged a close and lasting friendship. As his patron, Colin owned 15 Freuds which were eventually all sold. Nothing was too bizarre for Colin, however impractical, but he invariably looked elegant in whatever he wore.

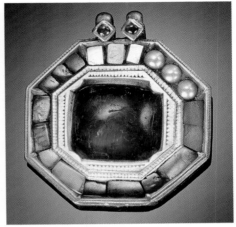

40. With ever an eye for quality and a bargain, Colin bought Edwin Landseer's *Death of the Wild Bull in Chillingham Park*. It hung in the hall at Glen until it, too, followed many a picture to the sale rooms.

41. The magnificent Tipu Sultan Pendant, the gem of Colin's collection. Throughout his life, he was invariably knowledgeable and far ahead of his time in whatever he chose. With his Indian jewellery he began with tribal pieces long before they were fashionable, then moved up to important Mogul creations.

42. Known as *The Whitehall Stairs*, John Constable's *The Opening of Waterloo Bridge* was sold by Colin to pay off the overdraft in Mustique. He claimed that he never minded selling a painting as he could close his eyes and see it at any time.

45. Wearing the fruits of his Sea Island Cotton crop, Colin stands before the ruined cotton house.

43. Colin at a children's party on Mustique. He was always good with the local children and often paid for their further education.

46. Hugo Money-Coutts drives Alan Whicker, the television presenter, during the filming of his documentary *The World of Whicker* (1970).

44. Barbara Barnes came to the Tennant family after the birth of Christopher and was to stay as nanny for 14 years. She left to go to Kensington Palace to look after Princes William and Harry.

47. Friends since their days at Harrow School, the youthful Patrick Lichfield and Brian Alexander. Brian was CEO of the Mustique Company for 28 years, while Patrick built a fine house in the south of the island.

48. Macaroni cheese on Macaroni Beach. Dommie Elliot (*right*), Anne, Princess Margaret and Colin pay homage to the great Italian dish.

50. Front and back – Princess Margaret poses for Colin while Patrick is photographing her from behind on Lagoon Beach, Mustique.

51. A working duo – Arne Haselqvist the builder, and Oliver Messel the designer. In all they built 15 houses on Mustique together.

49. Princess Margaret thanking the artisans who had been working on her house flanked by Arne, the master builder.

52. Basil Charles began as the barman at the Cotton House in 1971 and now owns several enterprises on Mustique, including Basil's Bar and the Raft Restaurant.

53. The share holding of the Mustique Company worked out on the back of an envelope. Colin's accounting methods did not impress the banks.

54. Nevill Turner, director of Previews International, Colin and the author, Nicholas Courtney, aboard the local schooner Whistler entering the harbour at Port Elizabeth, Bequia. They had just discovered the joys of Tequila on the crossing from Mustique.

55. Colin and Simpson Hamilton before the latter's classic sign prohibiting the turning of turtles and lobster fishing out of season. A keen conservationist, Colin also outlawed spear fishing. Consequently the reefs are full of fish and turtles inhabit Mustique.

56. Mustique in its pioneer days before the development in Endeavour Hills. The burned out wreck of SS *Antilles* can be seen between the sugar mill and the Cotton House.

Zetland who, like swallows, returned annually. These few visits were the start of the reputation that Mustique was the haunt of the aristocratic, the rich and famous. Princess Margaret came out to Mustique in February 1971, as she had for the previous two years and would do almost every year for the next three decades. For the few days prior to her visits Colin invariably became highly strung and difficult, while that particular year, she arrived tired and fractious after a series of articles had appeared in the Press on the state of her marriage. But from the moment of her arrival Colin danced attendance upon her, orchestrating the Royal progress, hour by hour, day by day, until she left when he collapsed, utterly exhausted. It was not long, however, before she responded to his attentions, and the magic of Mustique began to work.

In the early years, her visits were low-key as there were so few people around to involve in her entertainment. She would arrive with her protection officer and a Lady-in-Waiting, usually her cousin Jean Wills, or Janie Stevens, the former wife of Jocelyn, the owner of *Queen* magazine. Later, Anne shared the role when she too was appointed a Lady-in-Waiting at, according to Colin, the suggestion of The Queen Mother.

The daily routine was invariable. Princess Margaret rose late and wandered down to the Cotton House for a cigarette, possibly a drink, and always conversation. At that time, as Colin noted, 'She stood erect but lacked height, but had an hourglass figure with a lumpy bosom. All day she wore a whaleboned thronged garment, laced at the back with a short, frilled skirt of her own design. It appeared to be armour plated.' These remarkable garments were of printed cotton, with either green stripes or chintzy flowers. Colin once took a photograph of her under a parasol, leaning forward, while Patrick Lichfield snapped the back view.

A picnic was then taken to a beach, usually Macaroni Beach, where there was shade under the trees, and the table laid before the lunch party arrived. There was always a swim beforehand, when one of her 'court' would be deputed to swim with Princess Margaret. While she swam slowly in a determined breaststroke, head erect to preserve the coiffure, her companions developed a form of side-stroke so that they could swim and talk at the same time. There was never a minute without conversation. Princess Margaret hated sand on her feet and Colin would make sure that there was a basin of fresh water so that she could rinse them. It was typical of him to anticipate her needs, as indeed those of anyone who came to the island.

The swim was followed by lunch, consisting of the inevitable cold chicken in mayonnaise (always out of a vast Hellman's jar) and tired salad. Dinner was in either the Cotton House, with the Money-Coutts, or at Tennant's Tenements, with Arne and Anita, or the Paget sisters and the author. The same guests appeared every night, but it seemed not to matter. On one or two nights a band was imported, along with a few people from St Vincent, for a dance in the Cotton House. Colin had the flowers sent up from Trinidad, which he then arranged himself. With so little to do on the island it was necessary to eke out the treats, while at the same time making them all happen as if by magic. The result belied the effort and planning that went into the arrangements or, as Colin put it: 'It may look like frivolity but making these visits a success takes constant imagination.'

But the great excitement for Princess Margaret was the finalisation of the plans and the siting of her house. Oliver danced attendance too. She had told him what she would like to build and, as she recalled:

> He produced a plan and we mucked about with it at Glen. I explained to Oliver that I wanted to get the details of the house straight from the start and that I would do the interior myself, upon which he giggled. He always giggled when he was in doubt about anything, but he was in no doubt about my wanting to do the interior.

Oliver was a great addition to the party. He was very funny and a wonderful mimic, practised from childhood. At Eton he dressed up as his slightly older sister, Anne, wearing her clothes, makeup and a wig. He then interviewed his housemaster as to how 'her brother' was progressing. One of his favourite makeup characters on Mustique was the mythical super-rich, but complaining, Mrs Pforzheimer III.

Contrary to popular belief, everyone behaved with perfect decorum: everyone knew the rules and the boundaries and they were never breached. Tina Brown, who visited Mustique sometime later, skilfully observed that Colin and Princess Margaret seemed to fulfil a mutual need: 'His subtle understanding of the constraints on royalty makes it possible for the Princess to enjoy the illusion of escaping them without ever, as Tennant puts it, being "declassed", while her strict imposition to limits of informality stops him going over the top.'[lii]

By the end of March 1971 Hugo, through family pressure, stood down as Managing Director of the Mustique Company; Colin returned to London, and left the management of the island for the next four years to the author, a qualified land agent.

# Chapter 13

# LES JOLIES EAUX

Back in London, Colin and Brian Alexander continued to drum up business, create brochures and generally generate interest in Mustique. But all was not well at home with the eldest son, Charlie. After he had narrowly failed, twice, to pass into Eton, Colin sent Charlie to Clifton College, a lesser-known public school near Bristol. He was even more miserable there than at his prep school. The older boys bullied him mercilessly, particularly when they found out that his grandfather was a peer of the realm. A favourite ritual was to put the younger boys into a laundry basket and jump on it until they all screamed. In his wretchedness, Charlie's schoolwork was abandoned and, after just three terms, the school governors asked for him to be removed. Colin later admitted that the greatest mistake he made with Charlie was to send him from a strict boarding school to the progressive, co-educational boarding school called Frensham Heights in Surrey. But, for Charlie, he had found Nirvana. It was an extraordinary school, full of eccentric staff – once Charlie was taken to London by a master who wore a green bowler hat with a light on the top to hail taxis in the street. There were no real rules and no corporal punishment. The freedom went to his head: he grew his hair long and sometimes stayed in bed until one or two in the afternoon. He also began to smoke marijuana and take LSD, a particularly dangerous drug for one with a history of mental illness. These drugs were the beginning of the end for Charlie. There was one contemporary at Frensham who was to remain a friend of his for life, Joshua Bowler, the son of an actor and Colin's friend Henrietta Moraes, the muse of Lucian Freud and Francis Bacon. It had to be more than a coincidence that they were there together.

Charlie fell in with a bad crowd, becoming a founder member of a gang they called 'The Thieves Union', who went shoplifting every afternoon. One day he was caught and his parents were informed by the police. Though he swore that he would never do it again, once back at school Charlie carried on, though rather more warily than before. It was rare indeed that any pupil could be expelled from Frensham, but Charlie achieved it after just two terms.

Colin was deeply upset but the expulsion was nothing compared to the shock of seeing Charlie on his return: his hair was matted; he had not taken his clothes off for three months. He looked terrible and smelled worse. He refused to change his clothes, believing that evil spirits would take him over. He became deeply superstitious, from not walking on cracks in the pavement or walking under a ladder, to stepping backwards and forwards a hundred times before leaving the house. Worse, he thought that his brother Henry was unlucky and could not bear to travel in a car with him. That Henry passed into Eton and Charlie failed distanced the brothers further.

But Colin and Anne never gave up on Charlie, however maddening he had become, nor did they apologise for his behaviour. Charlie would stand on one leg at the top of the stairs at Glen with his eyes closed, being ignored by the grand dinner party below. When Princess Margaret was dining one night at Tite Street, Charlie had the urge to conduct his 'century hop' in and out of the doorway of the dining room. 'She just carried on eating as if everybody's son affected such odd behaviour'.[liii] One reason why Colin could understand Charlie so well was he could see much of himself in him at the same age. 'If things had been the same in my time at Eton in 1941, I might have done the same as Charlie. In my own youth one just didn't have to go that far to create an effect.' Colin felt that they had both suffered from many of the same things in childhood, not least their exceptional looks. He maintained that a part of Charlie's problem was the incredible beauty he had inherited from the Wyndham side of the Tennant family. His grandmother Pamela introduced it, passing it down to two of her sons, Bim and Stephen, and it had come out in Charlie. Colin truly believed that:

What lurks in the Tennant family is beauty. It does not matter what your features are like, as beauty is a separate quality to prettiness, handsomeness, presentability, or even sex appeal. There is a quality that is actual *beauty*. It came out in Charles. He was quite unconscious of it and made nothing of it. And he destroyed himself. It was not what destroyed him. Those were other things. I am comparatively good looking, but thankfully lack beauty. He was in some respects not quite as good looking as I am, but he had that beauty that I do not have.

What did destroy Charlie, however, was his move to heroin.

After the failure of Busuri Vici, Colin soon realised that his alternative idea of Oliver 'designing' the island was not practical. To show that he was serious in putting Mustique on a commercial footing, he appointed a London firm of planners, Llewelyn-Davies, Weeks, Forestier-Walker and Bor to come up with an overall development plan. After a year they produced a comprehensive study, costing many thousands of pounds, but soon after its completion, the bound volume lay in the Previews office purely as a sales tool, hardly ever to be referred to again. It was Colin who decided what and where everything was to happen.

That autumn Mustique was considerably enlivened by the arrival of Colin's erstwhile salesman from the Bahamas, Nevill Turner, to take charge of Previews International and to put the marketing of the island on a proper footing. Nevill's appearance coincided with the beginning of phase two in the Endeavour Hills, a large block of land overlooking the north of the island, with Bequia and St Vincent beyond. Colin had that knack of knowing how land should be divided and where to site the house. He had read about the expansion of London in the eighteenth century with what they called 'rookeries', where grand squares were laid out with large town houses surrounded by denser areas of less expensive housing, which made for a mix of style and people. As part of this 'rookery' idea these early lots were very small, barely half an acre, and consequently inexpensive, thus belying Mustique's 'exclusive' image. The price was US$1 per square foot. There was no stipulation as to the architect, although Colin was the one-man vetting board for all the house plans.

Even in planning meetings, Colin's wit was as sharp as ever. Two contiguous blocks of land were divided into six lots each and numbered from the outside in. This left two awkward-shaped adjacent lots both numbered six. When Nevill suggested that the lots be combined into one large lot, Colin typically said: 'Quite right, six of one and half a dozen of the other!' It was also suggested that the new road through Endeavour should be called 'Cardin Avenue'. One weekend on the neighbouring island of Bequia, when staying in his hotel, the Sunny Caribbee, Colin heard of a small boy who was selling little coconut boats made of half the shell, a piece of tin for the keel and a little cotton sail on a stick. When asked the price, the entrepreneur replied: 'cardin', which, after much repetition, was found to stand for 'according', as in 'according to who you are'. His pricing ranged from 20 cents for a local from Bequia, while a mainland Vincentian paid 50 cents, the English BWI$1, while the cost was over double, US$1 for the Americans!

Although neither the name, nor the variable price structure, was adopted, the early clients were an assortment of nationalities, ages and wealth. Colin's neighbours in Scotland, Michael and Kirsty Maxwell Stuart, bought a small lot. To Michael, the house that was designed for him looked so like a cowshed that he called it The Byre – 'at least it did not cost as much' was his gloomy comment. Murray and Belle Nathan, who had made their original fortune by buying Chinese pigtails for wigs, were American; John McLaren was from Toronto. Sir Harold and Lady (Mike) Cassel bought at the same time. Sir Harold was an eminent English QC and circuit court judge. They built an inexpensive house of woven bamboo on top of the water tank. Another early sale was to Hubert and Lucy Fisher from Memphis, Tennessee. They telephoned to ask if there was still land for sale. Fresh from brokering the largest wheat deal ever between the United States and Russia, they arrived the next day by private jet, stayed for a week and bought three lots on which to build a substantial house. Clearly, larger lots and bigger houses were the way forward.

By the winter season of 1972 Colin could see that his vision for Mustique was at last beginning to take shape. The houses on Endeavour Point were nearing completion, and a larger generator almost kept pace with demand. There were new clients ready to build in the Endeavour Hills, but apart from Princess Margaret, there was nobody particularly famous on Mustique. Yet the island's reputation as the exclusive haunt of the aristocratic, rich and famous grew, article by article, until it was universally believed. The reason for this exaggeration was, of course, Colin himself, who virtually single-handedly promoted the island and bolstered its standing by selling himself. He made it seem glamorous and fun: it was already very beautiful, and the difficulties of getting there made it exclusive. Journalists by the score were seduced as one glowing article appeared after another. It was even said that as Colin only wanted beautiful people on the island, those wishing to come or buy land had to send a photograph of themselves first for his approval. The story was, of course, apocryphal, but not out of the realms of possibility where Colin was concerned. What was certainly true was that Colin could not abide the vulgar, whoever they were, or however rich. Sir Rodney Touche, an early investor who bought and built on L'Ansecoy Bay, remembers Colin dealing with a man who told him proudly: 'I like your island. I looked it all over by helicopter this afternoon from my yacht'. Colin told him to go back to his yacht and sail away – or words to that effect: 'I do not like people who fly helicopters over my island without my permission.'

With Easter being early that year, the whole of the Tennant family were in Mustique for the school holidays. When it was time to leave, Colin chartered a nine-seater, twin-engined Britten Norman Islander to take them, with the nanny, Barbara Barnes, direct to Barbados, a distance of some 90 miles. Colin was always a nervous flyer, particularly in small planes. Half an hour after taking off, there was consternation on board when one engine failed, probably through water in the fuel. The pilot told them all to put on their life jackets and Henry, sitting in the back seat, to pull the life raft out of the hold behind him in case they should crash-land in the sea. A rescue plane was also called out from St Vincent with another life raft to escort them in. Anne and Barbara remained totally calm and sensible, each cradling an infant twin in their life jackets. Barbara made them all sing songs and told them jokes to keep their spirits up. Colin, who had put on his snorkel and mask, kept his spirits up from a bottle of rum that Charlie had spirited away from the Cotton House, and was rapidly becoming inebriated. All was going reasonably well on one engine until Henry pulled the ripcord of the life raft, which instantly inflated and filled the cabin. Everyone was pressed down into their seats and the pilot was squashed against the controls. Despite this, the Islander limped back on one engine and the pilot skilfully managed to land at Arnos Vale, the airport in St Vincent. On landing, the life raft had to be deflated before the family, deeply shaken by their experience, could squeeze out of the plane. Another plane was then ordered to take them to Barbados.

For Colin and Anne, this was a second brush with potential disaster. Previously, they had been flying from Tahiti to New York when the plane fell 12,000 feet in a steep nosedive. In an interview for the *Evening Standard*, Jeannie Campbell asked Colin what it felt like when the plane finally straightened out.

'Well', replied Colin, 'it was a feeling of relief, as if the end was coming and there was nothing left to fear. Then I said a lot of things to Anne, very quickly, which I shall never have to say again.'

'That you loved her?' Jeannie asked.

'Yes, that sort of thing, said Colin rather sheepishly.

It was to be a whole year before Princess Margaret's new house was ready in February 1973. She had called it *Les Jolies Eaux*, the pretty waters, a clever corruption of the name Gellizeaux, the early nineteenth-century owner of the little promontory. Two enormous packing crates arrived with all her furniture and, with the enthusiasm of a young bride, she looked forward to moving it all into her new home. Unfortunately the floor had been treated with the wrong sealant and the hot sun had turned it into a sticky, yellow morass. As she recalled: 'It was the most terrible task as it took thirty men with scrapers to get it off. There we sat in gloomsville, getting gloomier and gloomier. We used to come up every day through the kitchen door and unpack the packing cases and wash the glasses and china'.[liv]

Patrick Lichfield was in his element as he snapped away through the kitchen window at his cousin washing up in her yellow Marigold gloves. When the first wooden crate was empty it was taken away on the back of a tractor. At the end of the day Colin and Princess Margaret were returning to the Cotton House when they noticed the brand new staff quarters beside George Philip's house that had not been there that morning. They went to take a closer look and there was a charming little house with a corrugated iron roof covered in palm fronds, some steps up to the door and a window. The couple who had moved in were sitting under the porch on a swing chair with their small baby. As Colin and Princess Margaret passed by with a cheery wave they noticed on the side of the house:

HRH THE PRINCESS MARGARET
COUNTESS OF SNOWDON

stencilled on the side of what had been her old packing case! Before she left, Princess Margaret managed to move her possessions into her house, but she did not sleep there as there still was no electricity. To Oliver's chagrin, she furnished virtually the whole house from Ideal Home Exhibitions which she had visited, year after year, where she had been given individual pieces of furniture. Her harlequin dinner service, too, had been donated, place setting by place setting, on various official visits to the great porcelain factories. Rather than pictures, she hung plates on the wall. An inveterate conchologist, Colin made her a large shell looking glass as a house-warming present, which eventually disintegrated. 'The whole place was really terribly plain. There was a sofa facing the sea with a comfortable armchair on either side with a baskety kind of coffee table in front. There was no evidence at all of her being a Royal person other than a rather small reproduction of the picture of The Queen by Anigoni which hung beside her desk.'

It was at this time that Patrick Lichfield took the well-known photograph of Princess Margaret and her 'court' on Lagoon Beach. She is surrounded by Colin and Anne and their great friends, Judy Gendel (Montagu) and Dominic Elliot. In the back stand Basil Charles and the author; to the front is the Lady Bridget Sinclair, who had come out to work as a secretary. The photograph says much about the time Princess Margaret was on the island, where although much fawning took place, it was still very amusing.

One of the new houses was built by Arne for himself, a stone 'fortress' on top of a hill that was both large and grand. Typically Colin was jealous at the magnificence of the place while he had no house of his own, but the references to Henry VIII taking over Cardinal Wolsey's Hampton Court when he became too rich and powerful were totally lost on the Swede.

Mustique was still very low key, the entertainment consisting of a succession of people dining in each other's houses. Some of the houses were rented and a new generation of visitors appeared for Colin to stage-manage – often literally – when he made them perform at one of his spectaculars. He did, however, miss out on Bryan Ferry, who had rented Hugo's house. Colin had never heard of him, or Roxy Music, and was only impressed when he heard that his record producer, Chris Blackwell, had bought a larger private jet on the strength of his latest album, *Virginia Plain*.

Mustique continued to attract the attentions of the world's Press, including the prestigious American *Gourmet Magazine*. They sent their writer, Jan Chamberlain, and a photographer down in June during the 'off-season', in the middle of a drought, when the Cotton House was closed. There was no food, let alone anything remotely gourmet. No challenge being too great, a few local dishes were cobbled together out of almost non-existent ingredients. The rum punch, however, was strong and delicious, which can only have accounted for the article, which bore little or no resemblance to what Jan Chamberlain experienced. She waxed lyrical about the island, the architecture and, above all, the food and staff. 'White coated waiters move from group to group serving silver platters of mushrooms stuffed with *escargots*, fried coconut chips, plaintain slithers, and mangrove oysters'.[lv] The piece was pure fantasy, but was well received. An old copy happened to be in a dentist's waiting room and was read by Mick Jagger, who instantly responded to the idea of white-gloved servants serving him delicious treats. Somehow Brian Alexander had heard that Mick, Bianca, their daughter Jade and the nanny were having a beastly time in Martinique and sent a small plane to bring them all to Mustique, where the Jaggers rented *Les Jolies Eaux* for £400 the week. He was not impressed. The weather was erratic, the island still somewhat primitive out of season, and there was not a white-gloved waiter in sight. He and Bianca were, however, 'names', and their visit gave credence to the stories that circulated in the Press of the rich and famous staying on Mustique. Another visitor out of season was David Frost, with his then girlfriend, Diahann Carroll, who had the whole island virtually to themselves. Paul Newman sailed in for a day and a night, but not at the same time as Raquel Welch.

In the Royal calendar nothing still competes with the visit to Balmoral for the whole of August for the grouse shooting, the fishing, the stalking and Princess Margaret's birthday. From there she invariably wound her way through the hairpin bends to the Borders to stay at Glen, where there was always a lively party with plenty of entertainment. The guests were always chosen with care; a few familiar faces, the children and their friends, with a smattering of young men to pay court. The first week of September 1973, the mix that already included Drue Heinz, Colin's nephew Matthew Yorke and cousin Liz Paget, the (Richard) McGillycuddy of the Reeks and Lucia Santa Cruz had gone slightly wrong, as Dominic (Dommie) Elliot could not come at the last minute. Anne asked Colin to find someone else to make even numbers, not an easy task in early September. He telephoned 'Aunt Nose', his cousin Violet Wyndham, who had been staying a fortnight previously, to ask if she knew of a personable young man. As in the story oft told, she came up with a young man called Roddy Llewellyn, whom she had recently met at a dinner party. When he was tracked down to Fowey in Cornwall, Anne telephoned him and invited him to stay. As Colin recalled:

Roddy was always free, and living in awkward circumstances with

Nicky Haslam. He immediately accepted. I had no idea who, or what he was, but the minute I saw him in a dirty sweater and high collared shirt, I could see at once that he was what you would call 'just the ticket'. So too, of course, did Princess Margaret.

Colin paid for his rail ticket and sleeper, somewhat necessary for the impecunious research assistant at the Royal College of Heralds by day, and the cleaner of floors in an art gallery in the Fulham Road by night. On the morning of his arrival, Colin and Charlie drove into Edinburgh to meet Princess Margaret at the Café Royal with her children and their nanny, who had been driven down from Balmoral. Wearing his only tie as instructed Roddy, as he recalled, 'entered the Café Royal at 1 o'clock on the 3 September 1973.'[lvi] He was somewhat apprehensive but the attraction between him and Princess Margaret, as Roddy admits 'was mutual and instant'.[lvii] They arrived back at Glen sitting together in the back of the little minibus driven by Colin. It was certainly apparent that she and Roddy had established a rapport, and the moment they entered Glen, Anne instantly realised something had happened between them – she could not quite tell what. 'Heavens, what have I done?' she thought. 'I suppose no one knows what qualities people see in each other, but they do seem to make each other happy. None of us realised how strongly it would develop'.[lviii] From that moment on, Roddy, a virtual clone of Tony at the same age of 25, paid court to Princess Margaret. He sat beside her on the piano stool, turning the pages of the music score as she played; they sang in harmony the old music hall songs she loved. He was attentive, kind and fun; his dreadful schoolboy humour appealed to her too – a typical joke of his was: 'What did one cuff say to the other?' [Answer] 'I'm afraid'. Soon after their initial meeting he went for a walk with Anne and told her that he thought Princess Margaret had the most beautiful eyes. 'Don't tell me, tell her!' replied Anne. He soon did, during a walk with Princess Margaret and Drue Heinz. According to Roddy, they 'set off to walk to Loch Eddie when Drue soon realised that she was in the way. She dropped back then tactfully went back to the house' while they continued blissfully alone.

Ever attentive and caring, Roddy was the perfect antidote to Tony. During one wet afternoon at Glen some of the house party were playing gin rummy and Roddy was deputised to keep the running totals. When Princess Margaret asked to look at the scorecard, she saw that Roddy had written down a few irrelevant numbers and added 'I think you are looking very beautiful today!' She was clearly smitten by him, while Roddy greatly enjoyed her attention. Years later Colin admitted that he had hidden behind an arch on the main landing to witness any 'corridor creeping'. His draughty vigil was not in vain, but he would never have dreamed of discussing her relationship with Roddy. 'I did introduce her to Roddy', he said. 'But I never made any enquiries about how she felt about him, nor did we ever discuss intimate matters.' When drawn on the subject he surmised that 'She was very bruised by her marriage and Roddy was kind to her. His relationship with her changed. When they arrived here [Mustique], they were lovers but it was a matter of time before it became that of devoted friends.'

Colin and Anne continued to provide a 'safe house' for Princess Margaret and Roddy although, at that time, he did have a place of his own, and she and Tony still lived under the same roof at Kensington Palace. He, of course, knew of Roddy's existence and seemed to delight in making their relationship as difficult as possible. When, for instance, Roddy went out to Mustique the next March, 1974, Tony sent a telegram to her at *Les Jolies Eaux*:

POSSIBLE ASSIGNMENT IN MEXICO MAY DROP IN ON WAY OUT
SO LOOKING FORWARD TO SEEING YOU WILL CABLE DETAILS
LATER
FONDEST LOVE
TONY

The bi-annual visits to *Les Jolies Eaux* were eagerly anticipated by Princess Margaret, less so for her Ladies-in-Waiting and guests. In the early days before the swimming pool was built, the hapless few would sit on the terrace, often in scorching sun, there being no shade after the two remaining trees were cut down as their roots were damaging the drains and foundations of the house. There was nowhere to go and nothing to do before Princess Margaret emerged from her room at 11 o'clock for coffee. Once, her cousin and Lady-in-Waiting, Jean Wills, 'who was infinitely obedient, longed to go out for a walk and was caught sneaking out before the morning coffee. She was soundly berated'. It was typical. Colin often found that Princess Margaret was totally out of touch with her surroundings and friends. One summer, for example, she had been to stay with Jean Wills, and the following Christmas invited Jean to her annual

Christmas party where presents were handed out to friends and staff. Jean received hers and opened it in front of everybody to find that it was a revolting lavatory brush in the shape of a Disney dog. She was mumbling her thanks when Princess Margaret said: 'I'm so glad you like it, when I came to stay in the summer I noticed that you didn't have one.' Jean, mortified and almost in tears at the humiliation, hissed to Colin, 'Of course I had one. I would never put it out when she came to stay.'

At *Les Jolies Eaux* even Roddy felt trapped and sent pleading notes to Colin: 'Please come and talk to me', or 'Please can I come down?' At least he was able to design and plant her garden to give him something to do in the mornings. Throughout all her time on Mustique, Colin fussed around Princess Margaret, making sure that she was entertained, or when she was entertaining herself, that everything was in order.

Dinner, produced by Mrs Lane, a middle-aged, pan-faced cook, at *Les Jolies Eaux* was invariable. She would start with a pink shrimp cocktail with four large shrimps hooked over the lip of a V-shaped glass. Princess Margaret thought the pink sauce was something special and never knew that it was only a mixture of bought mayonnaise and Heinz tomato ketchup. This was followed either by chicken, or more often grey lamb swimming in thin gravy, ending up with ice cream. There were adequate wines, although Princess Margaret drank Famous Grouse whisky and water throughout.

Mrs Lane was a dreadful cook but it seemed not to matter. She had a daughter, Cloreen, who helped in the house. Cloreen took to religion and would go into Princess Margaret's room with tea to wake her then, waving her arms about wildly, she would dance about the room singing a hymn. 'Actually Princess Margaret didn't mind what happened very much down there, which was really quite a relief.' Mrs Lane resigned her Royal position leaving a note for her successor:

TAKE CARE NANCY WILLIAMS
ENJOY IT
HERE IS ALL YOUR KEYS

Nancy was, in fact, a man and served Princess Margaret faithfully for many years until, drunk one night (on her rum), he crashed her jeep through the sitting room doors. When Nancy was sacked Colin said to Brian 'I knew he would get into hot water'!

Solicitous and protective of Princess Margaret as he was, Colin also expended the same energy and tactics to the wooing of prospective clients. He could ladle out charm like Pooh Bear spooning honey from his jar. Later he would play the eccentric card if he thought that it would result in a land sale – one 'trick' was to walk into the sea fully clothed until he disappeared completely with only his hat floating on the waves to show how deep the water was – in fact it was only waist high and he was on his knees. To Colin, selling land was a calculated challenge which he relished. He created a gentle atmosphere, like a family picnic, where he would woo a visitor with chilled white wine, served from a portable paraffin fridge on the beach. 'After we ate', he recalled, 'I might sing songs pertinent to the conversation. Then I would undress and plunge into the sea [in his swimming trunks]. People are much more ready to talk business when they have their clothes off.' He genuinely loved to make people happy and to entertain them. Just like his mother, Pamela, he had the knack of knowing how to make a party or a situation work. Often 'They [the clients] would be swept up in the whole idea of living on Mustique, and that was when I would sell them land. They felt really liberated.' In those early days he made Mustique fun and very enjoyable and those who bought wanted to be a part of the scene.

By 1975 exchange control had put paid to the hope of any land sales from the United Kingdom, but the market was still strong in the United States and South America, particularly in Venezuela from whence came, to Colin and Mustique's lasting benefit, Hans and Maria Christina Neumann. Hans had left Czechoslovakia at the end of the Second World War and settled in Caracas with a special paint formula. There his paint factory grew, Tennant-like, into a huge chemical empire. He and Maria Christina had been introduced to Mustique by Colin's long-term mistress, Jill Goldsmith.

Colin had had the odd fling with many women in the past, particularly in Mustique, but Jill was different. Of Anglo-Irish extraction, she was the estranged wife of the ecologist, Teddy Goldsmith. With raven-black hair and striking, gypsy good looks, she was highly intelligent and right for Colin at that time, not least because she was a successful antique dealer in London, with a wonderful eye. While being totally possessive about her, Colin was also extremely generous towards her, showering her with gifts – he once bought back an expensive bracelet he had given Anne to give to her. He wrote her long and carefully constructed letters, often with two or three drafts, when they were apart. Anne appeared not to mind the arrangement 'so long', as she said, 'as I don't have to meet her'. Improbably, Colin once took Jill to a Club Med on an island in the Indian Ocean. Unfortunately she had broken her leg and was in plaster. The trip was an unmitigated disaster. On his return, Colin complained to *Anne* what a nightmare it had all been, to which she replied that she was not sure that she wanted to hear about his time with his mistress. Wife and mistress were, however, eventually introduced in the foyer of the Imperial Hotel in Delhi by a mutual Indian friend, Javed Abdulla. Javed lodged in Jill's house in London and once pointed out the four-poster bed that had been bought from a sale of English furniture at the auctioneers Christies in South Kensington. When Jill transferred her attentions to Colin, her former lover offered to buy the chosen bed with a modest estimate of £300–400 as a farewell present. Colin, meanwhile, heard of the plan, and was damned if he was going to sleep in her erstwhile lover's bed. Both men sent their representatives to the auction with 'buy bids', which meant that the four-poster was finally knocked down to Colin's man for tens of thousands of pounds. The affair lasted for well over a decade, when she broke it off to marry another.

Meanwhile Hans and Maria Christina had totally fallen for Mustique and bought a fine lot straddling Point Lookout beside L'Ansecoy Bay on the north-eastern corner of the island. Just as the first sale to Lady Honor was vital to kick-start Mustique, so the arrival of Hans Neumann was ultimately to save the island.

Mustique's reputation continued to grow, and on the outside everything seemed bright and breezy, but behind the scene all was far from well, and the cause of that malaise rested squarely with Colin. From the very beginning, he had run Mustique in his own, autocratic way as his own private fiefdom. As he picked up most of the bills himself, there was no one to tell him otherwise – Hugo had returned to Majorca and Gerald Ward, the other investor, was content to leave everything to Colin.

But Colin was fast running out of money. His expenses were phenomenal. Glen was costing the earth to maintain – after the oil crisis he found that it was cheaper to fly his whole family, with Barbara the nanny, to Mustique for Christmas than to open up the house. Charlie, who by then was on heroin, was costing a fortune, both financially and emotionally. The biggest drain on his capital and possessions was Mustique. When the author was the General Manager of Mustique, for example, the bank overdraft had reached its limit of £63,000, so Colin sold Constable's *The Opening of Waterloo Bridge, Whitehall Stairs, June 18th, 1817* for exactly the same amount. It changed hands again in 1987 for £3 million when it was bought by the Tate Gallery. It would be worth over tenfold in the art market nowadays.

But Colin realised that, to raise outside capital, rather than using his own money, he needed to reorganise Mustique with a proper management structure – the banks were not impressed with calculations on the backs of envelopes, which was Colin's way. Whatever his other faults Colin did have the knack of employing the right person at the right time. He had met John Golds, a former District Commissioner in Kenya before Independence, when he was Regional Controller for the Eastern Caribbean section of the Commonwealth Development Corporation (CDC) and living in Barbados. In 1969 Colin and Hugo approached him with the idea that CDC should put the basic services, such as the landing strip, electricity and water into Mustique, as they had done successfully elsewhere in the Caribbean. John visited Mustique and could instantly see the potential, not only for the island but for the benefit of St Vincent and the other Grenadine islands. Although he thought it unlikely that his masters in London would agree 'to such an upmarket project led by such a colourful personality as Colin',[lx] he personally thought it worth a try. As he suspected, he was turned down, most likely 'because the CDC did not wish to get involved with someone of Colin's well-published activities as rumoured in the UK Press'. Ultimately, John Golds was proved to be right when Mustique became exactly what he had envisaged.

On his early retirement from CDC John received three job offers: one from Colin to be Managing Director of the Mustique Company, another to take over the management of Cap Estate in St Lucia, and the third to run the North American and Caribbean operation of the shipping company, Ocean Transport and Trading Ltd of Liverpool. Not interested in any of these three offers in isolation, John put all three Chairmen together over dinner and they agreed that he would operate all three. For tax reasons, John moved to Mustique, which proved difficult – not least because it was agreed that Colin would visit the island only spasmodically over the next three years, to leave John free to put some semblance of fiscal control and discipline into the company without his continual interference. However, Colin's frequent visits to Mustique and John's stringent measures generated many heated rows between them. From the very beginning John realised that there was not enough money in the Company kitty to fund Colin's extravagances *and* provide good services for the investors. Many terrible scenes followed, often violent, as when the Managing Director's furniture was hurled out of the closed window of his office. To those who crossed Colin, conflict was inevitable. When Colin tried to replace John he found that banks financing the expansion of Mustique had made John remaining as Managing Director a prior condition of any continuing loan. Reluctantly, John could see that the only way that Mustique could survive, let alone move forward, as a business, was to remove Colin from any decision-making on the board. But his plans were soon overtaken by events.

As land sales had virtually dried up, and Colin was determined not to spend any more of his fortune on Mustique, the only way to sustain the Mustique Company was to offload their expenses onto the house owners. In the past, the Cotton House had been a useful sales tool, but without land sales there was nothing to offset the losses. So, in June 1976, Colin wrote to the thirty-four house owners informing them of his proposals for a service charge to cover the cost of running Mustique, such as the generating of the electricity (plus an increased tariff of what had been consumed), the maintenance of the roads and airfield, customs, police, education, and the village. Further proposals were to turn the Cotton House into a club for the benefit of the house owners, and create a separate department, under the General Manager, Jon Wainwright, to maintain and let their properties. This was followed by another letter with the details of the actual costs to each house owner, along with the proposals for the Cotton House Club and the US$25,000 joining fee. For the management costs of the renting and maintenance of their houses Colin proposed a 30 per cent fee.

The resulting storm of protest from the house owners was fierce and vociferous, particularly from those whom Colin had abused in the past. The initial dispute was spearheaded by Dr Bob Guthrie, a New York plastic surgeon, and his brother-in-law, Michael Holden, a broker and car dealer from New York and Connecticut. They pointed out that they were only responsible for the maintenance of their own sub-division and should not contribute to the cost of servicing undeveloped land, from which only Colin would derive the benefits of the sale. No one bought the idea of turning the Cotton House into a club.

Matters came to a head when the house owners met Colin at the Cotton House over Thanksgiving weekend. From the start Colin was abrasive and, according to Bob Guthrie, the house owners resented the imperious, high-handed way he told them that, as he had been subsidising the island for years 'they could take his proposals or leave'.[lxi] From the start, the house owners did not believe his figures. After the meeting, Sir Rodney Touche suggested to his co-owners that there should be a separate organisation to run the island services. He also suggested that Bob Guthrie should be Chairman. Both of these proposals were agreed and a house owners' association (H.O.A.) was formed 'to confine the expenses to services from which they actually benefited. Everybody joined, including Princess Margaret'.[lxii]

Bob went to Mustique wearing his Chairman's hat to meet Colin, who was immediately hostile. Unperturbed, Bob began by saying he could see that if Colin had run out of money, it was partially the fault of the house owners. Unlike every other resort in the world, they had all enjoyed a free ride at Colin's expense up to that time. He asked Colin to come up with a suggestion to solve the impasse. When none was forthcoming Bob then suggested a sharing operation whereby the association should pay a third of the running costs. Further, if Colin could not meet the remaining two-thirds of the annual cost, then the association would pay for it all and be reimbursed with every third or fourth sale. What they all wanted was for Colin to remain notionally in charge, as his presence would ensure that Mustique would remain the place that they all loved. According to Bob Guthrie, Colin dismissed this proposal out of hand, simply as he was not its architect.

In the end the house owners' association took over the running of all the island services. Colin handed over the generator and the whole of the electrical system on the island, along with the tractor and trailers for garbage collection. The association employed Rolf Linden (Junior), the Swedish engineer, and Jon Wainright, the General Manager of the Mustique Company, to manage their interests. Colin was enraged by what he perceived as Wainright's disloyalty and fired him. It was said that Colin engineered his work permit being rescinded by the immigration service and subsequently Wainright left to work for Rodney Touche in Canada. The house owners were content, although Colin came out of it bruised and disenchanted.

The perpetrators of the coup were never quite forgiven, although a harmony of sorts reigned for the rest of the time Colin was on Mustique. With this backdrop of unpleasantness, Colin's mind was, however, taken up with another matter somewhat closer to his heart: the celebration of his fiftieth birthday party

*Chapter 14*

# THE GREAT HOUSE, MUSTIQUE

It was billed as a latter-day Field of the Cloth of Gold as Colin celebrated his fiftieth birthday with a party on Mustique. And so it was, notwithstanding the background of the house owners' revolt. At 50 the theme was naturally to be all gold. The 'gold' encrusted invitation, that outlined the near-week of parties on Mustique at the end of November 1976, was hugely generous, at least for the British contingent, as it included an airfare and all the accommodation. True to form Colin invited mostly members of both his and Anne's families, along with a few close friends. In the end, there were thirty guests who flew out to Barbados where they stayed in the Crane Hotel, before being flown on a large charter plane to St Vincent the next morning. From there they were ferried to Mustique in a series of little charter planes, and billeted in various houses around the island. Most of the house owners who willingly lent their houses to Colin for his party were the same as had been the most vociferous in their condemnation of him and his pricing policies. While some were decidedly unhappy having allowed Colin to use their houses, and were subsequently not asked to the parties, there were enough houses to go round. Princess Margaret's own house party at *Les Jolies Eaux* included Reinaldo and Carolina Herrera, Prince Rupert Loewenstein and his wife Josephine, and Oliver Messel. For the Herreras it was a return match as Princess Margaret, Colin and Anne had stayed with them in Caracas the November before for her official visit to Venezuela. Colin and Anne stayed with the Channons at their main house, Clonsilla, with Phibbleston, their other house next door, bursting at the seams.

It was a scene of constant activity. Guests flew in from the United

139

States, the likes of Ahmed Ertigan and his wife Mica, with a party of their friends, arriving in the Atlantic Record's company jet. Hans Neumann and his wife, Maria Christina, flew up with a glamorous party from Venezuela. Colin's mother, Pamela, came, as did his half-sister, Catherine with her husband, Sir Mark Palmer. His cousins were there in force – Liz Paget, Zanna Johnston and her husband Nicky, Julian Tennant with his wife Miranda; Anne's sister, Sarah Walter and her husband David, and Anne's cousins too, with the likes of Lady Amabel Lindsay, and Lady Victoria Weymouth with her husband Nigel. Then friends, lots of friends, including Billy Whittaker, Patrick Lichfield and his wife Leonora, Brian and Elizabeth Lascelles, John Stefanidis, Henry and Margaret Vyner, and Anne's other great friend, Sarah Henderson. Rosie Baldwin, Jinty's mother, who was running Fort Liverpool as a guest house, was already on the island. There was a younger, glamorous group: Sabrina Guinness, Guy Nevill, a brace of Guinness boys, Valentine and Jasper, and Emma Soames. And then there were others, who nobody really quite knew why they were there: Lady (Bubbles) Harmsworth and her friend Scott Kalani Durdan, a male model for, amongst others, Pierre Cardin, and Charles Benson, the racing correspondent of the *Daily Express*, writing under the *nom de plume* The Scout. But for glamour and star quality there were Mick and Bianca Jagger. Mustique was finally living up to its reputation.

For the next four days guests were spoiled with lunch parties and grand soireés. There were entertainments, such as the trip to the wreck of the French liner, the SS *Antilles*. There was a dance in the Cotton House where Danna Gillespie sang and a local calypso singer went round the room making up limericks with guest's names. At a lunch party at Macaroni Beach Colin gave everyone T-shirts emblazoned with the 'Birthday Party' design of the invitation: at Arne's lunch party the rum punch was served from a large copper sugar pan. But all was leading up to the finale, the 'Caribbean Spectacular' at Macaroni Beach where the theme was, of course, all gold. In true Colin fashion, he had transformed the perfectly ordinary picnic place into a veritable Croesus' palace. The trees and the grass had been sprayed with gold: triumphal arches were made from plaited golden palm fronds. A portable generator purred in the distance as it powered the lights high up in the trees to bathe the whole place in golden light. Flaming torches lined the road.

Colin only just made his party as he had collapsed shortly beforehand from exhaustion and had to have an injection from the doctor to see him through the evening. Colin and Anne received the guests, he in a tight satin suit laced with gold, while Anne, in a beautiful turban, shimmered in gold lamé; her face and hands sprayed gold made her look as if she had stepped off the set of *Goldfinger*. Most guests had made a supreme effort: Carolina Herrara chryselephantine in a striped gold and white dress with an enormous feather turban, Maria Christina Neumann in silver lamé. Bianca Jagger stole the show with a gold creation reminiscent of *Gone with the Wind*, while Mick was a gilded Southern boy complete with a golden battered straw hat. Everyone made an entrance – Oliver Messel, wearing a mask of himself aged just 22, escorted Colin's mother, Pamela, followed by the guest of honour, Princess Margaret in a gold caftan and turban. But the real stars of the night were the local boys, whose oiled bodies Colin had dressed in gold tinsel cloaks with codpieces made from coconut shells sprayed in gold. It was a night to remember.

The next day there was a final lunch party at the Cotton House with an auction, mostly pieces that Colin had donated, in aid of the St Vincent Hospital. After four days of unrivalled fun, the British contingent was poured back to London. The guests agreed that nothing could compare with the simple elegance of that fiftieth celebration.

There was one guest who had extra cause to remember the whole series of parties on Mustique and that was Robert Mapplethorpe. Colin had met the emergent photographer in New York and invited him to Mustique to photograph his party, his very first outside commission. The fee was US$500. It was typical of Colin to hire him, he who could spot latent talent and was always willing to back his hunches to kick-start a career. The other memorable outcome of the party was that Mick Jagger decided to buy property on Mustique and chose the beach cottage and land on L'Ansecoy Bay.

Notwithstanding the jollifications of the week, the underlying problems of Mustique were as prevalent as ever. Colin was still short of money, the coffers of the Mustique Company were empty and the overdraft at Barclays Bank had reached its limit. While the steel band was tickling by the shore, negotiations whereby Hans Neumann would take over the Mustique Company were in the offing. John Golds had been to see him in Caracas to sound him out about taking over and instantly found him receptive to his idea. Hans was much in tune with Colin's vision for Mustique and could see that it was only a matter of time before he would be forced to sell, most likely to some unsympathetic organisation who would 'commercialise' the island. Initially Colin was unwilling to sell at all, then proposed a 50:50 split. But Hans would not hear of anything less than full control.

At the end of January 1977, Colin gave Hans an option to buy 60 per cent of the ordinary shares in the Mustique Company for US$1.5 million, the redemption of the preference shares owned by Gerald Ward and Hugo. Bob Guthrie said that the deal was kept private from his fellow house owners, and that 'had they known they collectively would have given Colin a great deal more for the shares'.[lxiii]

After a period of due diligence, during which Hans asked Brian Alexander to manage the island, and a non-returnable deposit of US$75,000 was banked in New York, the deal was struck. Hans brought in two partners, John McLaren and a Venezuelan friend, Alberto Vollmer, and so took over the Mustique Company. Colin was heartbroken to lose control, but was marginally mollified by the fact that he was free of the financial burden of Mustique, had money in the bank again and still owned 40 per cent of the Company, along with the site of the old Great House with its beach. He was magnanimous in passing over the control to Hans. On completion he wrote to him, 'It gives me real pleasure to think that you and your colleagues are now in charge of the destinies of Mustique. I am sure you will act wisely. The island is a treasure'.[lxiv]

Hans, too, was delighted as, in his hands, Mustique was safe. As he said:

> Colin and I understood each other. Some of the home owners were harsh, aggressive. He's an English gentleman. There was a clash of personalities. For Colin, form and content are what matter. Many didn't understand. And Colin can change moods like a child. It was better for him to make an offer to me, a kindred spirit who believed in the limited development of the island. We didn't want commercial enterprises here, hotels, a golf course ...[lxv]

Maria Christina, Hans' wife, recalled the occasion. 'Hans was the right person to take over. He had the same ideals as Colin. He never wanted to make money out of Mustique'.[lxvi]

Decades later, with 20:20 hindsight vision, Colin admitted that his greatest mistake with Mustique was to remain there after 1977. As he said:

> I should have given my life to something else, but back I went and

that was that. It was nice for the children in the holidays and there were some very grand parties. The Kents [Duke and Duchess of Kent] were there every year until she became too unwell. And I used to rather rashly move out all the pink sofas in the sitting room onto the beach and the parties were very much as you can imagine.

He decided to stay, build on his beautiful bay and enjoy Mustique without the financial worry. He had also acquired another interest, the beach bar and the shop by the port, from Rory Annesley. Rory was the very first to rent a property in Mustique. He arrived in early 1972 with Meg Stenham, the daughter of the Conservative Party Chairman, Lord Poole, having left behind three failed marriages between them in England. Together they took Blue Waters, Lorelei Robinson's house on Endeavour Point, and considerably enlivened off-season life. He had a ready wit – he once steamed off the beach after talking to Lord Orr-Ewing, former Parliamentary Under-Secretary at the Air Ministry, and Geoffrey Knight, Vice Chairman of the British Aircraft Corporation, muttering 'Just because the man makes fucking aeroplanes does not make him an authority on Proust.'

Mustique seemed to suit Rory and Meg, and they eventually decided to buy land and build a house, for which they asked Oliver to come up with the plans. The Gingerbread House was one of his best, being closest to indigenous West Indian architecture. Rory also needed something to do and acquired The Sand Dollar, a tiny beach bar started by the author with Rick Brammel (they wanted to call it The Sand Flies Inn but Colin would not allow it). He then expanded The Sand Dollar into a smart bar and restaurant built on some rocks on the edge of Britannia Bay. Rory, a loveable cove with great charm and a background in the theatre, also took over the shop nearby and stocked it with expensive items – like the tins of Beluga caviar imported for the wedding of Harrods' erstwhile owner, Sir Hugh Fraser. It looked like a branch of Fortnum and Masons, whereas simpler fare would have been more appropriate.

When the Gingerbread House was nearly completed, Colin decided that he wanted to dispose of the Sunny Caribbee Hotel on Bequia so, in a typical rushed deal on the back of an envelope, he exchanged the hotel for Rory's house, shop and beach bar. For Colin, it was a disaster. He was left with the expensive stock in the shop and its debts, but worse he had forgotten 'that he had signed a note with the bank accepting personal responsibility for all the hotel's debts.[lxvii] The Gingerbread House was then passed on to another Venezuelan, Diego Arias, without Colin ever using it.

Again, with Colin's love of innovation, he set about enlarging the beach bar by extending it out over the water with a restaurant. He called it 'The Raft'. When completed, he employed Basil Charles to manage it for him. Soon afterwards Emma Soames, who had been to the fiftieth birthday party, returned with two girl friends, one of whom was Virginia Royston, the widow of Viscount ('Pips') Royston, who had been heir to Anne's cousin, the Earl of Hardwicke. Virginia, very blonde and very extrovert, returned to Mustique to live with Basil with her two young children, Joey (who had inherited the Earldom from his grandfather by then), and Jemima. Together they ran the bar and restaurant for Colin. Basil would not put up with Colin's behaviour, which led to constant fights, often physical. In 1980, when Colin had had enough of Basil, he fired him, but Basil was one step ahead of Colin and exercised his right to buy the Raft Restaurant and bar for US$100,000, which he instantly raised through three house owners, Lucy Fisher, Bob Guthrie and Jim Heekin. Colin was fond of Virginia and reduced the price of the Beach Bar to $75,000 for Basil to give her 25 per cent as she had no assets. He was always protective of her, particularly after Basil had replaced her with another lover. Today, Basil's Bar has become a legend: it was even reproduced in the garden of the Goring Hotel during the wedding of Prince William and Catherine Middleton, they being habitués of Mustique.

Alongside the sale of the Mustique Company shares Colin also disposed of Tite Street for £500,000 to an Arab buyer, Sheikh Ahmad bin Ali Al Thani, the deposed ruler of Qatar. He bought it not for the architecture and original interior decor, but merely as he was fascinated by the electronic security blinds on the ground floor. The Sheikh never moved in and died six months later, whereupon it lay empty for years, save for a single housekeeper. Like the original Whistler house it was later altered out of all recognition into a mock Queen Anne town house. The developers wanted to pull it down and start again, but it was so well built that they could not demolish the shell and had to build around it. Colin, Anne and the family moved to a fine end-of-terrace house in Kensington.

Notwithstanding his changes in circumstance in Mustique and London, Colin's relationship with Princess Margaret remained constant. He was considered to be her 'official best friend', and in that respect he certainly was. When she came back from holiday, for example, he 'would go along to Kensington Palace', as he recalled 'and sit with her to look at all her holiday snaps. No one else did that kind of thing'. The only time that Colin was really cross with her was when once she was staying at Glen with Roddy, who had arrived in his white Ford Tansit van. For some reason, they decided to sneak away unnoticed, whereupon Colin sent his nephew, Matthew Yorke, down to the filling station in Innerleithen to bring them back to say goodbye to the staff.

When her official duties for The Queen's Silver Jubilee in February 1977 kept her in England, he wrote to her from Mustique:

> Madam
> A line to say, we miss you – very much. It is altogether rather quiet and spiritless this season. I suppose after the [fiftieth birthday] party, and what with the belligerence of the houseowners, a reaction is only to be expected. We need you to cheer us up, and give us something to really look forward to which is missing.... I am hoping to get a house started (with Oliver) for myself, now that I have been paid for The Gingerbread [House]. So all is by no means gloom, only flat without your Royal Highness.[lxviii]

As he wrote to Princess Margaret, with the Mustique Company loans paid off and money in the bank from the sale of the Gingerbread House, Colin embarked on building a house for himself on the romantic site on Plantain Bay nestling in the grove of mature coconut palms. For the new house, or palace, Colin had been originally been working on a Chinoiserie idea, but Oliver soon converted him to a Turkish theme based on the domes of Hagia Sophia. Not surprisingly, with the combination of the two gentlemen *architectus*, Colin and Oliver, the result was truly spectacular, although there were many tears when Colin 'interfered' with Oliver's plans.

It also cost a great deal of money. Colin wanted real coral stone from Barbados (as opposed to Oliver's faux stone made from concrete) but found that the only quarry had closed down through bankruptcy. Colin then bought the quarry and resumed operations.

The whole house consisted of a vast, single room behind an elegant hall with a double door. Four columns, shaped like the trunks of coconut palms, supported the dome that gave the room both height and grandeur. There was one bedroom with a large silver bed, and a dining room in a separate kiosk to the side, next to the kitchen wing. Sadly, Oliver never lived to see undeniably his greatest creation on Mustique finished, as he suffered a major heart attack in a London Hotel. His illness gave Colin the marvellous excuse to sever his ties with him, as the tears and recriminations from the distraught Oliver had become too much to bear. His departure left Colin free to finish and furnish the house with his own touches and embellishments, such as the copper palm fronds on the pillars that were later copied by Tommy Hilfiger when he built his own house three decades later.

The Great House ended up as a true work of art, a fantasy based on several Asian styles. Apart from the Turkish domes, the tiles were from Hong Kong and the front door was made up from carved tiles which were bought from Bali. 'Not a postiche, nor yet a pastiche', Colin claimed, 'but an invention'.

With the main house having only one bedroom, Colin built four wooden Balinese-style cottages for himself and his guests. But the one legacy from the demise of Oliver was Colin's introduction to Robin Guild, the noted London interior decorator. It was through Robin that Colin was introduced to Mitch Crites, a gifted scholar, dealer and entrepreneur in the Indian sub-continent (his conversion to Islam was marked by a 'dry' gallery opening in London.) The introduction was one of the most important in Colin's life, as Mitch's net encompassed the whole of India. It was as if he had been invented for Colin: he knew where everything could be found, and if it was not available, he could have it made, using the same, ancient techniques.

Mitch began by finding the most beautiful of all Colin's possessions, a white marble pavilion that was to grace the front of the Great House. It had belonged to the Maharaja of Bharatpur. Mrs Daniel Moynihan, the wife of the Senator on the Board of Regents of the Smithsonian Institution, Washington DC, told Colin that she was convinced that his pavilion had been associated with the Taj Mahal, which is likely, as it has the same coloured marble with pale ochre veins, and the Bharatpurs, just 50 miles to the west of Agra, were 'great thieves'. It is the most important Mogul building outside India.

The pavilion arrived from India in Mustique in 186 packages with Hari and Lal, two Indian craftsmen who were flown out at Colin's expense to erect it. Unfortunately they had not been paying attention when the temple was dismantled so were little help in putting it together again. They spent all their time praying until Colin sent them packing back to India. The pavilion was erected at the end of a vast pond that doubled as a swimming pool that had already been built. It was Colin's greatest possession and the one that he minded most on leaving. Patrick Lichfield's iconic photograph of Colin, flanked by two turbaned boys, was taken in front of the pavilion. Reinaldo Herrera, who 'styled' the photograph, said that the pavilion had the air of a *jeune fille debutante* compared to the Taj Mahal!

Through Mitch's influence, the 'Turkish' palace was quietly metamorphosed into a meld of Asian cultures, though predominately an Indian palace. He supplied carved sandstone Jali screens and a beautiful painted Pichwai textile wall hanging depicting the Lord Krishna entering a white marble pavilion similar in style to the real one outside, and a host of other quality artefacts. In India, and things Indian, Colin had found his true infatuation that would last to the end of his life.

Oliver died the following July, in 1978, and with his death ended a significant chapter in Mustique. His contribution to the island cannot be overestimated, where the theatre of his houses added a whimsical quality to the island. He taught those who followed about scale, proportion and designing houses for outdoor living. He knew how to site a house and frame a view through its arches. He was difficult to work with, and his projects ended up costing a great deal of money, always over budget. At times Colin wondered if the aggravation was really worth it, as with his own house, but in the end he was Oliver's greatest admirer. Although it was Princess Margaret who suggested him in the first place, it was Colin who recognised his genius and set the benchmark of the architecture on Mustique. The Great House he designed for Colin was truly great.

*Chapter 15*

G

# GLEN

With control of Mustique gone and his Previews office in Buckingham Gate closed, Colin cast around for alternative occupations. As a boy he had been fascinated by postage stamps and had put together a modest schoolboy collection. Seeing Hugo carry the mail every time he flew to St Vincent, Colin dreamed up a stamp to cover the cost of the delivery. There were four colours, red, yellow, blue, and orange. To kick off the venture, the Mustique surcharge stamps were stuck on to specially printed first-day covers beside a St Vincent stamp, franked in Mustique by the post mistress, Doreen Simon, who doubled as the school mistress. Another scheme was to print Mustique Island in the selvedge of sheets of St Vincent stamps and then have them made up into stamp books. These all went to Joe Urch, a stamp dealer from Bristol. They were not a success as they were ignored by true philatelists.

An early tenant of *Les Jolies Eaux* was a stamp dealer called Allan Grant. He met Colin at a drinks party on Mustique where the conversation naturally turned to philately. Allan, and his partner, Ronald Grover, could see that Colin would be a useful member of their team and invited him to join their company, Philatelists Ltd. Colin then enrolled at their philatelist school, Frithan House, in the New Forest for a month so that he knew what he would be talking about, not as a collector with tweezers and gummed hinges, but as a stamp dealer. Philatelists Ltd. had a good business whereby they approached newly independent governments, mostly of small islands, to set up philatelic bureaux. The company would then design and print each nation's postage stamps, donating (free) to the Government all the stamps they required, while they sold the rest of each issue to philatelists around the world. With Colin's connections in the Caribbean, he became an essential ambassador for the firm. Through Colin they set up the philatelic bureau in St Vincent and the Grenadines with the help of the Prime Minister, Milton Cato.

Travelling with Princess Margaret, Colin was also in a unique position to sound out other emergent governments of newly independent Caribbean islands such as St Lucia, Montserrat, Dominica, St Kitts, Nevis and Anguilla, and the British Virgin Islands for philatelic bureaux, and, partially through Colin, Philatelists Ltd. added other islands in the Pacific Ocean, including Tuvalu and Kiribati (formerly the Gilbert and Ellice Islands) and the Seychelles. To coincide with their Royal Wedding, Colin hosted an exhibition at the Hilton Hotel of the Prince Charles and Lady Diana Spencer issues from around the world. Loyally Princess Margaret turned out, she herself an inveterate collector of first-day covers.

Allan and Roy visited Mustique often on their travels. On one occasion they were dining with Colin and Anne at Basil's Bar when something upset Colin. A tantrum followed and, as was so often the case, he took it out on Anne; picking up a raw fish from the kitchen he smote her over the face with it, a variation of a 'slap in the belly with a wet fish', only more painful. Anne knew from long experience to stand absolutely still during a tirade for fear of something worse. As with so many projects in his life, after the initial buzz of setting them up, Colin became bored, or short of money, or both, and sold out, as happened with Philatelist Ltd.

Another departure in Colin's life was a venture into politics. Since the early 1970s he, along with his half-sister, Catherine, had been card-carrying members of the Scottish Nationalist Party (SNP) – as a Lady-in-Waiting Anne was spared membership of a political party that advocated devolution. Both sides of Colin's family had been steeped in politics, the Tennants virtually funding the Liberal Party at the end of the nineteenth century when Sir Charles, The Bart, was the Liberal member for first Glasgow, then Peebles and Selkirk.

While Colin was still at Eton, his mother Pamela had moved from Admiral's House to Phillimore Gardens in Kensington, West London to live with her aunt, Dolly, the Viscountess Gladstone. Aunt Dolly had been married to Herbert Gladstone, the youngest son of the Prime Minister and twenty-two years her senior. The widowed Aunt Dolly fancied herself somewhat as a Liberal grandee and even went so far as to have her knees lifted as she felt that they were all that could be seen of her when she sat on Liberal Party platforms. The operation, where a strip of skin was grafted like a sticking plaster across each knee, was not a success.

In the mid-1950s Lady Jeanne Campbell wrote to Colin:

After you left I had some long thoughts about our conversation and all convinced me that you should take this chance of going into politics. So much depends on timing and it seems from your point of view and Sir Anthony's [Eden]; this day January 24th 1955 – is a perfect day to choose!

From your standpoint – you are riding high publicly – that passes – and in the City you are not that involved in directorships and so forth to feel that the Commons would entail sacrifice.

From Sir Anthony's standpoint Winston [Churchill] will die soon and then he either succeeds or not. If he does succeed, he will surely want to cement tried political relationships rather than spending time helping young friends into the House. If you are already in the House he will be able to help you, and you may find yourself with office at the age he found himself with office!!!

If on the other hand he does not succeed, he will lose power, & heart, and not be able to help anyone. So dear Colin, talk to Clarissa [the Countess of Avon] today. I am sure you will never regret it. ...
With fond love,
Jeannie[lxix]

Nothing ever came of it. As Lady Avon said later 'He was totally unsuited to politics at that time.'[lxx] However, in the autumn of 1977 Colin put himself forward as a candidate for the SNP constituency of Roxburgh, Selkirk and Peebles. He had earlier hosted a Burns Night supper at Glen and contributed to party funds. For weeks before the selection Colin went to every SNP ward, where he spoke eloquently, pledging his support for devolution and his views on bolstering the Scottish economy. With the region being largely agricultural communities, and Colin knowing little of current farming practices, he found some of the meetings difficult. Margot MacDonald, 'she of the dampened fireyness says, "to give the laddie his due, he's been working quite hard!"'[lxxi] Tommy Neillands, Colin's head gardener, drove him to every meeting, and sat at the back of the hall. As he was everywhere around the constituency the organisers thought that he was Colin's most assiduous supporter and, to Tommy's great embarrassment, kept asking if he would like to ask a question. In the end, Colin received the most votes to become the SNP candidate, but it was thought that they would have a better chance against the Liberal candidate, David Steel if they chose an Edinburgh lawyer, Angus Stewart. Colin was made Chairman of the constituency.

Colin finally made it to the Palace of Westminster after his father died in 1983 and, on inheriting the title of Baron Glenconner, had the right to sit as a hereditary peer in the House of Lords. Colin initially thought of sitting on the Cross Benches representing the Scottish Nationalists, but his old Army friend, Peter Rees, (who was ennobled in 1987), wrote to him 'You must be true to your Liberal origins. What would Margot Asquith have said were you to defect?'[lxxii]

He finally took his seat on 1984, sponsored by his great aunt, the life peeress Lady Elliott of Harwood (The Bart's daughter by his second marriage) with the ceremony witnessed by Princess Margaret. He did not, however, make his maiden speech until November 1992 where he spoke on the plight of the banana trade in St Vincent and St Lucia. Many congratulatory letters followed. Lord Palmer thought it a 'brilliant maiden [speech] which was so well received on all sides of the House',[lxxiii] while another peer complimented him on speaking 'without notes – most rare. How dare you be so clever!'[lxxiv] The Resident Representative of St Lucia, Philip Rouse, also sent his congratulations 'which contributed greatly in informing Parliament of the danger that threatens these Islands'.[lxxv] The next year he spoke on the drugs trade in St Lucia.

While Mustique was settling down and with the move to his new house in London complete, Colin was still facing an ongoing crisis with his eldest son, Charlie. From the beginning of his drug habit Charlie, thinking heroin to be glamorous, was determined to become an addict. He started at the age of 16 and, like other addicts, his looks remained at that age virtually for the rest of his all-too-short life. Towards the end he became completely ravaged, with no vein untapped, including his eyeballs. He had continued his unconventional education with a succession of private tutors after the disaster of Frensham Heights, and there was absolutely no chance of him ever finding employment. Colin and Anne tried everything to cure him. Charlie was sent to a clinic in Edinburgh for ten months where there were group therapy sessions every Friday, but he still managed to be supplied with drugs whilst there, so the treatment failed. He went to another clinic in the United States but the cures lasted only until he returned to London and his suppliers. Both parents were in despair, although neither ever gave up on him. Charlie stole items from the house and sold them to fund his habit. He once took the countess' coronet that had belonged to Lady Winchelsea and Nottingham to Spinks. Virginia Sykes-Wright, then a young assistant, recalled this 'totally beautiful blond god', Charlie, coming into the gallery with a tin box, out of which he produced the coronet with its purple velvet cap and pearls. He said that he wanted £600 for it, which Virginia thought exactly the market value, and gave him the money. Her head of department recognised it instantly and told her to contact Colin. He came down straight away with the £600 in cash and bought his coronet back, with the instruction that if Charlie ever brought in anything else to sell, he was to be given the money and he would reimburse them. It was the start of a professional relationship between Virginia and her colleague Simon Ray that lasted to the day Colin died.

Colin indulged Charlie, and paid for him to travel. He spent long periods in New York, where he consorted with the likes of Andy Warhol and Robert Mapplethorpe, and stayed for months at the Imperial Hotel in Delhi where Colin thought that opium was not as harmful as heroin. When he visited Thailand he was caught entering Heathrow with 7.4 grams of opium with a street value of about £37. He was arrested and spent the night in a police cell. The next day the magistrates remanded him in custody for seven days and he was sent to Ashford Prison. There, he was put into overalls and shared a dormitory with five others, one of whom was said to have axed an old lady to death. Suffering from 'cold turkey' without his drugs, he was made to scrub floors. When he appeared in court a week later he was given a £200 fine and a conditional discharge as he already had 'a place to go for treatment' and the promise of a job on a cattle farm in Africa (which never materialised). Whilst in hospital his friends continued to supply him with heroin. Like some remittance man Charlie was sent to Australia to work on a sheep station. He turned up the first day in silk cowboy shirt, green velvet trousers, snakeskin high-heeled boots and mirror sunglasses. The farmer took one look at him and said, 'Jeezus will you look at that' and sent him away. Charlie did fare better while staying with Colin's half-brother, Toby, on his farm in the Borders.

Knowing the responsibilities and the expense of running an estate, Colin realised that Charlie would never be in a fit state to take over Glen and decided to pass everything over to his brother Henry. Henry had started at Eton but left to go to the Edinburgh Academy, where he did well academically. He was certainly in tune with Scotland and country ways. Colin's decision to disinherit his eldest son was not taken lightly, but he could see that, in Charlie's condition, he could not have begun to manage his inheritance and Glen would undoubtedly have been disposed of immediately he inherited, and the money squandered. Colin believed that it would be in safer hands with Henry. As it turned out Henry, who married Tessa Cormack, the granddaughter of the Liberal Peer Lord Davies, whom he had met travelling in Ecuador, has been the saviour of Glen, keeping it going and making it work against all the odds. As part of the deal whereby Charlie signed over his future rights of Glen to Henry, Colin agreed to look after him medically for the rest of his life and for him to inherit the West Indian properties. There were some spells when Charlie was better but, as he grew older, the improvements were for fewer, and for shorter, periods. At one stage he was so bad that Anne banned him from their houses, fearing his influence on her other children. Also, he had the habit of leaving lighted cigarettes on the furniture, 'little charred sausages' as Colin called them, and she was frightened that he would burn down the house.

One of Charlie's better periods of improvement happened while staying with Rosie Baldwin on Mustique, where he even talked 'of being Mustique's Mr Whippy in a tuneful electric ice-cream van'.[lxxvi] His stay coincided with yet another visit of the Royal Yacht *Britannia* bearing The Queen and The Duke of Edinburgh on their tour of the Caribbean that coincided with the Commonwealth Conference in the Bahamas. Everyone on Mustique, especially Princess Margaret, was in a rare state of apprehension, particularly as the weather was changeable. The Royal party came ashore and were received by Princess Margaret, Colin and Anne under a triumphal arch. The local children put on a short pageant before they all repaired to *Les Jolies Eaux*. At the picnic Colin arranged at Macaroni Beach, Charlie was seated next to Her Majesty. He gaily told her that he had recently been staying in one of her houses. Intrigued, The Queen asked which one. 'HMP Ashford, Ma'am', replied Charlie with a mischievous grin. At Her Majesty's pleasure.

Colin laid on a party at the Cotton House that night where he, Princess Margaret, Jean Wills and Christopher sang to the tune of 'My Bonny Lies over the Ocean' a sycophantic song they had composed on the Queen's tour, with the refrain:

*Your peoples are over the ocean,*
*Your peoples are over the sea,*
*You honoured them all with your presence,*
*You started your trip in Belize.*

The song failed to liven the stiff atmosphere. The evening was, however, saved by a performance of 'Alphonso the dancing dwarf'. This was a clever routine whereby Arne, with his arms inside a T-shirt, formed the head, torso and legs of the 'dwarf', with his hands in a pair of clogs for his feet, while Nevill, standing close behind, put his arms through slits in the back and out through the sleeves of the T-shirt as the dwarf's arms. Their bodies, not on display, were hidden behind a screen above a table on which Alphonso performed a clog dance to the great amusement of all.

Charlie was back in the news again the next year when he stole some photographs of Princess Margaret taken at a party at Glen. As every year, Colin had arranged an extravaganza whereby most of the house guests performed for the other 150 invited guests, such as neighbours, estate workers, and tenants – who at one stage included members of The Incredible String Band, a talented folk group who rented cottages on the estate.

One member of the house party was John Phillips, the songwriter and leader of the American group, The Mamas and The Papas, who told Colin about a long-sleeved T-shirt printed to look like a dinner jacket, complete with a black bow tie and white carnation. For Colin it was a must-have item. Frantic calls to Los Angeles followed and a dozen were air-freighted overnight, picked up at Heathrow and carried to Edinburgh to arrive moments before the male chorus opened the show with a rendition of 'Chattanooga Choo Choo'. Then Prince Rupert Loewenstein and Michael Szell, with Jade Jagger, May and Amy, tripped onto the stage dressed as sugar plum fairies, followed by Bianca Jagger who danced the *danse de faune*, only the performance was the *'danse du phone'* when a telephone rang and she answered it at the end of her performance. Roddy Llewellyn, dressed as a wizard, sang 'What I See in Your Eyes' to a skull, followed by the author, who danced a highland fling in a kilt that slowly came apart and fell to reveal a large green fig leaf – pinned to flesh-coloured tights. Colin, in his usual role as master of ceremonies and appropriately dressed in a top hat and frock coat, introduced each act, culminating with two masterful performances from Princess Margaret. In one, dressed as the

Valkyrie Brünnhilde complete with horned helmet, blonde wig and spear, she mimed a spirited aria from the *Die Walküre*, the second opera in Wagner's *Ring Cycle*. In the other performance, dressed in a sleek black dress, a feather boa and a curly blonde wig, she appeared as Sophie Tucker, the 'Red Hot Momma'. Again she mimed two songs before metamorphosing as Mae West, when she parodied all the seductive gestures of the old movie goddess. It was these photographs of Princess Margaret that Charlie sold to a friend for just £20, which appeared soon after in the *Daily Mail*. Anne sued for breach of copyright, and won large damages, which she donated to charity.

The house parties were always the greatest fun and happy affairs. Colin was inevitably at his most original best. There was always great wit around. One guest, the artist Teddy Millington-Drake, looking at a purple-clad hillside, declared that the heather was very pretty but 'I do so wish it was blue', to which Colin replied: 'Of course you're right, it should be blue'. Taking Teddy's remark in hand, the next year he bought vast numbers of brightly coloured paper flowers and decorated the hillside by Loch Eddy for a party. On another occasion, one overcast morning Prince Rupert Loewenstein came down to breakfast in a loud tweed suit that resembled a Russian salad, saying: 'I thought the day looked grey so I would cheer it up by wearing this suit!'

With Colin's mercurial temperament he was never content to stay in one place for long. He and Anne were inveterate travellers, and had an exotic holiday each year to places such as Mozambique and the Comoros Islands, Mauritius, Madagascar, Tanzania and one year in Saudi Arabia, as the guests of Sheikh Yamani.

Sheikh Yamani, the brilliant international lawyer and Minister for Oil in the Saudi Arabian Government, sailed into Mustique on *Nabila*, the largest private yacht afloat belonging to Adnan Kashoggi. The Sheikh was at the height of his power, being the most prominent minister in OPEC, and had recently survived a horrendous kidnap in Vienna at the hands of the notorious Carlos the Jackal, in an operation now thought to have been funded by Gadaffi. At first Sheikh Yamani refused to come ashore, so Colin ignored him, but relented when the Sheikh sent a message that he wanted a tour of the island. His visit caused a great stir. The ex-SAS soldiers employed to guard the Sheikh were to be seen practising their martial arts on Macaroni Beach. The private secretary was sent to Martinique to collect the week's petty cash for the yacht, all US$400,000 of it, and Claire Turner, Colin's secretary, was deputed to look after a 14-year-old guest for the day. She asked him if he would like to go for a walk, or a swim, or perhaps for a ride? 'No', the youth replied, 'I want a woman.' Then, pausing for a moment as a woman walked by he added 'I'll have that one!' It was Bianca Jagger.

Back in England Colin read that Sheikh Yamani was going to a conference in Edinburgh and invited him to stay at Glen, which he readily accepted. As it was late autumn, the central heating was turned up to full blast. Everyone was sweating with the heat save for the guests, who spent the whole time in heavy fur coats.

In return, Sheikh Yamani invited Colin and Anne to stay in his summer retreat in the hills, some distance from Riyadh. Never at a loss to find an original present, Colin brought one of the richest men in the world two honeycombs from the hives at Glen. Colin and Anne set off from Heathrow to a barrage of Press cameras, looking every inch the handsome jet-set couple, and arrived, as Colin recalled, 'at the somewhat disappointing summer mansion made of concrete [where] we were in a rather uninspiring guest cottage that looked like a container'. The fellow guests included the very grand Prince and Princess Borghese from Italy. They stayed for five days, in the searing heat, with nothing to do except sit around the swimming pool. Anne could not even sunbathe as it was indiscreet to show her ankles since it 'would inflame the servants'. Towards dusk, men in big flowing garments 'in whites and brown and navy blue' joined all the house guests in a huge sagging tent with Turkish carpets and huge cushions. Then, quite late at night, they were suddenly joined by Sheikh Yamani and his ravishing wife, Tammam al-Anbar. Colin was captivated by her and her hair. 'It was really like a raven's wing, black, rippling down her back, but like a bird's feathers, shining, shining. She had a wonderful figure and eyes to match.' One evening, as a joke, Sheikh Yamani picked out a sheep's eye and handed it to Anne like a grape on a skewer. After dinner Colin and Sheikh Yamani danced together every night to a blind Egyptian pianist. The inevitable shopping trip followed and, having been thoroughly entertained, they 'flipped back to London and that was the end of that adventure'. They returned home laden with 'uninviting gifts of rather tawdry silver belts'. Apart from the heat Colin revelled in those five days, quoting long passages from *The Rubáiyát of Omar Khayyám*, which he had not thought of since his days at Eton.

For Colin there was always the annual holiday with Anne and the younger children (Charlie was variously in his house in Fulham or in a clinic, while Henry was starting at Edinburgh University). Like his mother, Pamela, Colin was always imaginative with these holidays and in 1979 he took them, with Barbara the nanny, to the United States. It was typical of Colin to include Austin Lewis, a boy from Lovell Village in Mustique, who was a friend and contemporary of Henry's, to drive the minibus he had hired in Phoenix, Arizona. Once out of the city, Austin took over the driving and immediately drove into a cactus – he had only ever driven in Mustique before, so Colin had to drive the whole way.

They went first to the Grand Canyon, where only Anne descended to the bottom on a mule. A trip to a dude ranch followed, before driving to San Francisco where Colin had hired an enormous double-decker Winnebago. The first stop was a theatrical costumier recommended by his friend, John Phillips. He eventually found the warehouse and parked the huge bus outside on a 'No Parking' bay and went in, leaving Anne and the rest outside. It was not long before two policemen drove up on their huge Harley Davidson motorcycles. They swaggered over to the motor home, the San Francisco skyline reflecting in their dark glasses. As they slowly took off their gloves they told Anne in their Californian drawl that she was illegally parked and had to move the 'van'. Anne remonstrated that she could not drive it, nor could Austin or Barbara. The cop repeated that it had to be moved: Anne said that only her husband could move it as he had the keys and he was inside. Eventually Christopher was sent in to find Colin. Five minutes later the stalemate was broken when Colin appeared dressed as a fairy. It was a wonderful apparition. He wore a pink tulle ballet tutu over a pink satin leotard, pink tights and pink pumps. A large pair of feather wings sprouted from his shoulder blades. The cops' jaws dropped as Colin advanced. As he tapped the sergeant on the shoulder with his pink wand, he dropped he keys into his hand and sweetly asked if he could move the vehicle. The cops looked at each other, turned as one, and drove off. They had met their match! Disaster struck when Colin drove down the switchback streets, totally out of control, knocking off the wing mirrors of the parked cars.

Not all of Colin's travels were purely for pleasure, as with the two philanthropic tours of Ghana and Thailand. One night he was dining in London when his neighbour told him that the Third World needed outside labour, not money to develop, as the money invariably went to a numbered bank account in Switzerland, whereas manpower, working alongside the locals, produced the best results. Colin grandly said that he had 300 men at his disposal, to which his neighbour responded that he should use them for some good in the world. The next day Colin telephoned his partner, Gerald Ward, who was Chairman of the Young Men's Christian Association (YMCA) to inquire if they had any interesting projects on offer. Gerald came up with the building of a post office in the jungle in Ghana. Colin agreed to go and take six others so long as it was a clinic, not a post office that they built. At his own expense Colin flew Eldon Lewis and two other Mustiquians from Lovell Village, along with Carib, the taxi-driver from St Vincent, Junior, the Swedish electrician, and Basil, to London, where they were joined by Colin and the author to fly on to Accra. They hired a car and drove down along the coast to the slave castle of Elmina, then up to Kumasi where they were all received by the King of Ashanti, seated on the golden stool under a vast umbrella in the Manhyia Palace. That night Colin left the windows in his hotel room open and the light on as he went out to dinner. When he returned there were two Rüppell's griffon vultures perched on the end of his bed. He thought that it was an omen and that he was about to 'be gathered', but they flapped off into the night.

From there the party drove to the small town of Ho in the Upper Volta region, where they stayed in a YMCA hostel. It was deeply uncomfortable (the pillows appeared to be filled with 'dinosaurs' toenail clippings'), but very hospitable. Every day for a fortnight they went to the village of Hlefe, not far from the shores of Lake Volta. It was an extraordinary experience for them all, not least the dismissive attitude of the West Indians towards the Ghanaians. When the clinic was virtually built the *togbe*, or chief, gave a 'topping out' party. The virgins of the village danced, they prepared wonderful local dishes and not so wonderful palm wine. Colin, dressed in the tribal polychrome robes and a gold crown with a semi-erect phallus, was made an honorary *togbe* – though, to his disappointment, he was not allowed to hang on to his regalia. At the end of the trip they returned via Rome, where they all stayed with Milton Gendel, Judy's American widower, on the Isola Tiberina. At the farewell dinner back in London, the Mustiquians, who had never left St Vincent and the Grenadines before and consequently had never seen things that are taken for granted in the West – an escalator, sleek cars, streets of smart shops, the antiquities of Rome – were asked what they remembered most about the adventure. Carib, the most sensitive of them all, said that there was a 'painted bus in Accra that had the same name as one in Kingstown back home'.

Three years later Colin repeated the exercise and took another party to

Thailand. Again he had consulted Gerald, who put him in touch with the YMCA in Geneva. They operated some refugee camps on the Laotian border and Colin was given permission to go there to help. This time his party included Brian and Arne, along with Basil and Junior again, with Winston King, who was responsible for the agriculture on Mustique. They flew to Bangkok where the local YMCA top brass were very unhelpful, as they did not want a bunch of amateurs running around and upsetting the place. Basil and Winston, being black and resembling American GIs from the Vietnam War, were left behind, while the others moved north to Changmai, then under a military governor. Only Junior, with his special engineering skills, was allowed to go up country to the Laotian border to repair broken generators and electrical installations. Returning to Changmai he was caught in an ambush. The party then drove back to the capital where they all indulged in the flesh-coloured delights of Bangkok before flying home via Hong Kong. Colin paid for the whole trip, which cost a great deal of money but, apart from Junior's work, was totally unproductive at the end.

Often a holiday was tacked on to, or preceded, an official visit with Princess Margaret. Colin and Anne made a round-the-world tour in 1978 that coincided with the independence celebrations of Tuvalu, a minute speck of an island in the Pacific Ocean. The visit was not a success because Princess Margaret developed viral pneumonia before the official ceremony and was flown to Sydney to recover. She was due to go on to the Philippines and Hong Kong, but these visits were cancelled and Colin and Anne were asked to deliver a personal note of apology from Princess Margaret to Madame Imelda Marcos, and to explain the reason in person. Recognising a shopaholic when she saw one, she had a department store in Manila opened up at midnight for them to take anything they wanted. Anne thought the whole thing rather vulgar and found a couple of fabric badges for the twins to sew onto their jeans. Colin, on the other hand, predictably went mad with delight as he ran from department to department like a demented child in a sweetshop. Crates of 'loot' were shipped to Mustique for the new house.

Never one to spend her own money unless it was absolutely necessary, Princess Margaret grabbed any of the official engagements going in the Caribbean as her, and her Lady-in-Waiting's, airfares were then paid by the British taxpayer. Thus, she was able to fit in a week in Mustique before going, with Colin and Anne, to Dominica for their independence celebrations, and again to those of St Kitts Nevis and Anguilla. She was not, however, required for the granting of Statehood of St Vincent and the Grenadines. Colin had been part of the Associate Statehood celebrations ten years before, when Britain gave the government control over its internal affairs of the islands. It was a time of great celebration, so much so that David Wilson remembers Bequia being virtually deserted the day after, and those people he did see moving were doing so very slowly indeed. On Mustique Colin threw a party for the locals with a few invited outside guests that included James Mitchell, the MP for the Grenadines. The village turned out and enjoyed themselves hugely, all except for Hubert Trimmingham, a man in his mid-nineties. When James went to see him the next day to ask why he did not join the party, Hubert replied: 'If the white man wants to give me something, then he can bring it to my house!' Colin always had an exceptional relationship with the village.

The Statehood celebrations a decade later were equally spectacular, and included a reception at Government House to which Colin and Anne were naturally invited. After dinner the police band were playing a medley of tunes in the background. After a short break they struck up again playing 'All Through the Night' by Cole Porter. Colin, who knew the words, started to sing along with the band, but Milton Cato, the Premier, thinking that it was the new national anthem of St Vincent and the Grenadines, leapt to his feet and stood rigidly to attention!

The older Princess Margaret became, the more she looked to new cerebral friends to entertain her. Professor Sir John (Jack) Plumb, not of *Cluedo* fame but the erudite Master of Christ's College, Cambridge was one, and through her, he too became a friend of Colin's and Anne's. Colin maintained that he was in love with him, but then he said that about many such men, with absolutely no foundation. Sir Oliver Millar, Surveyor of the Queen's Pictures, was another friend who organised jolly trips to various Royal residences for them all. Once, accompanied by Lady (Pru) Penn, they all went to the Queen's House at Greenwich where, to Princess Margaret's fury, she and Colin jumped into the State Bed together. Her letter of apology to Princess Margaret, written in verse, was a triumph. Another time Colin went with Princess Margaret to Rome where, accompanied by Milton Gendel, she went to look at the churches, for which she had a great liking and a prodigious memory. Colin stayed with Milton, while Princess Margaret was entertained by the Ambassador. As it was an unofficial visit, various members of the embassy staff were deputed to entertain them.

When foisted on one of them for lunch, the 10-year-old daughter of the hosts was told to say the grace they had taught her earlier. At the table she became tongue-tied and whispered that she had forgotten what she had to say. 'You remember', whispered her mother, 'just repeat what daddy and I said before lunch', whereupon the little girl piped up: 'Oh God, why do we have to have this difficult woman to lunch?'

*Chapter 16*

# THE RITZ

With the Great House up and running Colin used it to the full, entertaining a succession of guests and his family. As before, his parties were legion. For one at Basil's Bar he had bought a blow-up sex doll and tossed it into the sea. As she drifted away he shouted, 'Look, a woman's drowning', whereupon the place emptied as the men dived into the water to save 'her'. They were rather deflated when they found what they had rescued.

'We liked to be spontaneous', Colin recalled. 'We had one tableau where I told everyone that an exotic lady from the East was arriving. She was carried in on a litter, hidden under a mosquito net.' Four local fishermen, their semi-naked bodies painted gold underneath gold tinsel cloaks (left over from the fiftieth birthday party), carried in the bier covered with a mosquito net. Colin advanced with a machete, announcing: 'The Princess has come to us at last, but she has to be freed from this awful cocoon which has kept her prisoner for the last 1,000 years!' With that he slashed the muslin with the machete and Bianca Jagger emerged wearing something diaphanous. To kick off the dancing, Colin organised a Paul Jones. When the music stopped, one myopic female house-owner found herself opposite Cliffy, the painted tractor driver, and complimented him on his beautiful gold suit. Certain sections of the media delighted in 'revealing' the drug-fuelled sex-parties on Mustique. While Colin's guests were responsible for their own actions, and some inevitably used drugs, they were never condoned by Colin, who had a total abhorrence, having seen first-hand what they had done to Charlie. As for the orgies, if they happened, they happened behind closed doors.

Nakedness on Mustique was not the norm, although of course topless bathing was virtually *de rigueur* when it was fashionable throughout the world's beaches. Colin went through a short 'streaking' period and would drop his trunks at the earliest opportunity. At one picnic on Lagoon Beach with Princess Margaret, Roddy, and the author, Colin asked her if she minded if he removed his swimming trunks. She replied 'So long as I don't have to look at *it*.' So Colin stripped off and covered his groin with his cotton panama hat. Roddy then removed his trunks. The only man left clothed was the author, who reluctantly removed his trunks too. Princess Margaret, needless to say, remained fully clothed in her creation. After a swim and a walk along the beach, Colin then took Roddy's camera and photographed Princess Margaret with the naked Roddy and the author, she hiding their 'modesty' with the skirts of her bathing costume. Princess Margaret then photographed the three in various poses. The scene was interrupted by the arrival of a trailer-load of construction workers who had come for their afternoon 'sea bath' – their wild guffaws could long be heard as they retreated to another beach. Fearing that the photographs could be misconstrued, Colin took the film out of Roddy's camera. Taking a great risk, he had the negatives developed in the chemist shop at Innerleithen and kept the prints in his desk in London.

Ten years later the photographs appeared in the *News of the World*, where drawn coronets were strategically placed. A week later the photographs appeared in colour in *Paris Match* where Union Flags were used, only they were flown at half-mast. For the first time ever, the author's wife went to buy the Sunday newspapers in the local corner shop. There she met a friend and remonstrated about her buying the *News of the World*. 'At least *my* husband is not naked on the front page!' she replied. A great aunt of the author's saw them and castigated the proprietors of the paper for airbrushing out the swimming trunks to make it appear that they were all naked, while Nigel Dempster, the gossip columnist, merely used the story to show how lean the diet on Mustique was in those early days. Roddy sued the paper for breach of copyright and won substantial damages in an out of court settlement. Few believed Colin when he said that he had nothing to do with the sale. After he died Anne destroyed the prints, but not before showing them to the twins in front of the author. Today, nudity is not tolerated publicly on Mustique.

With Colin at the Great House, the island under Hans Neumann's overall stewardship, and the management of the services in the hands of the House Owners Association, Mustique struggled on. When Brian Alexander was asked to continue managing the island, he declined, feeling that 'Mustique was dead in the water'. Consequently Hans, at John Gold's suggestion, brought in the former Governor of Montserrat, Dennis Gibbs. Colin disliked him and his colonial manner. In the meantime Nevill Turner, who had decamped to St Lucia to restore and run a hotel, returned and, with Brian and Arne, secured the marketing of Mustique worldwide, so replacing Previews International. With John Golds and Brian, Nevill then put together an overall strategy for the marketing and future of Mustique. They came up with a plan that a total of only 120 lots should be sold. As Nevill said 'The idea of scarcity suddenly presented itself. The plan gave us the unique selling point of privacy, exclusivity, urgency – better buy now before it is all gone.' Hans adopted the proposal in its entirety. For the first time in the development of Mustique there was a coherent policy and marketing strategy that could be followed, as opposed to the former whim of one man, Colin. The report did, however, give him full credit for his 'way of doing things, particularly his style and good taste'.[lxxvii] At the eleventh hour Mustique had turned the corner of decline. Although Colin was not directly involved with the renaissance, his presence on the island, and his 'ways', all contributed to its eventual success. Colin was synonymous with Mustique, and it was still considered to be 'his' island which, for many, was a strong reason to buy land there and to build.

But whatever the easy bonhomie and bluster that Colin presented on the outside, inside he was deeply troubled. He needed constant reassurance that he was well-loved – there was even a 'Colin we love you party' at Basil's Bar where the guests wore T-shirts with COLIN printed on the front. He was deeply touched when everyone sang 'For He's a Jolly Good Fellow'. But then all his life he needed constant assurance that those around him really cared for him. Even when family and friends did love him, as with both his parents, he would not believe them, and would still react disgracefully against them. Emotionally, he was a bully. Whatever anyone gave Colin by way of love, whether it was Anne, the children, or the rest of his family and friends, it was never enough. He was invariably disappointed with everybody, particularly his parents, C. Tennant, Sons & Co. and the Mustique Company Board, imagining (wrongly) that they had let him down. This only increased his internal anger and frustrations towards them, which subsequently manifested itself in towering rages.

It was not long, however, before Hans asked Colin to be Chairman of the Mustique Company. Hans realised that, as Colin was living on

Mustique it was, like the Hoover principle, better to have him on the inside of the tent rather than out. It was a clever move, too, to have him on board and let 'Colin take the front seat and have the kudos of being king of the island'.[lxxviii] Also, he could use his house for entertaining prospective clients and keeping existing clients happy. But the major decisions were still made by Hans. Steve Rubell, the co-owner of Studio 54, the New York nightclub, loved Mustique – his live-long memory was watching the sharks mate on Black Sand Bay – and wanted to buy Arne's house, Fort Gustav for US$1 million. Hans did not want him or his like on the island and vetoed the proposed purchase. Colin was all for him. Likewise the former President of the Philippines, Ferdinand Marcos, and his wife Imelda, wanted to buy land and build, but Hans would not have them either. Colin was further disappointed when, after Marcos was deposed, he wanted to rent the Great House for an enormous sum, but Princess Margaret told Colin he was not to let to the deposed President.

Inevitably, Colin fell out with Hans, but by that time Brian had agreed to take over as Managing Director of the Mustique Company. He was to stay for twenty-eight years. At least Colin had an ally at 'court'. It can only have been frustrating for him to see Mustique developing into what he had envisaged, but failed to achieve for himself. The rich and famous beat a path to his door as they swallowed up the remaining lots on the island. They built large houses and gave opulent parties. The houses were rented for vast sums of tax-free money, bringing in generations of new blood from all over the world. Mustique moved up several notches. Mick Jagger enlarged the Beach Cottage at L'Ansecoy Bay in the Japanese style. Another early client was Harding Lawrence who, with his wife, Mary Wells, built a vast Italianate villa, The Terraces. They were the dynamic couple. He had run Braniff Airlines, while she was the owner of the hugely successful advertising agency, Wells Rich Greene, and was the only female CEO of a publicly quoted company on the New York Stock Exchange. They ended up in Mustique having left Acapulco after some Columbians occupied their house and, as Mary said, Harding had ruined the place 'by flying millions of tourists from the United States there on Braniff Airlines and by building hotels for them.... Acapulco was great when it was little and sexy and, when I heard about Mustique, it sounded like my dream of a private island, and perfect.'[lxxix]

During the ten-year 'interregnum' after Colin had partially sold out to Hans, celebrities passed through the door of the Great House in such numbers as to be indistinguishable one form the other. Colin, for example, greatly admired Raquel Welch's beauty. As he recalled:

> Her wrists and ankles were ravishing and so was the rest of her. But it's rare for everything to be perfect, and she had nothing much to say. She was a nice enough woman but totally self-absorbed. She spent the whole of her time doing yoga. She came several times to Mustique. Her husband of many years was a Frenchman, André Weinfeld. He was *par excellence*, very Jewish and very amusing. She did not appear to have any friends. I went to her birthday party once in New York where the only other guests were her hairdresser and PR man.

There were, however, two permanent guests at the Great House: a couple of St Vincent Parrots (*Amazona guildinii*). Their generic name came from the Reverend Landsdown Guilding who had been rector of St George's Anglican Church in Kingstown at the beginning of the nineteenth century. He was a fine naturalist and a wonderful artist whom Colin greatly admired, and subsequently owned many examples of his work. The two parrots had originally been four, but they started to quarrel and one was killed. Colin separated the remaining three, giving one to Basil, who called it 'Mr T', although no one had the remotest idea what sex they were. 'They were magnificent birds, the most noble birds I have ever seen', Colin recalled of his two parrots, who flew about the palm trees and came when called. They made their nest in one of the guest cottages but it was actually Colin's mother, Pamela's, bedroom. 'So when she approached it they swooped down and attacked her because they presumably supposed she was a marauder, nay even a marauderess.' Thereafter they had to live in a cage where they eventually died aged 15 years.

On one occasion the Government veterinary surgeon, Dr Earle Kirby, visited Mustique to discuss the plight of the St Vincent Parrot with Colin. He went to the Great House and was on the beach looking out over a very low spring tide. There, just showing above the water, were three distinct pottery rings. He leapt into the sea and started to push away the sand with his hands, soon to be joined by Colin. They pulled up a bottomless pot, then another underneath, and a third below that. They managed to extract a total of six pots altogether. What they had discovered was the earliest known example of 'pot stacks' in the Caribbean. The early inhabitants of

Mustique tapped into the freshwater lens on the sea shore before it leached out into the sea. These WOR (white on red) decorated pots dated from the fifth century AD. Today some of them are in the Mustique museum.

The one client who set the mode of Mustique above all others was Patrick Lichfield. He had admired the island since his debut photoshoot in 1967 and had returned regularly. He loved the anonymity of the early days. As there was no television, cinema or radio no one knew if anyone was famous or not. Colin, whom he described as 'the classic English explorer, unsuitably dressed and indomitable',[lxxx] recognised what an asset he would be to the island and gave him a special price on his small plot beside Princess Margaret's land at Gellizeau. Oliver then designed a fine house for him named Obsidian after the bay it overlooked. Patrick brought another dimension to the island. He invited a succession of grandees to stay, some forming the core of the house owners' cricket team with the likes of Charles Balfour and an assortment of peers, Tommy Arran, Tim Tollemache, Anthony Tryon and Shaun Normanton, all with their glamorous wives. He captured the spirit of Mustique in his being, and through his camera lens.

Although Colin was no longer at the helm of Mustique, the island continued to attract the famous and the attentions of the Press. After Mick and Bianca Jagger's divorce, Bryan Ferry rented a house with his then girlfriend, Jerry Hall. It was there that she met Mick, whom she subsequently married in an unofficial Balinese ceremony. Shortly afterwards, another rock legend, David Bowie, and his wife, the model Iman, bought a lot and built a magnificent house in the Balinese style. The house is now owned by the publisher, Felix Dennis.

But Colin's life was not, however, entirely centred on Mustique. There were long periods between visits that were spent either at the house in Eldon Street, later Victoria Road, in London, at Glen, or abroad. As before, much of his time was taken up by Princess Margaret. When Roddy Llewellyn, Prince Rupert Loewenstein and his wife, Josephine, were staying with Colin and Anne, the subject of Princess Margaret's fiftieth birthday came up. After a short discussion they decided that they should give her a party, and that Paul and Ingrid Channon's large house on the Embankment in Chelsea (now owned by Roman Abramovich), with its ballroom and large courtyard would be the best venue. The party was to be small and intimate, with only close friends and a small band. When this reached the ears of Lady Penn, a Lady-in-Waiting to The Queen Mother, she and fourteen other friends organised their own dance, which was held on 4

November at the Ritz Hotel in London. There were 200 guests that included most of the Royal Family. Colin felt that he had been cold-shouldered. He lamented: 'I made some enquiries but received only vague replies. Clearly our party had been brushed aside as it was not thought appropriate for Roddy to co-host such a dance.' He and Anne received late invitations, while Roddy's arrived only two days before the dance. He was adamant that he was not going, but Colin and Anne insisted that he should. Colin forced him into a dinner jacket and took him out to dinner in a nearby restaurant.

The hosts gave a private dinner in the Louis XVI Room which included The Queen and The Duke of Edinburgh. Their dinner party was making its way to the ballroom when Colin, Anne and Roddy arrived. There: 'Everyone in the long corridor turned aside, including The Queen. So we walked straight through, without being greeted, onto the dance floor. I danced with Princess Margaret, and Roddy with Anne. Then, by prior arrangement, Princess Margaret disengaged herself from me to dance with Roddy, and I swept off with Anne. And that was that.'

The incident was to have profound consequences. It virtually marked the end of Princess Margaret's relationship with Roddy as, shortly afterwards, he met, and subsequently married, Tania Soskin, a fashion designer. Thereafter, Princess Margaret 'carried a flagpole for Roddy for the rest of her life'. The other cost to Colin was that the hosts and the Royal Family blamed him for the whole Roddy charade, and he was not to remain unpunished. He and Anne were left off the guest list of the wedding of the Prince of Wales and Lady Diana Spencer. Nor were they alone. Reinaldo and Carolina Herrera were asked by Princess Margaret to stay at Kensington Palace over the Royal Wedding. On the morning they were standing in the hall, she beautifully dressed in one of her creations, Reinaldo immaculate in his morning coat and silk top hat, waiting for Princess Margaret to appear. Her car was purring outside when Princess Margaret swept down to greet them. 'When are we leaving?' asked Carolina. Ignoring the question, Princess Margaret replied 'Oh, I have arranged a television in the sitting room. All the staff are coming to the wedding, so they have left some sandwiches for you.' With that she was in her car and swept off to Buckingham Palace, leaving them speechless. Notwithstanding this misunderstanding, Carolina undertook to dress Princess Margaret, which greatly improved her appearance for the rest of her life.

Colin was finally reconciled with The Queen when they met at a party where they discussed Barbara Barnes, their loyal nanny and friend, who had just been recruited by the Princess of Wales to care for the future Prince William, and later Prince Harry.

By the mid-1980s Colin began to bring his life on Mustique to a close. With his mercurial temperament, it is surprising that he lasted so long. He became more and more difficult, and alienated more and more people who never forgave him. Hans and the rest of the board members found him impossible to deal with, and he was the despair of the House Owners Association. The end came when the H.O.A. approached Colin and Hans to buy out the majority shareholding in Mustique, to which they agreed in principle. Colin then became impossible over terms, and in his dealings with Hans. He had learned a lesson from John Ponsonby, who had worked for him in the early 1960s, that

> if you were expecting to be sacked or going to leave, make yourself as difficult as possible, because if you left under a cloud it was always accompanied by a heavy rainstorm of money. If you left quietly, or voluntarily, you were given a rousing party and you left in sunshine, in dry weather, but without much in the way of compensation. So towards the end of my time in Mustique I kept on bringing up massive, outlandish schemes, like creating a big marina down by the lagoon, which I knew would annoy them.

In the end, Colin sold his remaining 40 per cent of the Mustique Company to Hans to give him 100 per cent of the company, keeping 50 acres around the lagoon for himself. Hans, in a separate deal, then sold on 75 per cent to the house owners with the proviso that no house owner should have more than 5 per cent. Brian, ever loyal to Colin, pleaded with him to keep 10 per cent of the company, but he dismissed the idea out of hand. He was sick of Mustique, and particularly the board members of the Mustique Company, and would not hear of it. 'He just wanted out.'[lxxxi] Colin put it another way: 'It becomes wearisome to listen to people complain, and in the long run it just wasn't worth listening to them.'

Later, in St Lucia, while reflecting on his years directing Mustique, Colin marked up a passage from *A Lost Lady* by Willa Cather, obviously drawing a parallel with his own involvement in Mustique:

> The Old West had been settled by dreamers, great-hearted

adventurers who were unpractical to the point of magnificence; a courteous brotherhood, strong in attack, weak in defence, who could conquer but could not hold. Now all the territory they had won was to be at the mercy of men like Ivy Peters, who had never dared anything, never risked anything. They would drink up the mirage, dispel the morning freshness, root out the great brooding spirit of freedom, the generous easy life of the great landholders. The space, the colour, the princely carelessness of the pioneer they would destroy and cut into profitable bits, as the match factory splinters the primeval forest.

The following year, Colin finally cut his links with Mustique (apart from the acreage he retained in the south) when he sold his house to Sergei Kauzov, the ex-husband of Christina Onassis. Colin's only two regrets were that he had to leave the Indian pavilion behind and his house was pulled down by the Russian only to build something similar, only much larger.

There is a saying in St Lucia that a man is allowed to cry only twice in his life; when his mother dies and when a storm takes his house away. Travelling with the architect Lane Pettigrew, Colin flew over the Great House and saw it completely demolished, except for four columns and the central dome. With tears streaming down his cheeks, Colin turned to Lane and said: 'The things that should be forever, are the most easily forgotten'. Colin never knew that his dome still exists, sandwiched between the layers of the new dome.

Reflecting on his contribution to Mustique, Colin believed he was in some way an artist

if it be an art to create a form of lifestyle. Looking back, I did create a certain lifestyle in Mustique that has appealed to a wide range of people, and has continued to appeal. Today, Mustique has never been stronger. Others have followed possibly with a greater organising ability. I think Mustique has been a success because of my particular traits that I have reproduced there. It is not swanky of me to say so; it is just what happened. Mustique was an entirely natural reproduction of certain aspects of my life. We did not set out to do it deliberately, and, had we done it by the book, it certainly would not have worked. It was reported as a continual house party, but of course it had an underlying, serious commercial background.

Shortly before Colin died, the Canadian singer Bryan Adam's mother, Jane, wrote to thank him 'for being yourself – a visionary' and making it possible for her to end up in her son's house in Mustique in 'such beauty and tranquillity of this island.' She went on to write: 'I am sure that it is a far cry from what you might have planned, however it is forever yours, whatever people may do to it later. With admiration of your work and dreams, Jane [Adams-Clark]'.[lxxxii]

To which Colin replied:

*Dear echo of a far off cry*
*Though echoes may not answer why.*
*Your lovely letter makes me ask,*
*Whatever did I do to bask.*
*It was a gift, and not a theft*
*I simply paid the bills, and left.*

Jane's sentiments were a fine epitaph to all Colin had achieved on Mustique, although Colin's witty reply was uncharacteristically self-deprecating. But just as his Mustique door was closing, so another door opened when he bought the Ruby Estate in Souffrière, a ravishingly beautiful plantation in St Lucia. With its purchase, so began the final phase of Colin's life.

*Chapter 14*

G

# THE WATERFRONT, SOUFFRIÈRE

'Did you know that there are twenty-seven different varieties of mango trees here?' Colin would ask. The 'here' was Ruby Estate, just above the town of Souffrière to the south-west of St Lucia. What is more, he could identify every mango tree on the estate and the individual fruiting properties of each one. He knew exactly when they ripened, and just how they tasted. 'This is an early one', he would say as he walked up around the plantation, 'and this one is so juicy that you have to eat it in the sea.'

Henry Tennant, very tall, red-headed and beanpole thin, was staying in the town where he was studying transcendental meditation, and taking a correspondence course in mathematics with a view to going to the University of the West Indies in Trinidad to study tropical agriculture. It was while there that he had heard that Michael de Boulay was selling the 387-acre Ruby Estate growing, beside the mangoes, coffee and cocoa. There was a reasonable house, with the usual outbuildings, and a sugar mill. During the negotiations to buy Ruby, Colin met Lyton Lamontagne who was then working in Barclays Bank in Castries. Tall, with striking patrician good looks, Colin took to him immediately and offered him the job of managing Ruby, which he instantly accepted. He was just one of dozens of young people who owed everything to Colin, who started them all off on their new, and often highly successful, careers. Lyton was to stay with Colin for many years until he branched off on his own (with a substantial loan from Colin). He and his beautiful wife, Eroline, now own a supermarket in Souffrière, and the magical Fond Doux Estate with its award-winning hotel and restaurant just outside the town. While John Golds, who was living at Cap Estate on the north coast of St Lucia, suggested that he should develop Ruby, Colin was adamant that he should keep it solely agricultural for Henry to grow fruit and vegetables. The development would come later, elsewhere.

However wonderful Ruby was, it came at a price. The money came from the sale of Black House Farm, with its good grouse moor, on an outlying part of Glen. At that time the sale of agricultural land attracted no capital gains tax so long as the money was reinvested in farmland. By an oversight, the Act of Parliament did not specify *where* the new land had to be, so Ruby in St Lucia qualified for roll-over relief in Scotland. Toby, Colin's half-brother, wanted to buy the farm and grouse moor. He had always been passionate about Glen, where he had spent the happiest of childhoods roaming the estate with dog and gun. Colin had already received an offer from Tom Renwick, his farm manager, but before accepting it he offered it to Toby. Toby wanted to know what Colin wanted for the land; Colin wanted him to come up with a figure. Toby could not make up his mind and, impatient as ever, Colin accepted Renwick's offer. What upset Toby further was that Renwick then sold on the land to the Forestry Commission, who covered it with useless pine trees. The rift between Toby and especially his wife, Lady Emma (sister of the Duke of Devonshire), and Colin never healed, even in death. But the money went to good use for Colin bought The Birks, a 500-acre farm overlooked by Glen that had never belonged to the estate, and Ruby. With that purchase began Colin's love affair with St Lucia, and in particular, the town of Souffrière.

In tandem with his dealings in Mustique, St Lucia and London, Colin continued to play a large part in Princess Margaret's life – he always said that he lived by the three Ps – the people, the Press and the Princess, and he made sure that he was on the best possible terms with all three. The arrangement with Princess Margaret worked both ways – he looked after her, while she included him in her more exciting Royal tours, always accompanied by Anne in her official capacity as her Lady-in-Waiting. In September 1983 Princess Margaret went to the United States by way of Mustique. Colin was invited too, which gave him such enormous pleasure that he recorded the whole visit on the back of a large envelope.

The party left Mustique for Barbados in a little charter plane. '"Always takes an hour, whatever they say", said a grumpy Princess Margaret not yet awake', wrote Colin. On the plane to Miami, Princess Margaret and Colin finished *The Times* crossword. Although there was a vast amount of luggage in the hold, the whole party and staff were carrying endless brown paper parcels and packages with fragile lampshades, broken porcelain, and the like, which made them look more like raggle-taggle gypsies than a grand Royal progress.

At Miami they were herded into a queue for the X-ray machine until Inspector Phillpott, the Scotland Yard Detective, heavily armed, slipped round the side and explained who they were, just as Princess Margaret was about to be frisked. At Dulles, the airport for Washington DC, they were met at the steps of the plane by their hosts, the British Ambassador, Sir John Wright and his wife, Lady Wright, who whisked them straight to the Embassy. Colin was 'particularly relieved' to find an invitation in his bedroom 'addressed to myself from the White House to the Saturday dinner, so dreadfully hoped for, I do confess'.

That first night they were joined by 'the Minister, Mr Thomas at dinner – a delicious succession of lobster, chicken and kiwis'. The highlight of the visit was, of course, the dinner with President Reagan and his wife, Nancy. Colin and Anne went in the first car as a decoy where they were harangued with shouts of 'Murderers, British murderers' at the White House gates from a group of demonstrators, no doubt recalling Princess Margaret's alleged remark about the Irish being pigs some years before. They arrived at the top of the White House staircase where Princess Margaret introduced her party to the President and Mrs Reagan, and then signed 'the book', she first, followed by Anne. When Princess Margaret's Private Secretary, Lord (Nigel) Napier, tried to sign, the official pen had run out of ink and 'his stately autograph flourish was reduced to a series of scratches'. It was left to Colin to decide whether to skip this formality, or wait for a new pen (no one around had one), and so miss being introduced to the other guests in the wake of the Royal retinue. 'Deciding that no one would catch my name anyway', he recalled, 'but that posterity would have plenty of time to decipher my signature, I waited and signed clearly (just above Nigel and below Anne, more or less obliterating his effort) and was not introduced'. This meant that he missed out on the official White House photograph, which greatly upset him, but he was united with some old friends – Carolina Herrera, Lynn Wyatt, Drue Heinz and Lee Annenberg whose husband, Walter, Colin recalled with pleasure, raised 'my status by loudly proclaiming "You have built a very nice house in Mustique."'

There were four tables of eight, and Colin sat between a Miss Leibling and Mrs Carter Brown, whom he found the more challenging until she told him that she was an habitué of these evenings at the White House, as her husband, John Carter Brown III, was the Director of the National Gallery of Art. She added that she thought the child Amy, the young daughter of President Jimmy Carter, was 'definitely precocious and would amble into these galas and draw up a chair beside her father, pull out a book and sit there reading, while occasionally prompting her neighbours with "eat up your spinach" before shimping back to her homework.' Mrs Reagan chose the British Ambassador and the Russian ballet dancer, Mikhail Baryshnikov, while Princess Margaret drew The President and Senator John Warner, by then 'free of Elizabeth Taylor and a great lady-killer', wrote Colin 'though I haven't yet heard if PM proved susceptible'. All agreed that it was a marvellous party.

Keeping his ear close to the ground in St Lucia, Nevill Turner heard that there was a beautiful copra estate for sale right between the Pitons, the twin volcanic plugs just to the east of Souffrière, called Jalousie. Nevill then obtained the exclusive selling rights and offered it to Colin, who sent Henry, still living at Ruby, to look at it and report back. Henry said that it was one of the most remarkable places in the Caribbean. As it was only really accessible from the sea, it was totally unspoiled and deserted. Best of all it had three-quarters of a mile of beach frontage. There were two marching estates, Jalousie and Beausejours, totalling nearly 600 acres. They were owned by two Americans, Jean and Anne Daugherty, scions of the Bowater paper family, who had several estates around the Caribbean. They had tried to sell Jalousie through Previews Inc. in the 1970s for US$600,000, but there were no takers. In 1980 the trustees put 476 acres back on the market at $440,000, where again no one was interested, even at that price. When Nevill took up the sale, he advised the trustees that, in the current market, the price was too steep and reduced it to $375,000. Colin danced around at the end of Nevill's string to the day after his option expired. In a rare capricious act Colin bought Jalousie direct from the American owners in Oregon, so denying Nevill his commission. He simply marched into their lawyer's office in Castries with a certified cheque from the Royal Bank of Scotland for the asking price of EC$1 million (around £200,000) and bought Jalousie and Beausejours estates there and then. Colin later sold Ruby to Michael de Boulay's aunt for EC$850,000, not far short of the price of Jalousie.

Soon after the purchase was complete, Colin embarked on a project that was so typical of his whimsy, so brilliant, so bizarre. It was to change his life forever. He bought an elephant. Through this one purchase, he announced to the world that he was about to create another 'Mustique' thereby, as he said, 'putting St Lucia on the map', for just as Mustique was known internationally as 'the place where Princess Margaret has a house', so Jalousie became known as the place where there was an elephant roaming free. Ironically Princess Margaret hated elephants.

Colin was on a jolly with Anne and the twins in Brighton when he announced his elephant purchase and asked them to suggest a name for the 7-year-old female. As they were passing a BUPA hospital, Amy suggested 'Bupa', and the name was adopted immediately. The saga began when Colin mentioned to his philatelic co-director, Allan Grant, that he wanted to buy an elephant and it was he who introduced him to his near neighbour and friend, John Chipperfield, one of the famous circus family. John is the son of the legendary Jimmy Chipperfield who, with his other son Richard, was responsible for changing how animals are observed in captivity. Jimmy set up the first safari park at Longleat, the Wiltshire home of the Marquess of Bath. For the first time it was the spectators who were 'caged', in their cars, while the animals roamed free. While his father developed the parks, Richard caught up most of the animals for the Chipperfield-run enterprises around the world. When he was killed in a car accident mid-safari in 1975 his younger brother, John, took his place in Uganda. There he caught all manner of animals, including the 4-year-old Bupa – her capture undoubtedly saved her life as subsequently the Ugandan Army severely depleted the elephant population by using the animals for target practice. Bupa was sold to Dublin Zoo where John found her three years later, up for re-sale. The deal was struck – Colin said that she cost the same as a second-hand long wheelbase Land Rover – and she was shipped to Longleat to await transportation to St Lucia. From Longleat she was crated and taken to Tilbury Docks, where she was loaded onto a Geest banana boat accompanied by her handler, Keith Harris.

The boat docked in Castries to the north of St Lucia on a Saturday, and the dockers were excited at the news that there was an elephant on board. On Bupa's crate was a notice DO NOT FEED, which was ignored by the 19-year-old Kent Adonai, who was standing in for his stevedore father. Kent kept going back to Bupa's crate and feeding her a hand of bananas at a time. He had completely fallen for her and from that first moment decided that he would spend the rest of his life with her.

Colin noticed that Kent had exceptionally large ears and thought that they would make Bupa feel at home. The next day, at Colin's direction,

Kent then jumped on the lorry taking her to Souffrière, where she arrived in the square during Matins. With the news that an elephant was outside, the churches emptied mid-sermon. Colin had flown out two Indian mahouts to look after Bupa, but Keith could see that Kent had a rapport with her, and that the Indians were superfluous. 'Bupa was quite remarkable', said Keith Harris, 'She took all the travelling, particularly the sea voyage, in her stride. I spent six glorious weeks with her, Colin and Kent before returning to Longleat. She settled in beautifully to her new surroundings, and she obviously took to Kent.'[lxxxiii] The affection was entirely mutual – she would never stay in her own quarters at night and would always move behind the little house where Kent lived on the estate to be near him.

Bupa's arrival was to enhance Colin's life twofold. While she never failed to amuse and delight him, she equally importantly brought Kent into his life and, as Colin always said, 'with Kent came fun'. They were to remain, first as master and elephant boy, then great friends, for over twenty-eight years. As the years went by Kent was to play an increasingly important, and indispensable, role in Colin's life. Kent always acknowledges, rightly, that he owes everything to Colin, quite literally (see Envoi). Illiterate, Colin sent him to London to learn (only partially successfully) to read and write. As Kent, whose first language is patois, said 'Everything I learn was from Mr Tennant. Mr Tennant was my life. He educate me completely. He taught me how to speak with people, how to present myself. Everything.' He even learned from Colin how to eat fish with two forks, reminiscent of the opening line of John Betjeman's poem, *How to get on in Society*, 'Phone for the fish knives Norman'. Colin and Kent could well have been the last two in the world to eschew the fish knife on the grounds that it was 'non-U'. There was always the frequent speculation that Colin and Kent were lovers. The suggestion is ridiculous, as those who knew Colin and the many mothers of Kent's numerous children would all testify.

With her great sense of humour, Bupa was a constant joy. Since elephants are, of course, herd animals, she undoubtedly missed the company of her own kind and, to compensate, she teamed up with a pig, who became her constant companion. Bupa's favourite ploy was to make a slide. All morning she would fill her trunk with water, then spray an incline on the hillside until it was a thick morass of mud. Then she and the pig would slide down the slippery slope on their bottoms, over and over again, squealing with delight until the mud dried out. Sadly, her companion was killed when Bupa sat on her.

Much of Bupa's life was spent in the quest for food. No one was safe on the beach carrying a white paper bag, synonymous to her with some delicacy. She would advance on the hapless person and pluck it out of their hands and consume it, whatever the contents. Often she was disappointed as it held only a camera, or some precious possession of the fleeing owner. Cleaning out her quarters, Kent would sometimes find extraneous items in her dung. Sunglasses and keys were commonplace, but he once found a wallet with US$2,000 in cash. When a hotel guest complained to Colin that his elephant had trodden on her sunglasses, he retorted that she was very lucky: 'Just think, you can go home and tell everyone that your glasses were broken by an elephant on holiday!' Living almost exclusively amongst humans, Bupa had many human traits. Once a woman went for a swim off the beach and left her baby in a Moses basket in the shade of a coconut palm. While she was swimming, the sun moved round, exposing the infant. The baby began to cry volubly whereupon Bupa very gently moved the Moses basket back into the shade with her trunk, then wandered off. The mother, seeing an elephant with her infant, nearly had a heart attack.

Bupa knew the charter yachts that anchored stern-to to the shore with the warp tethered to the coconut palms. At dawn she would pull in the yachts, stand on the rope, then scavenge for food in the galleys with her trunk through the open porthole. Often she would untie the yachts just for fun. The villagers of Morne La Croix, above Jalousie, were no admirers of Bupa or her antics. A favourite ploy was to spray dirty water on their clean laundry as it hung out to dry. Nor was she above going into their houses, opening the refrigerator doors and removing the contents.

With Ruby sold and the house on Jalousie unsuitable, Colin moved into a single room over a shop overlooking the waterfront in Souffrière. It was very primitive indeed, with no kitchen, bathroom, electricity or even running water, hence no lavatory. For all his ablutions Colin walked over the road and used the washroom of the Texaco filling station. Colin always said that he thrived on hardship, but this was pushing adversity to its very limits. When the filling station was closed he used the eight-seater open-air latrines, literally a long plank with holes set over the sea, where he sat with the poor of the town. The place was said to be haunted at night, but the ghostly bottom hand-wipe was not some nanny ghoul, but children with a large leaf on the end of a long bamboo pole! Colin made great friends with his fellow defecators, mostly the Rastafarians, and arranged for them to join his band for the Castries carnival. Kent took two days to walk Bupa along the road to Castries, where he joined Colin and his latrine friends, who had been kitted out with Indian costumes bought in Delhi. Bupa had a huge saddlecloth made from hundreds of strings of polychrome beads, misspelling her name as 'BOOPA', and a fine Indian ceremonial head cover. She looked wonderful and she knew it, enjoying the two days of carnival as much as the rest of the band. Not surprisingly, they won first prize.

But not everyone was enamoured with Bupa, or indeed with Colin for keeping her. The *Born Free* actress Virginia McKenna wrote to Colin in her capacity as a trustee of Zoo Check to say that they had received many complaints from visitors to, and residents of, St Lucia. She continued that Zoo Check would be prepared to return Bupa to Africa but, to meet the costs of repatriation, they would have to rely on the publicity to generate the funds. She concluded with: 'it is unnatural for a female elephant to live solitarily and, over a period of time, this can cause psychological problems and stress. They need to have the companionship of other elephants for their well-being'. However, it is certain that Bupa was completely happy with her lot at Jalousie, bonding with the pig and humans, in particular Kent. She would have become aggressive if not content. To return her to Africa, with a change of diet and no immune system to cope with the unsterile food and water sources in the wild, was a utopian dream of conservationists. Bupa remained *in situ* to the delight of nearly all.

But events sadly overtook the stalemate. Towards the end of February 1993, Bupa was fed large amounts of discarded bread dough. Over the following fourteen hours the yeast fermented in her stomach 'producing excessive gas, the stomach distended causing depression in the cardiovascular and respiratory systems'.[lxxxiv] In other words she died of asphyxiation. Colin later admitted that the day that Bupa died was one of the saddest in his life: both he and Kent were devastated. After removing her tusks, one of which Colin gave to Kent, she was buried close by the site he had chosen for his house. There was a well-attended wake for her, where her many admirers gave heartfelt eulogies.

The story of Colin's beloved elephant began with John Chipperfield catching the 4-year-old calf in Uganda: it ended with him accompanying Colin, Christopher, the twins Amy and May, Kent, the author, and a *Hello!* photographer, Lawrence Lawry, to South Africa to seek a replacement for Bupa. The resulting *Hello!* article hardly ticked the 'no publicity' box. They found several possibilities at a safari park near Johannesburg, and Colin chose one of a pair. The party moved on to the Kruger Park to show Kent elephants in the wild. On their return to London, John, a world-expert in moving animals, found that under CITES regulations at that time, a single elephant was not allowed to be transported, and the St Lucian government would not allow in a pair of elephants in case they bred and overran the island. Today the live-long memory of Bupa always brings a smile to the face. But then that is what elephants do.

# Chapter 18

# HILL LODGE

Before anything could possibly happen at Jalousie, a proper road had to be built from the main highway to the plantation. For this, and the subsequent development, Colin looked to Arne Hasselqvist, who had served him so well in Mustique over many years. They formed a loose partnership as Arne brought in heavy machinery to begin the initial construction, while Colin tipped in 'buckets of money'. Colin returned to Scotland for the whole of August, leaving Arnie with a bulldozer and his chequebook. When he later flicked through the counterfoils, which he rarely did, Colin saw that there were two cheques made out for US$300 each. When Colin tackled Arne, he admitted that they were for work done for him privately. Their long association ended forever at that very moment. Colin was clearly upset for, as he said, 'Arne had been a very close friend: he travelled with me often, and was a very hard worker. In Mustique practically everyone I employed was entirely honest, but not Arne, who was cheerfully dishonest, not deeply, but certainly just below the surface, where most of his drainpipes ended.'

Arne and his son Lucas moved to the Bahamas where he started again, building a resort. The cottage where they were living caught fire and father and son escaped. Seeing no flames, they both went back into the house to retrieve their possessions, but were overcome by the toxic smoke from the foam-filled furniture. Both were killed instantly. It was a tragic end of one who contributed so much to Mustique.

Although Colin was totally at home in the West Indies, he also had a great affinity with India, and all things Indian. From the early 1980s onwards he travelled with either, or both, of his two companions and dealers, Mitch Crites and Maharukh Desai, to all parts of the continent. He felt comfortable in India and was a very good traveller. They would often go for many, many hours at a time in an Ambassador taxi, usually without air-conditioning, and stay in modest hotels where he was happiest. He never wanted to meet grand people, although he was once invited to dine with Ratan Tata, whom he found 'socially penetrating and ruthlessly entertaining' in his penthouse in Mumbai. Colin was particularly fascinated by the strange and mysterious aspects of India. Once with Mitch in a market in Hyderabad they saw

> an amazing looking, and beautiful, young man, quite wild, with steaming hair and a transfixed expression, naked to the waist, and in his arms carrying this newly-born baby. He was followed by a girl looking much the same. They must have been gypsies or perhaps some caste of snake charmers from the desert. His chest had been slashed with little blades hundreds of times so the blood was trickling down and dripping onto the baby. No one noticed them go past.

Typically, Colin's comment was how psychologically damaged the baby must be, and that it 'couldn't have happened in Golders Green!'

Another time, driving through the suburbs in Mumbai with Kaizad Toddywalla, Colin noticed two stalwart, military looking figures on the pavement amongst the seething crowd. They were dressed more or less as officers, with a kind of Sam Browne belt, but on closer inspection, they were not actually military personnel. Kaizad told him that they were eunuchs. 'Very conservative families still use them' he was told. Colin recalled that

> these two males, dressed as a kind of female, but then again as males, were standing taller than the crowd and thought to be very superstitiously lucky. People have to make way for them and give them luck money. Not much, but little bits of money. And apparently they are still preserved in, as it were, very conservative families who are deeply religious and old fashioned and still have eunuchs in their harems.

Colin and whoever he was travelling with always had such adventures.

Once, with Mitch and Maharukh in Tamil Nadu they went to a primitive vegetarian restaurant where the food was served on a banana leaf. While the others tucked into their vegan lunch, Colin brought out a large salami and asked for a knife to cut it. Silence descended over the room as Mitch hurried him out. Later, in Chenai, Colin remembered that he had left his suit behind in the hotel, so Mitch telephoned to have it sent on. The manager said that he had indeed found the suit and that it was no trouble to send it, but 'he had also found the 'pig' [the salami] which had been ritually burned'.[lxxxv]

Strangely, Colin was not interested in sightseeing in India. On their first visit to Agra he and Mitch were passing the Taj Mahal, which Mitch obviously wanted to show him. But Colin just shouted 'Keep driving until we reach the shop!' As elsewhere, shopping was Colin's real love in India, where the thrill of buying was acute. He shopped at every level. At one end of the scale he bought inexpensive clothes for the carnival bands in St Lucia; the other end of the scale went right up to expensive pieces of antique jewellery and artefacts. Colin owned, for instance, some of the most important *lingams* – a representation of the Hindu deity Shiva used for worship in temples – in private hands. One, a group of rock crystal *lingams* on a red marble base, was displayed in the Smithsonian Museum in Washington DC. He owned others, including a spectacular lapis *lingam* on a floral marble inlaid base. As Mitch said, 'He had the best eye for art – faced with a vast array of goods he could instantly filter out the rubbish and go straight for the best piece'. Maharukh was in the same mind. 'He had a great eye and great vision. He would make up his mind instantly, yes or no, and would never haggle over the price.'

Colin began by buying southern Indian tribal silver jewellery long before it became known, or remotely fashionable. When he had the largest and most important collection he sold it, and moved on to more classical Mogul pieces. He became obsessed with Tipu Sultan, the great scholar, soldier, and poet of Mysore and always wore his white jade amulet on a chain around his neck. But his most prized possession was the magnificent Tipu Sultan pendant, 'octagonal, set with a large central cushion flat back cabochon Columbian emerald, with border of topaz, blue sapphire, zircon, cat's eye, ruby, coral, diamond and pearl'.[lxxxvi] Unlike some of his other collecting phases, Colin remained passionate about his Indian jewellery and would wear it on every possible occasion. He particularly enjoyed the Mogul emerald ring bearing the name of Prasanna Coomar Tagore, and whenever there was an appropriate opportunity, a lunch or photographic session, he would don a heavy gold anklet, the symbol of an important Maharaja, and a gold necklace, bearing long spikes like chillies.

In April 2010 Colin put five of his best pieces into the *Arts of the Islamic World Sale* at Sotheby's in London. The sale was not a success for him, although a few pieces were later sold after the auction, far below the bottom estimate, while one of the best pieces, a seventeenth-century 'Mughal gold inlaid and gem-set bazuband, later set as a brooch by Cartier'[lxxxvii] was sold to an Arab sheikh, but it took months for the money to be processed. It was a double disappointment for him, as he desperately needed the cash and hated to see his precious pieces dispersed. But the lasting legacy of his Indian collecting and dealing was his close friendship with Maharukh. Colin would stay with her in Goa, and she would visit him often in St Lucia. With their common interests, they delighted in each other's company.

Colin never needed an excuse for a party, but when there was one, like his sixtieth birthday in December 1986, he went all out in expense and originality. The planning lasted a year. He began by chartering the *Wind Star* 'a sleek, four-masted sailing yacht accommodating 148 guests' while she was still being built and, as the week-long party would be her maiden voyage, Colin secured 'a very good deal' in exchange for the publicity. The birthday party itself was to be the Peacock Ball at the Great House in Mustique and, for the 'fineries and fripperies', he naturally went to India. Colin took a family party of Anne and the twins, along with Lyton (who became known there as the 'black sahib') and the author, to help him through the jostling humanity of Delhi Airport. As it turned out there was a brand new, virtually deserted arrival hall. From the Imperial Hotel daily forays were made to the shops of Delhi. Mitch had given Colin an introduction to Mrs Gulshan Nanda, the Deputy Head of the Central Cottage Industries Emporium. Here Colin had 'died and gone to heaven', as his arm-length shopping list was taken care of, item by item. He ordered two vast *shamianas* (side-less tents supported on four poles). Both were ravishing, the one painted pink with lilies and decorated with gold thread, for the day; the other telephone-black with a constellation of stars in silver thread, for the night. Even the tablecloths and napkins were ordered to be made up in the special theme-pink linen.

'What size are your tables?' Mrs Nanda inquired with a slight tilt of the head.

57. Princess Margaret accompanies herself on the piano as she sings to Roddy Llewellyn. A thoughtful Anne Glenconner, her Lady-in-Waiting looks on in the drawing room at Glen.

58. The house party at Glen where Roddy Llewellyn (left) first met Princess Margaret (centre), September 1973. Lucia Santa Cruz, (far left) is next to Drue Heinz (seated), Anne, Sarah Armstrong-Jones, PM, Christopher, David Linley and Henry, with Matthew Yorke and Colin behind.

59. The shooting of the tick – Colin takes a 'pot shot' at the tick that Roddy had removed from Princess Margaret's dachshund, Pipkin.

60. Basil Charles and Lady (Virginia) Royston. Together they took over the beach bar and restaurant on Mustique.

61. All that glitters was gold, well almost at the 50th birthday party. Colin, dressed chryselephantine, with Princess Margaret and Leonora Litchfield.

62. Dress rehearsal for Princess Margaret as a Valkyrie, for the evening performance when she mimed an aria from Wagner's Ring Cycle. She is 'protected' by the twins, May and Amy, suitably clad with outsize horns and heavily armed.

63. The belle of the ball, Bianca, dressed as Scarlet O'Hara, with Mick Jagger. They had been to Mustique for several years running but only decided to buy a house immediately after the party.

64. FOR SALE One exquisite Temple. It was possibly the finest of its kind outside India. Made from the same marble as the Taj Mahal, it broke Colin's heart to part with it when he left Mustique.

65. Things were not done by half in Mustique where the rum punch was served out of an old sugar boiler for a party. Nigel Weymouth, (*standing far right*) Patrick Litchfield, Zanna Johnston, Carolina Herrera, unknown. Billy Whittaker is seated in front of Bianca Jagger and Nicky Johnston.

66. Colin favourite possession. The Indian temple, erected at the Great House, was possibly the finest of its kind outside India.

67. Aerial view of The Great House, Mustique. The flat central Turkish dome atop a well-proportioned house was Oliver Messel's last, and possibly finest, creation in the Caribbean.

68. 'Dr' Mick Jagger attends a 'pregnant' Jerry Hall at a fancy dress party on Mustique.

69. Colin's lifelong interest in philately led him to produce his own Mustique stamps (*bottom left*). He tried to create a market by printing 'Mustique Island' on the selvage of St Vincent and the Grenadines stamps but they were eschewed by serious collectors.

70. Colin with the American actress, Brooke Sheilds, at the boat house on Loch Eddy at Glen. She was amongst dozens of stars of stage and screen who were totally charmed by him.

71. Cutting from *The Daily Express* after Charlie Tennant was fined for possession of opium. Although a serial drug addict Colin and Anne never gave up on him.

73. Mick Jagger with Colin at a house party at Glen.

74. With their film-star looks and social fame, Anne and Colin were 'caught' by an *Evening News* reporter as they departed for Saudi Arabia at Heathrow.

72. Anyone for sheep's eye? Colin and Anne stayed with Sheikh Yamani and in his wife, Tammam al-Anbar (*right*). He and Colin danced together every night to a blind Egyptian pianist.

75. The honorary *togbe* of the village of Hlefe in the Volta region of Ghana where Colin and a team of Mustiquians had built a clinic. He is seated beside the chief surrounded by the tribal elders. Carib, the former Mustique taxi driver stands behind Colin, with the author to the left.

76. Anne with Madame Marcos, wife of the President of the Philippines. A Lady-in-Waiting to Princess Margaret, Anne delivered the Princess' apologies in person when illness prevented her from visiting whilst on a World tour.

77. The inveterate shopper, Colin doing a basket run in Tuvalu, South Pacific.

78. The Queen receiving a bouquet of bougainvillaea from Lady Jemima Yorke during her second visit to Mustique in 1978. After her first visit in 1964 the anchorage was renamed Britannia Bay in honour of the Royal Yacht.

79. Anne and Charlie in happier times at the Cotton House, Mustique.

80. Hans and Maria Christina Neumann. He is recognised as the saviour of Mustique when he took over control of the Mustique Company, but kept alive Colin's vision and ideals for the island.

81. Colin's invitation to dinner at the White House for Princess Margaret, 'so fervently hoped for', was a great relief when it was waiting for him in his bedroom at the British Embassy, Washington DC.

82. The arrival of Bupa, Colin's Ugandan elephant, at Castries Docks, St Lucia on a Geest banana boat. According to her handler, she took her travelling completely in her stride.

83. After Bupa died from a surfeit of buns, Colin took a party to South Africa to find a replacement. The venture failed as a single elephant was not allowed out of South Africa, and a pair of elephants was not allowed into St Lucia in case they bred and overran the island.

84. The Jalousie Plantation, Souffrière in St Lucia shortly after Colin bought it in 1982. There were no roads to the estate so everything had to be carried in by hand or come by sea.

85. Amy, May and Christopher ride on the back of Bupa. Not many children can boast an elephant amongst their family pets. Kent immediately bonded with Bupa, and she with him.

Allowed to roam free over Jalousie, she had the most endearing habits and a wicked sense of humour, such as spraying clean laundry on a line with dirty water, or setting yachts adrift tied to coconut palms on the shore.

86. *El Colino*, matador! Colin 'fighting' a bull in Gulmarg, Kashmir, during the buying spree in India for his 60th birthday party.

87. Christopher and Charlie in happier times in Mustique for Colin's 60th birthday party.

89. A seasoned shopper, Colin would always seek out the best. It was said that he would go into the front door of a shop and end up either in the stock room at the back, or in a factory. Here he is accompanied by Tessa Tennant on a hunt for textiles.

88. Lyton and Eroline Lamontagne arrived in a pony and trap at the beach party at Jalousie where Colin introduced them as the plantation owners from the neighbouring estate. They are amongst the many who were helped by Colin to a more prosperous life.

90. Colin and André Weinfeld flank a cut-out of his wife, Raquel Welch, at a party in Bequia. It was as close as she came to the parties for most of the week until she actually arrived at the Peacock Ball, after Princess Margaret.

'I don't know', replied Colin, 'they have not yet been made.'

'Then how can I make up the tablecloths if I do not know the size?' said Mrs Nanda, tilting her head the other way.

'Just make them up', said Colin, becoming impatient.

Sensing an imminent explosion the author interjected: 'What Lord Glenconner means is that he will cut the tables to suit the cloth.' Mrs Nanda shook her head from side to side in agreement.

Carl Toms, the famous stage designer and erstwhile pupil of Oliver Messel, had designed costumes for all the ladies of the 'court', including one for Princess Margaret, and these were consigned to Mrs Nanda to be made up. When Princess Margaret saw her creation, she was quite overcome, saying that she had dreamt of having a dress like that since she was 6, while another admitted that when her husband saw her draped in the limp, diaphanous muslin toile of her dress, it quite revived their marriage.

Dozens of Indian costumes were ordered for the rest of the guests. There were 'kurtas and Aligarth trousers and turbans and ghagra/cholis and harem dresses in a whole range of sizes and styles'[lxxxviii] – one was in spinnaker proportions for a female guest. There were costumes too for the attendants in the chosen pink, with great wands and staffs with peacock feathers, peacock handbags and peacock feather fans. Colin's own costume remained a secret, the only clue being that once again it was to be chryselephantine. All the guests had to do was to provide their own jewellery, owing to a 'mishap' in Delhi.

Disaster nearly ended the whole enterprise when Colin and the others went to a market that specialised in faux jewellery. They travelled in two Ambassador taxis, one of which needed a push start. Colin naturally overdosed on the wonderful array of baubles and beads. He paid for them with a large US dollar bill and received a little change in rupees. For some reason the vendor upset him, and Colin pushed his purchases back at the man, grabbed his money then pushed him in the chest and strode out, taking the rupee change as well. The vendor remonstrated, and where there were just a few people milling around beforehand, following the incident the market suddenly multiplied a thousand-fold with excited Indians. Colin leapt in the car that worked, followed by Anne and the twins, leaving the others to cope in the broken car. Colin's only reference to the incident was his cure for the poverty of India: 'Give everyone a comb. You feel so much better when you comb your hair!'

With everything safely in Mrs Nanda's capable hands, Colin took the party to Agra to see the Taj Mahal. On the way they stopped for lunch, buying some *chapattis* beside the road. 'Just what ordered the doctor', declared Colin. And then it was on to Srinagar to stay on a houseboat, the *New Peony*, on Lake Nagin. It was a fun time with the inevitable shopping for carpets and more baubles, and excursions on the lakes. One day Colin bought the contents of a flower seller's *shikara* and filled the houseboat with the blooms; on another he paid for everyone to have a massage. One night was spent above the snow line in the mountains at Gulmarg. As the party erected their tents a group of Punjabis appeared on little ponies and gathered around the camp, gazing at Colin and company as if they were observing primitive tribal people. In a way we were. In true Paget fashion we all sang to keep warm. The whole trip was very generous on Colin's part and a great success.

Colin's final preparation for the party was to have a little cosmetic surgery done to himself, when he had his upper and lower eyelids lifted. He appeared after the operation looking like a panda in reverse, with black circles from the bruising around his eyes on white skin. Fortunately the bruising subsided leaving him, Dorian Gray-like, a decade younger. His teeth, however, were a constant source of discomfort, and a horrendous expense. His first bout of implants for the party, which was never successful, cost him £40,000. After more tens of thousands of pounds were spent over the years, he had to wear false teeth, but none were satisfactory or ever fitted comfortably. In later life he found them too painful to wear, which made him difficult to understand, and look frighteningly cadaverous. On a visit to Glen in 1999, he was showing his grandchildren how, as a boy, he caught trout in the burns. Having collected the worms, he then took the smallest hook he could find and expertly tied it onto the cast in front of the fascinated children. He then put the end of the cast between his teeth to tighten the knot. He was just about to bite the end off the cast when, remembering the cost of his choppers, he yelled: 'Kent, come quickly and bite this!' Kent's pure-white gnashers made short work of the fine nylon. He was then deputed to stand behind Colin to catch the little trout as Colin expertly whisked them out of the pools.

At last, the week of the parties started at the end of November 1986 when, at Colin's expense, the London contingent flew out to St Lucia to join the *Wind Star* berthed alongside the dock at Souffrière. The coveted guest list bore a strong resemblance to that of his fiftieth birthday, being mostly made up of his and Anne's family members, with a few dozen of their close friends. All the children were there. Charlie, charming as ever, danced around on methadone, having come off heroin. Henry and Tessa, came too, with their son Euan, along with a few of their friends. Henry and Tessa were, in fact, amicably separated after Henry had announced he was gay, so he was there with his actor friend, Kelvin Omard. Christopher, on his gap year after school, flew in from Mexico with his three travelling companions, while the twins, Amy and May, were allowed an early exeat from school. Barbara Barnes, their erstwhile nanny, was allowed to leave her Royal charges, Princes William and Harry, for the week. Anne's sisters, Carey Basset and Sarah Walter (she with her husband David), were there as part of the 'court', with an assortment of their boys, along with two of Anne's oldest friends, Sarah Henderson and Margaret Vyner. There were clans of Coke cousins, mostly Norfolk-based, and their friends, and cohorts of Tennant and Paget cousins, like coveys of grouse, a mixture of old and young birds. Whole families, headed up by the Guinnesses, descended on *Wind Star*. Princess Margaret had her own coterie, including her son, David Linley, with Susannah Constantine and some of his friends, Roddy and Tania Llewellyn, Jack Plumb, Norman St John Stevas, and a Lady-in-Waiting or two, Jean Wills with her husband John, and Janie Stevens. There were new friends, like the writer Ken Follett and Barbara, his politician wife, who passed around vintage champagne on the outward journey. There was a brace and a half of decorators, John Stefanidis, Michael Szell and Robin Guild. But it was primarily a family affair, with nary a private jet amongst them, although Prince and Princess Rupert Loewenstein and their daughter, Dora, had the use of one. However, those who might have come 'privately' faded at the last minute. Neither David Bowie nor Mick Jagger made it, although Mick's wife, Jerry Hall, joined the party later. Reinaldo and Carolina Herrera missed the celebrations too, as she finalised the deal for her new scent.

Colin was deeply attached to the town of Souffrière and the first night his guests mingled with the townsfolk for a huge 'jump-up'. The next day the *Wind Star* sailed to Martinique, returning the day after for a barbecue lunch at Jalousie. There, in the bay, they discovered another ship, the *Maxim's de Mer*, sister of the Paris restaurant, riding at anchor. She had been chartered by Raquel Welch and her husband, André Weinfeld, to escort the American contingent – somewhat depleted of celebrities as the week clashed with Thanksgiving. She, however, was not on board, being tied up somewhere in Los Angeles. All on *Wind Star* looked down, literally, on the *Maxim* where 'no amount of interior Art Nouveau tarting up could belie her minesweeper origins'.[lxxxix] She had, in fact, been bought by the Brazilian millionaire Francisco Pignatari for his new wife, Ira von Furstenberg, but the couple divorced before they had a chance to use her.

The barbecue at Jalousie was no ordinary picnic. A fourteen-strong steel band played throughout; bets were taken on which small boy could tip the first coconut from the top of a lofty palm. Bupa joined in the fun and swam in the sea with the guests. Then the spectacle: Lyton and Eroline, dressed *aux* Rhett Butler and Scarlet O'Hara, arrived in a horse-drawn buggy and were introduced by Colin as the esteemed owners of the next-door plantation. The *Wind Star* then sailed to Bequia with the *Maxim* (instantly dubbed the *Mal de Mer*), following at a respectful distance in her wake. A dozen Mini Mokes were there to take the teams on a treasure hunt around the island and back to the Frangipani, Sir James Mitchell's hotel in Port Elizabeth. Star of the show was Dianne Brill, dubbed the Queen of the Night by Andy Warhol, whose ample *embonpoint* raised the temperature on both sides of the divide of the two ships. She was to feature the next night when it was the turn of Raquel Welch to play host to Colin's guests on the *Maxim* whilst anchored off Mustique. But still she failed to show – even for her own party. Princess Margaret was not amused.

The next night, in a scene worthy of a sixth-form school dance, there was high excitement on board the *Wind Star* as the guests prepared for the Peacock Ball. Tessa had been appointed wardrobe mistress and had kitted everyone up in their Indian finery and frippery: there was even a seamstress on board for those last-minute alterations. A moment of panic set in when the lighting men from Los Angeles had not turned up to illuminate the Great House but, just as the first guests arrived, they had finished 'washing' the walls with a pale magenta and the roofs with pale blue, like some vast, extravagant birthday cake. Each coconut palm had been individually lit, throwing shafts of light to the cloudless night sky. The whole scene was totally magical. Guests walked through a guard of honour mounted by pink-clad, turbaned attendants from the village and Souffrière, each holding a vast fan of peacock feathers. Beneath the 'night' *shamiana* Colin, sporting a white and gold bejewelled creation, with Anne resplendent in an appropriate peacock-blue silk dress, welcomed everyone. He was also wearing the crown that he had bought some years earlier with Mitch, and a ruby bird-shaped brooch, bought at the same time in Agra when he had eschewed the Taj Mahal. His eyes were bright and sparkling, and he wore a smile that showed his feeling of total, utter and complete happiness. It was the culmination of everything in his life, for which he had every reason to be proud.

When all but one of the guests had arrived – the one of course being Raquel Welch – Princess Margaret and her 'court' assembled in Anne's bedroom ready to move off. When it was certain that La Welch was not going to turn up, the Royal procession advanced, headed by Anne's two sisters, Prince and Princess Rupert Loewenstein, Jerry Hall, and James and Minnie Coleman from New Orleans. Then came Princess Margaret, with Carl Toms a respectful yard behind, while David Linley, wearing a white peacock headdress, with Susannah Constantine, brought up the rear. They processed to Colin and Anne in the receiving *shamiana*, to deep curtseys and bows along the way, after which everyone found their *placement* (or *place à table* as Princess Margaret would say firmly: '*Placement* is what maids have when they are engaged in a household.') Dinner was well under way when Raquel Welch arrived, the lone dissenter from Indian costume, wearing 'a grey shirred metallic evening gown and shoulder-length evening gloves'. For the second time in as many days Princess Margaret was not amused.

On Mustique that night there were five princesses – Princess Frederick from Lovell Village, Princess Margaret from Kensington, Princess Josephine and Princess Dora from Loewenstein, and Princess Tina, who came (that night) from the Indian pavilion. The marble had been illuminated by golden light, which caught the 'smoke' as it sifted out of the lattice work. She appeared, gyrating, down the steps with a full glass on her forehead and a tray of drinks balanced on her tummy, to the wonder of all. As the guests filtered back to the *Wind Star* and their houses, all agreed that it had been the most wonderful of evenings, not seen before and most likely not to be seen again.

The festivities were not quite over as Princess Margaret 'gave' (Colin paid for it, as he did all the other parties) a lunch party the next day where the *shamianas* from the night before were re-erected at Macaroni. There were coconut shies, hooplas, and a hot tub, and all the fun of the fair, with some dressed as clowns and funny hats. There was no Raquel Welch until she made her entrance when the pudding was nearly consumed. As *Vanity Fair* recorded:

Miss Welch was all smiles as she greeted her hostess. Princess [as she was known locally] inhaled deeply through a long cigarette holder protruding from the corner of her mouth, exhaled, pointedly looked at her watch, wordlessly establishing the time, and then returned the greeting with a stiff smile. One-upmanship was back in the royal corner.[xc]

That night there was a farewell dinner where the satirist John Wells delivered his ode to Colin that ended:

> *... God to bless*
> *The author of our happiness –*
> *This Prospero, magician king*
> *Who makes enchanted islands sing;*
> *So charge your glasses, friends to honour,*
> *Our reckless host, dear Lord Glenconner!*

Colin, ever one to downplay a situation, replied that however much his guests said that they would never forget the party, they would. In that, he was unquestionably wrong. Nobody knew, least of all Colin, what his party cost – certainly several hundred thousand US dollars, including US$30,000 for extras on *Wind Star*, for the bills for the mini-bar in the cabins and the stolen pornographic videos.

*Chapter 19*

G

# JALOUSIE PLANTATION

While they were basking in the glow of the effusive letters of thanks for the party, disaster struck the Tennant family. Anne was in her house in Norfolk one Sunday morning when she received a telephone call from Central America: 'You come, your son die.' Christopher had gone back to Mexico and, against Anne's instructions, he and his three friends had each bought a motorbike to continue their trip to Belize. They had been caught smuggling their bikes across the border and Christopher's was confiscated. He then rode pillion behind one of the others, without a helmet, and when the bike crashed into unmarked roadworks, Christopher was thrown off, landing on the road on his head. He was taken to a local hospital and left to die. Shaken to the core, Anne telephoned Colin in London, who instantly turned to his most powerful ally, Princess Margaret. By chance, Nigel Napier, her Private Secretary, was in his office that Sunday morning and alerted the Foreign Office. From that moment on events moved very fast. The FO contacted the British Army base in Belize, who sent a helicopter (as they would for any injured British subject) with a surgeon to the local hospital, where he found Christopher in a coma, his head wounds open and untreated. His ear was severed. The Army surgeon believed that he was just two hours from death. From there Christopher was airlifted to the Army field hospital, where they removed a clot from his brain, and he was then flown to Miami, just as Colin and Anne arrived by Concorde. For three weeks Christopher remained on a life-support machine, before being brought back to the Wellington Clinic in London by air ambulance, along with two surgeons and a nurse. Anne had taken out travel insurance for Christopher for a modest premium at the start of his journey – the best investment of her life.

From there it was a two-year nightmare. The world's authority on coma patients told Anne 'If your son lives at all, he'll only be a vegetable. I'd go home and forget him.' It was too much for Anne. She found a Dr Clarke, who had pulled his own son through a lengthy coma. He examined Christopher and thought that he had 'a fighting chance' of recovery by using the 'Coma Kit' he had developed, but it would be a long and hard haul. His method was to stimulate the five senses by shocking them with 'nice and the nasty' – a sweet-smelling rose alternated with the lining of his old trainers, or sweet and bitter tastes, or rough sandpaper and a soft feather. Anne, Barbara, family and friends alternated the sessions, fifteen minutes every hour, for nine hours a day. Christopher finally came out of his coma after a hundred days and eventually pulled through to make a remarkable recovery. He had to learn everything again as if he were a baby – what saved him when he could not swallow whilst in his coma was Barbara bringing in a baby's bottle to feed him. Anne and Barbara were written up in *The Lancet* on how, as lay people, they thought a coma patient should be treated. Christopher went on to marry first, Anastasia Papadakos, by whom he has two daughters, then Joanna Lissack in 2011.

Once Colin found someone he admired and liked working with, he remained loyal and employed them over and over again. One such was the legendary interior decorator John Stefanidis, whose work Colin had admired when he stayed at the British Embassy in Washington DC. John had stepped in to advise on the Great House and Balinese cottages in Mustique after the rift with Oliver, and was then engaged to work on the house Colin had bought in Victoria Road in Kensington, London.

Victoria Road was Anne's favourite house, but as John Stefanidis said, 'it was one bedroom short so that the two elder boys, Charlie and Henry, could not stay at the same time' – although they had officially long since left home. After Christopher Glenconner died in 1983, part of his estate that was inherited by Colin was the freehold of Hill Lodge, where his mother Pamela had lived since the early 1950s. In her mid-80s, the house had long been too large for Pamela since the departure of the many 'Hill Lodgers', so Colin took it over and moved her into the comfortable annexe, known as The Red Cottage. But Pamela did not enjoy her little cottage tacked onto her old house for long, for she died in 1989, aged 86, after a short illness and was buried at the Paget home at Cranmore.

The money from Victoria Road went into making Hill Lodge one of the most remarkable houses in London, again under the hand of John Stefanidis. It was large, commodious, and opulent. Anne never really took to it, as she felt the drawing room redolent of a station hotel, but kept her bedroom very much as in Victoria Road with the fabrics, 'Veronica' and 'Lady Anne' designed by John for her. The drawing room was redone more to her taste. As John recalled: 'Colin had the most marvellous eye. He would buy things for the house, visualising the spot where the piece would go, and invariably he was exactly right. He would make up his mind instantly'. No expense was spared, as with the purchase of the wonderful ceramic chimney-piece by Alfred Stevens, 1869, in the drawing room, with its caryatid figures by James Gamble. It had never previously been assembled – its twin went to Dorchester House in Park Lane, and is now in the James Gamble room in the Victoria and Albert Museum.

As Colin and Anne were homeless in London (although there was always Anne's farmhouse at Burnham Thorpe in Norfolk and Glen for the twins' school holidays, and Christopher was still in hospital) Princess Margaret had them to stay at Kensington Palace for what turned out to be a year and a half. Just as she moved herself into *Les Jolies Eaux*, so she donned the Marigold rubber gloves and moved them out of Victoria Road and, when the time came, helped them into Hill Lodge.

Hill Lodge was a perfect house for entertaining, and the first big party that Colin and Anne threw was for Amy and May's coming out dance. Typically it was not a stiff black tie affair, but a 'Tropical Evening' where guests were exhorted to wear tropical dress for what turned out to be a true West Indian jump-up, complete with steel band and jerked pork in the large garden. Jerry Hall came dressed as a beautiful bird of paradise, with a huge yellow feather tail. It was for all ages. Such was the success of the twins in their 'Season', that they were chosen to represent Britain at the International Debutante Ball in New York.

It is often said that with advancing age the years come round quicker, but Colin was as committed and busy as ever throughout his sixties. He continued to go to Balmoral for Princess Margaret's birthdays. Always affable to the young, particularly if they were pretty and lively, he took greatly to the Princess of Wales and Sarah, Duchess of York. He would always come down to dinner early, where he met up with them in the drawing room. He found them thick as thieves while they found him very good company. They confided in him, the Princess saying that when it was their 'turn' they would sweep away all the tradition and stiff court behaviour in all the Royal homes. With that she bounced on the little tartan chair that tradition dictates no one sits on, as Queen Victoria was the last person to sit there. Not anymore. Their conversations continued at picnics around the estate, Colin even keeping as a souvenir a baked potato that had been cooked by The Queen, and delivered by the hand of the Princess of Wales. The following year, in August 1990, he and Anne were back at Balmoral for Princess Margaret's sixtieth birthday. Notwithstanding his mounting overdraft, he still found £3,000 for 'an Empire French three-colour gold toothpick case'.[xci]

There was also a party for Princess Margaret's birthday that was given by two of her Ladies-in-Waiting, Anne and Janie Stevens, along with four other close friends, Prue Penn, Drue Heinz, Diane Nutting and Tania Llewellyn, at Spencer House in London. It was a magnificent affair for which the dining room had been decorated by Michael Szell.

Back in the West Indies, with Mustique and Ruby gone, Colin put all his energies into preparing Jalousie for development. Lyton was managing the estate – whatever there was to manage with the only income coming from copra – but also assisting Colin in his quest for outline planning permission, to which there was great opposition from certain quarters. Derek Walcott, the St Lucia-born Nobel Prize laureate for literature, condemned the idea of the development as a sacrilege, comparing it to 'opening a take-away concession in Stonehenge'. His poem condemning the proposed development, 'Litany to the Pitons', contains the lines:

> *Merchants and traitors*
> *Makers of waiters*
> *Whores out of waitresses*
> *Deep our distress is.*
> *Jalousie is one of*
> *The Seven Deadly Sins*[xcii]

Many, like him, believed that the area should have been kept as a national park. Colin argued that where a national park would employ only a handful, at most, of local people and remain unvisited, his development would employ hundreds and bring in much-needed foreign investment. Colin enlisted the help of Lane Pettigrew, a talented architect who had been working on the Club Med resort at Vieux Fort in the south of St Lucia, close by the international airport, which he also designed. In return for a plot of land at Beau, Lane put together a development plan for Jalousie. Colin was fortunate that he had great allies in Sir John Compton, Prime Minister of St Lucia, and Sir James Mitchell, Prime Minister of St Vincent and the Grenadines, who were great friends and confidants. The two premiers had discussed Colin's proposal and the objections to his project. The turning point came when Sir James sent a postcard from a conference in Switzerland showing a perfectly harmonious village at the base of some mountains, and wrote on the back 'If you build in the valleys it does not affect the mountains, just like Jalousie and the Pitons.'[xciii] Soon after this, Colin received assent for his plans.

Jalousie was haemorrhaging money (around US$100,000 a year) which again took its toll on Colin's collection of pictures, among them the fourteen by Lucian Freud, which he sold for £100,000 to the art dealer James Kirkman. James later became Lucian's agent. Colin said that he did not mind selling them, which he did, as 'they would be enjoyed by others around the world'. James insists that the price was the market value at the time, but Lucian thought it an act of betrayal and fell out with Colin. Years later they met by chance on the street (Lucian lived around the corner from Anne's flat in Holland Park), and they made up over tea.

Having funded Mustique out of what was in effect his own money, Colin was determined that he would not make the same mistake in St Lucia and was on the lookout for a backer. By chance, Colin met an Iranian, Kamran Ahgadpour, travelling to Geneva on a British Airways flight. It was an auspicious meeting. Kamran was the personal assistant to Prince Abolfath Mirza Mahvi, the grandson of the last king of the Qajar dynasty of the Persian Empire. Mahvi, known as *Shazdeh*, meaning Prince, was a considerable force and highly respected in the world of high finance. The Shah had made him his economic adviser and through him brokered deals with the world's leading aircraft and oil conglomerates, such as the Pan American International Oil Company and Siemens, who built two nuclear power plants in Iran. After the revolution in 1979 the family's assets in Iran were seized, but the *Shazdeh's* considerable holdings outside the country remained intact. These included *M Group Resorts* which, as its name implies, is a resort development company with hotels and casinos around the world.

Kamran set up a meeting with Colin and his boss, the *Shazdeh*, and the board of the M Group. Colin was more than excited at the thought of a partner being a member of a royal family (even if it was a deposed monarchy) of such great wealth. Likewise Kamran had no trouble in persuading the *Shazdeh* that he should treat with Colin, as he liked investing in developing countries, and relished a challenge. After brief negotiations, Colin sold Jalousie to 'the Iranians' (as he always referred to them) in what was to be, in the end, a disastrous deal. What was on the table was US$500,000 cash for 90 acres around the beach frontage with a 10 per cent holding in the subsequent development. When Colin met the Iranians' lawyers, they changed the deal to include another 100 acres behind the original parcel of land at no extra cost. For six hours Colin pleaded with them to revert to the original agreement, but he was desperate for the money and signed at 11 o'clock at night. The bank was pressing him and he could not adhere to the old maxim 'sell when you want to sell, not when you have to'.

At first everything started well. The *Shazdeh* came, with his friend known as the 'Swiss Miss' complete with her *dirndl*, to Jalousie where Colin and Anne found him very 'jolly'. He eventually sent out his son, Pascal Mahvi, to mastermind the project. As he wrote in his autobiography, Pascal found the project 'preposterous', until he saw Jalousie itself:

> The property is a beautiful, virginal waterfront backed by two vivid green mountains: the Pitons, St Lucia's national symbols. But it's isolated with no roads in or out. We'll have to rely on boats to move thousands of tons of construction supplies, equipment and 2000 labourers six days a week for two years, and, unless the government builds a road to the location, the resort employees and guests will never get there – if we ever get there. This is sure to make the cost of development astronomical.[xciv]

Pascal's prognosis was correct. The M Group had budgeted on US$14 million for the development, but in the end it turned out to be nearer $44 million. Colin, as expected, was to see no more cash. He introduced Pascal to Lane Pettigrew and the two took to each other immediately. Lane was commissioned to come up with some sympathetic designs for Jalousie which the three of them took, during a hurricane in Castries, to the Prime Minister, Sir John Compton. At the next Cabinet meeting the proposal was approved unanimously and work went ahead.

All his life, Colin had been the most exceptional 'ideas man' with wonderful vision, but he was completely out of his league dealing with these world players. He introduced a firm of Brazilian contractors to Jalousie, but where he should have received US$1 million in commission, they fobbed him off with tiny favours – a Toyota jeep or some container transport for his furniture. While the bulldozers rumbled away Colin was up to his old tricks again, asking for concessions after the deal was signed, and began to make demands. He wanted to be Chairman of the board of the operating company, which was denied. He wanted an office in Souffrière. They insulted Colin by giving him a converted garage with a table and chair. Colin needed a role, and 'the Iranians' finally gave him the decoration of the drawing room in the main building which they called, to his lasting annoyance, the 'Lord's Room'. It was an exact replica of Clarence House, built as the residence of the Commissioner of the Royal Navy's Dockyard in Antigua in 1804. He brought in Michael Szell to help him. The furniture from the Great House in Mustique, including his mother of pearl-covered piano, a table made by David Linley, and heavy West Indian ebony pieces, were lent to furnish the room. Surprisingly, with this amount of talent involved, the room lacked the charm of what he had created with the Cotton House, and Colin blamed 'the Iranians' – at the opening party he was so angry that they had put glazing bars in the doors that he smashed one with his cane.

The Iranians wanted Colin out. In yet another disastrous deal Colin insisted that they formalise his 10 per cent holding. When the Jalousie lawyer came back with the deed they had given Colin 10 per cent of the B shares which were, of course, worthless as the A, or preference, shareholders would take all of the profit, if any. Colin was insulted and, instead of going to court to ratify the 10 per cent of the holding company, just threw the shares back at Pascal saying he did not want them and stormed out.

Colin had long held the idea of developing the land and beach of Malgré Tout that marched with the west side of Jalousie. For this he set up the Malgré Tout Development Company with Lane out of an office in Souffrière that had once been Thelma's Grocery, and before that the magistrates' court, complete with two jails. Colin then secured a government lease on all the land (about 25 acres) above the beach, save for an acre and a half that belonged to eighteen members of a family called Alexis. A river ran through the middle of the property. He and Lane then put together a development plan for a health spa, a beach bar with wonderful onion-top roofs, and twenty-five cottages, which was approved by Cabinet. It was a magical plan. Colin took a little house on the property, where he had a dalliance with Analana Phillips, a green-eyed beauty whose diaphanously clad portrait he had painted by the waterfall some way upstream of his river. It was there that Colin once entertained David Hockney and Gregory Evans, although on that occasion the scene went unrecorded on canvas. Hockney later recalled the visit with pleasure: 'My memory is a little hazy, although the waterfall is quite vivid. It was rather spectacular, almost like a Hollywood film set.'[xcv]

The whole Malgré Tout scheme fell apart when Primus, a member of the Alexis family, refused to sell their parcel of land. Colin could have gone ahead without it, but chose to pull out. It was an expensive and bitter blow.

From the end of the 1980s Colin was spending most of the year in St Lucia, finding it too cold to live permanently in England. He took the lease on a house above the Beau Estate, typically spending a great deal of money on it, so that in time his family could stay there when they visited. But the house was 600 feet above sea level, and the long walk up the steep hill became too much, so he handed it back to the owner, Michael Jacques, a Tai Chi and Kung Fu expert. Jacques sued Colin over damage he claimed to have been made to his property, and repeatedly lost in the courts. Still resentful, even after Colin's death, Jacques continues to vilify Colin, ludicrously branding him a drug dealer and a pervert in a booklet.

Colin had fallen out with 'the Iranians' before what was to be called The Jalousie Plantation Hotel was finished, and had retreated to concentrate on the development of Beau. But no sooner had the hotel been completed than it was beset by a series of disasters, not least management problems and a world recession.

There were, however, a few bright diversions in Colin's otherwise solitary life. Being safely ensconced in St Lucia out of harm's way, Colin was always a welcome addition to any party in Mustique. Often he would just fly down for lunch (if the invitation was grand enough) so that he did not have to stay with anyone. He went to David and Iman Bowie's 1990 Christmas party, Colin sporting another golden crown – perhaps that of a disposed monarch – with Anne wearing a bright magenta sari. It was all very enjoyable and low-key, consisting mostly of the other owners and their house parties, rather than a grand jet-set occasion. Paul Channon wonderfully came as a Turkish wrestler complete with baggy trousers, bare chest and a false curly moustache. Colin described the party in his letter of thanks:

Dear David,

Your party was so dazzling & brilliant. I can shut my eyes & see the house throbbing with fantastic crowds, magical music, lights and reflections; you & Iman giving us such a lovely welcome in the drawing room ... the tiers of terraces thronged with dancers, diners and drifters. It was just as Mustique should be, & I was delighted to be there & so grateful to be your guest,

My thanks to you both for such fun and pleasure.

Colin

A few days later Colin and Anne were back again for New Year's Eve with Mick Jagger and Jerry Hall, who gave a similar party with an Indian theme. Again, Colin summed up the party when thanking his hosts:

Dear Mick and Jerry,

New Year's Eve 1990 will always be the night of Mick and Jerry's brilliant party in Mustique. There was a most magical feeling as we came in – the isle was truly 'full of noises, sounds & sweet airs, that give delight' [Caliban, *The Tempest*] – & <u>what</u> a sweet welcome you gave us, surrounded by so many goodly creatures that for once one felt how beauteous mankind is – with the stage so brightly lit by the once-in-a-blue full moon.

1991 has been rather a letdown but nothing will dim the dazzling interval between the last two acts, when we revelled and marvelled in your enchanted paradise....

It was a perfect New Year's Eve and we were most grateful to have been there,

With much love and thanks,

Colin

With the Gulf War at its height it was thought imprudent for Princess Margaret to travel abroad on holiday. Colin wrote her an amusing letter telling her of all the 'treats' that she was missing in Mustique, to which she replied: 'when there is a foul war on, it's better to muster at home. One feels pretty useless being so old and far away, but we plug along'.[xcvi] Having missed her holiday on Mustique, Princess Margaret's friends, in particular Drue Heinz, rallied round to give her other 'treats' in New York and in her villa on Lake Como in Italy.

Chapter 20

# THE CHATTEL HOUSE

At the beginning of the year Colin and Anne were faced with another tragedy when Henry died of AIDS. Just four years after his and Tessa's wedding on Mustique, and the birth of their son, Euan, Henry 'came out', but found the strength to rearrange his life, largely through his Buddhist faith. As mentioned earlier, he had taken up with a fellow Buddhist, an actor from Antigua called Kelvin Omard, and spent the remaining two years of his life travelling with him around the world. Anne came to terms with the set-up adding 'Henry and Kelvin are not lovers. Kelvin has been an angel to my son. He is very sweet and has decided to look after him. He is part of the family.' When Henry was diagnosed as being HIV positive, rather than keeping it a secret he declared it publicly in the hope that it might help others in the same plight. Anne was distraught. Charlie had reverted to heroin, Henry was dying of AIDS and, although Christopher was out of his coma, he was still learning to live again from scratch. As she said in *The Man Who Bought Mustique*, the documentary about Colin, she knew that both her elder sons were dying and Christopher faced an uncertain future; she needed 'a lot of strength' which she found through her Christian faith and friends. Sixty of their closest friends responded when Jack Plumb and the author organised a dinner in the Great Subscription Room at Brooks's to show just how much they cared for her and Colin.

At the end of his all-too-short life, Henry moved into the special unit at St Mary's Paddington, where he was twice visited by the Princess of Wales. There he died peacefully and was given a Buddhist funeral, then a memorial service at St George's Church, around the corner from Hill Lodge, that was attended by family and the throng of loyal supporters of

Colin and Anne, led by Princess Margaret.

Although Christopher went on to lead a near-normal life, Charlie drifted in and out of heroin addiction. He did, however manage to live drug-free for the last six years of his life. In 1993 he married Sheilagh Scott, who had taken a house on the estate at Glen with her former husband and two children, whilst Charlie was living close by in the chauffeur's cottage. She was 'a counsellor working with alcoholics and was credited with helping him overcome his drug habit',[xcvii] or as Colin put it: 'she had a wonderful bosom, where he [Charlie] finally came to rest'. Their son, Cody, was born the next year. But the years of serial drug abuse finally took their toll, and Charlie died in 1996 of hepatitis C, aged just 39 years. The Press, of course, had a field day, turning the triple tragedies into the 'Tennant curse', saying that the family was 'jinxed'. Colin dismissed it all, countering their claims with the fact that the Tennant family had suffered far worse in the First World War when ten out of sixteen first cousins were killed. 'We weren't brought up to throw in the towel. We were brought up to bite bullets and to fold towels neatly'.[xcviii] Colin was never one to show his feelings publicly, but in the documentary, *The Man Who Bought Mustique*, he was filmed making a speech in the community church where he asked the congregation to remember the villagers who had died since he bought the island and, with his voice breaking with emotion, added: 'I would also like you to remember Charlie Tennant, and Henry Tennant, who loved you all deeply'.[xcix]

Today there is a memorial to Henry and Charlie at Glen, set in a folly on the way to Loch Eddy. The epithet reads: 'Like bright shining comets, they burned out so young, touching everyone they met.' The words were inspired by Hale-Bopp, the comet that lit up the night sky for months after Charlie died.

Apart from the great emotional toll on Colin, in life the two boys had cost him dear. Charlie had never worked, apart from a brief spell as a reporter on an underground magazine, *The Chelsea Scoop*, in the late 1970s. Meanwhile Henry became a devotee of spiritual practices which were never revenue generating. Consequently their lives were wholly funded by Colin. By 1987, Henry and Tessa were living amicably apart – Tessa with Euan at Hill Lodge, and Henry in a small cottage south of Brixton. When Tessa was offered an internship in an environmental investment company in Boston, Colin sponsored the three-month placement. Just four months later, she co-founded Merlin, the first environmental investment fund in Europe, possibly the world. Henry, meanwhile, was travelling around the world, with his friend Kelvin, again at Colin's expense.

In another disastrous deal with the Mustique Company, Colin sold 40 acres of his remaining land in Mustique for US$1 million to set up Charlie and Sheilagh in a house in Edinburgh, keeping back a 10-acre toehold around the lagoon for himself. More pictures and treasures went to the sale rooms and in private deals, as the Royal Bank of Scotland appealed for him to reduce his overdrafts that had reached over £2.25 million. In the end, his decision to sell Hill Lodge was not taken lightly, but he was living in St Lucia, Anne had her house in Norfolk, the children had all but left home, and the house was too large and expensive to run. A buyer, the property developer Peter Beckwith, was eventually found and Colin was back in funds. The price was reduced from £4 million to a little over £2.5 million. Anne had just two weeks to move out.

Colin said goodbye to Hill Lodge, another of his creations, and sent his and Anne's furniture and treasured possessions to Glen to be stored in an isolated wooden building that had originally been a roller-skating rink, then converted to a racquets court. Towards the end of November 1993, Charlie had gone into the building and had left the door open and the place unlocked. It is thought that some boys from the village were playing in the building, and it was they who set it alight. In minutes it was reduced to a pile of ash. Many irreplaceable treasures were lost, particularly Anne's personal mementos. Colin said that he most minded losing a beautiful snuff box, made out of a conus shell (*Conus litteratus linens*) with gold mounts, by Louis XIV's goldsmith, Barnabé Sagaret and dated 1746 – he had obviously forgotten that he had sold it to Wartski, the renowned Grafton Street jeweller for nearly £300,000 in 1985. Gold boxes were not something that Colin ever collected, but this truly exquisite and exceptional box obviously appealed to him for its subject matter, quality and beauty. Amongst the treasures he did lose were a valuable eighteenth-century Chinese chess set, the set of James Cook's *Voyages* (large folio volumes bound in red Morocco that had originally belonged to the Duke of York) and a mechanical mouse, made for the Chinese market. Larger pieces went too, including a fine eighteenth-century Italian tortoiseshell chest, gilded bronzes, and two gilt looking glasses with sconces that had come from Wilsford. Fortunately all the pictures from Hill Lodge were saved as they had been moved into Glen. Nothing was insured, for Colin maintained that he 'always worked on the premise that if you cannot afford to lose it, you should not insure it', which is why he 'never insured anything'.

Back in St Lucia Colin addressed the problem of finding somewhere to live. Instead of building something small and wonderful, he hit on the idea of living in a local 'chattel house'. After Emancipation, labourers were not allowed to own land, but they could own a house. Thus they only built houses that could be moved. Colin asked Kent, who was now managing Beau since the departure of Lyton Lamontagne, to find him something suitable. In a trice, Kent came up with a chattel house that was for sale in Vieux Fort, the town 40 miles to the east. He negotiated the sale and arranged for it to be taken apart and transported to Beau, where it was re-erected on a knoll overlooking the sea.

The single-roomed house suited Colin ideally: it was on his land so he could keep a close eye on the estate, and it was primitive. There, he lived a Spartan existence, sleeping on a piece of foam rubber on the floor and, with no running water, he slipped over the border to Jalousie to use the restaurant's lavatories – shades of the Texaco filling station. He took a 'sea bath', watched by Kent to see that he was all right, every evening at 7 o'clock. Later, with his usual flair, Colin made the 'shack' into comfortable quarters, adding another chattel house. The result merited a feature in *Architectural Digest*. There, he described it as 'rat hole *orné*', but it was a rat hole designed with style, flair and insouciance, and the *orné* was far from ordinary. Nor was comfort necessarily a virtue in Colin's decorating scheme. He took 'special delight in noting that his favourite chair, of solid mahogany with a cane seat from St. Vincent, is so uncomfortable that no one but a masochist would sit in it'.[c]

Colin had long admired, and become knowledgeable about, West Indian furniture. He had bought many good pieces, originally for the Great House, in Mustique from Michael Connors in New York. Other pieces were bought locally from St Vincent and St Lucia. Kent became enthused with the project and rooted out many important pieces which were difficult to buy as the sale had to be agreed by the multifarious owners, some living abroad. Once, Kent was caught, in the middle of the night, removing the whole end of a chattel house in order to extricate some large piece when he could not secure the whole family's permission to sell.

With Lane Pettigrew firmly on board as a partner and architect, and Kent to manage the estate, Beau should have taken off there and then. In return for three extra lots around his house Lane, who was overseeing the early development of Jalousie, brought the services (water, electricity, telephone, cable TV) to the boundary of Beau, surveyed the estate, laid out the roads and lots, and obtained planning permission, with more besides. Colin had the most wonderful ideas for Beau. He wanted just a few lots, with houses interspersed in a botanical garden – he and Lane travelled to India and Malaysia constantly looking to import rare, flowering trees, even exotic butterflies. But nothing came of these ventures. He was going to build a clubhouse and a spa, but all this, too, came to naught, save for the mirrored ceiling he bought in India for US$75,000 for the spa. As Lane said: 'Colin was a creative genius, full of originality and flair, yet he lacked the strength, finance and willpower to see anything through to fruition.'

Colin remained on bad terms with 'the Iranians', but was tolerated by the company that operated the hotel. He would wander around the grounds being pleasant to everyone, who naturally thought that he was the owner. As one general manager said, 'There is a perception that he is a major player in Jalousie, which is not true, but he has done a great service with his family name.'[ci] In a ludicrous deal Colin allowed the Jalousie workers to come through Beau (rather than go many miles around to the main entrance) in return for breakfast every day, a copy of the *New York Times* digest (which contained an American crossword that was difficult for the English to solve), the use of a bedroom in the hotel for Anne and Princess Margaret for a number of years, and for him and Lane to use their access to the main gate.

Colin may have lacked physical courage, but nobody could possibly have accused him of lacking moral fibre. Just when everything seemed to be conspiring against him, not least the banks, he picked himself up and began a new venture. He had long held that visitors throughout the Caribbean staying in large resort hotels with international cuisine never experienced anything of the country, least of all local food. For the residents, and the visitors to Jalousie, Colin created an authentic St Lucian rum shop and a restaurant serving local West Indian food. After the success of his own chattel houses, Colin bought four others to convert into the bar, an office, dining room and the shop, which he painted in merry pinks, blues and yellows. Closing the square of the courtyard was Colin's *piece de resistance* – the kitchens encased in a pink and blue edifice, two storeys high, that was an exact copy of Oliver Messel's set for the Broadway musical, *The House of Flowers*. He was particularly proud of the sign that proclaimed: 'Rum Shop. Licensed to sell intoxicating liquor: Lord

Glenconner.' The whole place was a triumph, and an instant success. Colin kept the prices low so that the local people could afford to patronise it, which also achieved his aim of integrating the tourists with the inhabitants. It was so typical of Colin to give it an original name: Bang, so that when he was asked where it was, he could say 'Bang between the Pitons!' Typical, too, was the opening.

Two hundred guests, including all the St Lucia Cabinet, with Sir John and Lady (Janice) Compton turned up for another of Colin's spectaculars. True to form, the place was decorated in style, complete with a vast silk parachute with appliquéd pink elephants. With the guests assembled, a boy arrived with a flaming torch to announce that a carriage had been sighted and was heading their way. It was no carriage but a sleek limousine bearing Princess Margaret and Anne, in her role as Lady-in-Waiting. She was handed a pair of scissors on her arrival and, with a practised snip, cut the golden ribbon and declared Bang open. At that moment one of the waitresses dropped a pile of plates – bang! Lane then announced that there was a present for Colin and six locals brought in a large box. Colin tapped one side with his 'magic' wand and one of the pretty waitresses popped out. He tapped the other side, and out popped May, whom he thought was back in London. Surprise! It was a marvellous party, though nearly a valedictory one for the ministerial boat struck the Petit Piton on its return to Castries.

Although Bang was not a multimillion dollar operation, it was at least a successful one and its fame soon spread amongst the yachting fraternity and the locals. Colin was fortunate in having Amy to help him run it in the early days, and she was to return often. Kent of course was in his element, always knowing exactly where to buy the supplies and what price to pay. The menu was simple and delicious, with such local delights as callaloo soup, grilled fish caught that morning, jerked pork, and soursop ice cream. Colin was there morning, noon and night doing what he did best, meeting and greeting. He also did some of the cooking himself. On Wednesdays there was a jump-up where three local boys, *The Elastic Band*, did amazing acrobatic turns, swallowed fire and limbo danced under an impossibly low, flaming pole, after which the guests danced to a steel band. The event proved to be extremely popular amongst the hotel guests from all around Souffrière, and with the locals, some even coming from Castries. Here Colin was in his element. He was the master of ceremonies (when his voice gave out, Kent took over, copying all his mannerisms). When asked if he was a frustrated showman he merely replied: 'I am not frustrated.' He was adept in pulling people in to his gala night. A favourite ploy was to say: 'What a pity you're leaving, I am having a party on Wednesday.' The hapless 'yachties' would then alter their plans, thinking that they would be joining the rich and famous at a private party, only to find that they were amongst a hundred other fee-paying revellers.

In its heyday there was always something going on at Bang. At Easter Colin revived the Easter Bonnet Parade, an institution he started in Mustique. On the first occasion Colin and Bianca Jagger were judges of the bonnets, they themselves wearing hats fashioned out of round cacti. Everyone was invited to participate, particularly the children, for whom there was also an Easter egg hunt. Colin recalled: 'It was a lovely, lovely time, of course, and very popular here. Gradually all these ladies and lots of children were able to deck their heads up with more and more flowers and palm leaves. In the end they got good at it and quite sophisticated. All won prizes', either chocolate Easter eggs or bottles of scent which he had gone to Martinique to buy.

What Bang really did for Colin was to give him an interest, made him a (comparatively) small amount of money, and allowed him to meet all manner of people. Colin was frequently labelled a snob, but this is unfair, although he was perennially impressed by Royalty and grand people. But he certainly knew his place – he would, for example, accept an invitation to shoot with the Duke of Buccleuch, but would never dream of asking him back to Glen, any more than he would ask the Duke of Edinburgh, with whom he annually shot grouse at Balmoral, and pheasant in Windsor Great Park. He did, however, have the 'common touch' and would, and could, talk to anybody, if he so cared. He always had a particular affinity with the local people and they with him. 'In the West Indies people are not neurotic, so they don't notice my neuroticism. They have a simple fatalistic attitude to health and death.' He was extremely generous to those he liked, often paying their children's school fees, or medical bills. He particularly liked the children, who referred to him as 'Papa Tennant' while he was universally, and affectionately, known in St Lucia as 'Mr Tennants'. The locals were fond of him too, although they would not hesitate to rob him given the chance. Kent was always very protective of him, and loyal, constantly bearing the lash of his tongue. 'He treat everybody the same', Kent confided in the documentary on Colin. 'But if he do it [shout] to be different or to show off, I would not even be around him. Everybody have their ways. That is why I am not offended.' Kent was to be at his beck and call for the rest of Colin's life.

But in 1995 the bitter blow came when the hotel once again closed. Not only did Colin lose his clientele for Bang, the closure also blighted the land at Beau. As Colin said, 'Who wants to buy a piece of land next door to a defunct hotel?' But he struggled on.

Princess Margaret was at last able to reciprocate some of Colin's generosity over fifty years when she gave him his seventieth birthday at Kensington Palace. The guest list was made up, as usual, of family with a smattering of friends, who sat down forty-eight to dinner. It was the usual happy meld and format – John Wells composed another ode and John Nutting made a speech while a few more came in after dinner.

Always looking for fun for himself and others, Colin took *The Elastic Band*, his two acrobats Cletus and Marcellus, and of course Kent, to the Edinburgh Fringe Festival. It generated a great deal of publicity for Colin and Bang, but little by the way of revenue, even though there was standing room only every night – there were just four chairs.

Colin returned, without Kent, to England for another facelift. He made the excuse that he thought people would not do business with him if he looked too 'old'. He was also shaken when an old woman walked all the way from Souffrière to see him. Looking him squarely in the face she said 'Mr Tennants, I come to find if old age catch thee!' With that she walked back to the town. The facelift went terribly wrong and septicaemia set in. He was alone in Anne's flat in London and nearly died. Thereafter he vowed never to travel without Kent, which suited Kent well – as a consequence he went to Bali, India, Malaysia, the Galapagos Islands and, towards the end, to Italy.

# Chapter 21

# THE TENTS, LAGOON BAY

After years of expense and frustration, Beau finally took off, or rather lifted slightly off the ground. Jalousie had returned from the dead, having been taken over by Hilton, and on the back of that, Beau was once again an attractive proposition for potential investors. Colin began with a land sale to Richard Tudor, an English doctor. Colin had not lost his selling touch. The Tudors, who were on their first trip to St Lucia, made up their minds to buy immediately, having fought their way through the undergrowth to their site 'with the most fantastic views'. Lane then designed them a five-bedroom house in 'Caribbean Georgian style'. Dr Tudor was followed by the Russian pianist, Vladimir Ashkenazy, who built a Scandinavian-style house, and Gabriel Van der Elst, a Belgian Baron. Later came Marco Minucci, a coin dealer from Padua. Sadly Colin ended up hating them all, and they him, except for the Tudors who remained constant and true friends.

The documentary of Colin's life up to that point was a film waiting to happen. The ITV Channel 4 had commissioned a series on the Caribbean, and two freelance directors, Joe Bullman and Vikram Jayanti, had been to Mustique to see if there was a film to be made there. In the course of their research, they found that they

> had missed the real story by 20 years, and its name was Colin Tennant.... his eccentricity, his flamboyance, his tantrums, his disastrous business sense, his terrible family tragedies, and above all his charm and sense of fun. It was obvious that he had been the life of the Mustique party, and was still its soul.[cii]

While they were waiting at St Vincent airport, Colin suddenly appeared. They introduced themselves and said that they wanted to make a film about him. Colin readily agreed, and a date was fixed when Princess Margaret would be on Mustique. As it was to be a retrospective view of him in Mustique, Colin asked the author to come out to help. Colin had his own agenda, and took over the directing. He wanted to be portrayed in a film celebrating his life in St Lucia, airing his views about the community, his fondness for the locals, and his sense of the past. The producers were distraught at this update of the *World of Whicker* thirty years on. They knew that they had no useable footage, and any attempt to direct it their way was met with a tirade. Their break came when the scene moved to Mustique. Colin said something that he thought was amusing, which was not recorded. He told the directors from that moment on, when he was with the film crew, they must film him constantly. They took him at his word, and with this licence to record everything, they had their film. Colin, over-strung and hyperactive, railed against everything and everyone – the house owners, particularly the Mustique Company board, who he saw as the cause of his exile twenty years earlier. 'Smug, small-minded people, mostly inept', he called them. He singled out Walter Noel, later to be exposed as running one of the feeder funds in the Bernie Madoff scandal, and his wife, Monica, whom he described as 'worms, and terrible snobs' while they said such charming things about him in a separate interview. The film built up to the lunch for Princess Margaret under his *shamiana* on his remaining land in Mustique, beside the lagoon.

Instead of building something suitable, Colin, to be different, invested in three large tents from India – a saloon, a bedroom for himself, and one for Anne. Three wooden bases were constructed for the tents. In a marvellous piece of theatre, one tent was erected, Colin directing operations for the camera while Kent quietly showed the large labour force what to do. In a marvellous scene Colin chased the Noels and their house party off his land with a stool. As always, Colin was in a state of high excitement and exhaustion when Princess Margaret was on the island, which doubled again with the filming. It had rained heavily all night and the morning of the lunch dawned grey. Eventually the setting was ready and Princess Margaret and the Herreras arrived. From then on the sequence moved through a perfectly ordinary picnic to the 'entertainment', when large screens of tantric images were unrolled. There Princess Margaret was treated to a surprise attack of naked maharajas and gods, some blue, and courtesans with nipples like nails. Princess Margaret looked on amazed. 'What are they doing?' she asked. 'Well, more than wrestling' replied Colin.

The resulting documentary, *The Man Who Bought Mustique*, was shown to mixed critical acclaim. The film was nominated for a BAFTA award and, had it won, Colin surprisingly (as the subject, not the maker) would have gone on stage to collect the award. It was shown at other film festivals, including the Sundance, around the world. But Vikram had the last word when he wrote 'He [Colin] is strangely unsentimental about himself, and as a great showman, he'll know that he might just have given us his greatest performance yet.' Colin loved every minute of the film, gazing at himself on the screen in absolute wonder when it was first shown on television.

The reviews of Colin in the film were mixed. Most, like Stephen Holden, the *New York Times* film critic (a longer version of the film played at The Film Forum in New York for five weeks where it became a 'cult movie') thought him dreadful – 'Human expression doesn't get much chillier than in the gusts of icy contempt wafted by a British aristocrat in high dudgeon,'[ciii] – while Jonathan Foreman of the *New York Post* found it 'One of the more entertaining documentaries to come along in some time.' When it was shown on British television, reviews were also mixed, in equal quantity. Camilla Redmond of *The Guardian* went so far as to praise the directors for having 'accomplished the unusual feat of capturing a living, breathing dinosaur on film'.[civ] Those who knew Colin well were amused by his performance, but the majority of viewers did not like what they saw, and his antics on screen only reinforced their negative ideas of the aristocracy.

Colin was conscious of the steady decline of his friend, Princess Margaret, which began so slowly that it was barely perceptible. It started when she made over *Les Jolies Eaux* to her son, Viscount (David) Linley, on his twenty-seventh birthday. Initially all appeared to go reasonably well with the change of ownership but, as February was the height of the letting season, David understandably needed the money rather than to indulge his mother. But the house was never the same after the 'old guard', the likes of Colin and Roddy, had moved on, although Princess Margaret soldiered on without them. Her decline accelerated after the first of the strokes occurred when she was dining with Harding and Mary Lawrence. It was at a large dinner party that included, amongst others, Princess Margaret's amusing

Irish 'walker', Ned Ryan, and Anouska Hempel, wife of Sir Mark Weinberg. The dinner had only just started and Princess Margaret's hosts invariably produced their best wines when she was dining, much to the delight of the other guests, although she invariably drank Famous Grouse whisky, later Robinson's barley water. On this occasion, one of the two butlers had just finished pouring the Château Pétrus 1959 (described by Michael Broadbent MW as 'fairly deep, mature looking; an incredible bouquet, rich, fishy in the Chambertin sense, full, deep, velvety, rich, rich, rich; dry finish.') when Princess Margaret suffered a mild stroke during the first course, which somewhat upset the proceedings. The island doctor, Michael Bunbury, was summoned and the party broke up. Hosts and guests left, leaving Ned, who solemnly drank his way around the table, understandably not wishing to waste a drop of the precious wine.

Princess Margaret used to stay at Jalousie to see Colin on her way to Mustique, but it was not the same as in the old days. Finally, David sold the house to Jim Murray, a sympathetic American from Virginia who had made his fortune from mobile telephones. He appreciated the house and sculpted it back to the original Oliver Messel creation by removing the warren of tiny bedrooms, and then completed Oliver's grandiose plans with gate houses and pavilions. Princess Margaret was fiercely loyal to David and said that she did not mind him selling her house, but in reality she did.

It was on her last visit to her house that Princess Margaret scalded her feet. The official version was that she had inadvertently turned the tap that directed the flow of very hot water, heated all day by the sun, from the showerhead to the bath spout. There were those, Colin included, who were convinced that this was a cry for help. But this is totally wide of the mark. According to Anne, who nursed Princess Margaret for three weeks after the accident, she was, in fact, washing her hair under the shower within the bath. With her hair over her eyes she instinctively felt for the lever that operated the flow of water, but instead turned the temperature control, thereby shutting off the cold water. The near-boiling water then cascaded onto her feet. It is, however, likely that she suffered a small stroke at the same time. Although she was probably depressed, and had been drinking – David and his wife, Serena, had left, and some prospective buyers of *Les Jolies Eaux* who had visited the house had upset her – self-harm was certainly not in her nature. Whatever the reason for the accident, the effect was to send her health spiralling downwards.

Princess Margaret did attend her joint birthday party (her seventieth) with Queen Elizabeth The Queen Mother (her hundredth), the Princess Royal (her fiftieth) and the Duke of York (his fortieth) at Windsor Castle on Midsummer's Night 2000. Colin and Anne were naturally invited amongst nearly 1,000 other guests, whose names were all in a little booklet, which Colin annotated:

QUEEN ELIZABETH THE QUEEN MOTHER – *Perfectly formed, endwarfed, v-aged, flourishing: (Royal Bonsai)*

THE PRINCESS MARGARET, COUNTESS OF SNOWDON – *Looking quite sweet in her wheel chair. Sarah Spencer made her dress. 'PM chose a furnishing material!' S.S. enhanced it with embroidery.*

PRINCE AND PRINCESS MICHAEL OF KENT – *red: Valkyrie*

Colin wrote later:

The ball at Windsor celebrated the last convolutions of the rule of class, & the aristocracy. There were no outsiders. No fairy godmothers to bless, no wicked stepmothers to curse.

The Duchess of York stood bewildered and uncertain. Camilla was excluded, as was L$^d$ Snowdon. The Princess was in a wheel chair and The Queen Mother has become a bonsai, an ornament on the *bureau plat* [writing desk].

The following year Princess Margaret's health continued on its downward trend. Colin saw her for what was to be the last time in May of 2001, when they lunched together, and he was distressed how the latest stroke had affected her. Never shy of voicing his opinions, he gave a scathing interview, castigating the Royal Family for their lack of understanding Princess Margaret, her illness and her mental state – unfairly as it happened, as the Prince of Wales was most solicitous, telephoning Anne for regular updates of his aunt's condition.

Colin and Anne would talk every day on the telephone and, through her, he kept abreast of the news of Princess Margaret. He kept notes of her last months and recorded how, towards the end, Anne was one of the very few she would see. She did not want men to see her in her state, not even

Roddy. 'Towards the end', Colin claimed, 'Anne was a closer friend than I was, because she needed a woman at the end of her life.' In fact Anne had been a close friend since childhood but, being two years younger, temporarily lost touch when Princess Margaret embarked on the Season.

At the end, in early February 2002, Princess Margaret was taken to King Edward VII Hospital, where she died after a final stroke. Colin did not return to London. Her funeral at St George's Chapel, within Windsor Castle, was on 15 February 2002, the same day, fifty years on, as her beloved father's funeral. She was cremated and her ashes were placed in an urn beside her parents' tombs.

Colin was heavily criticised for not attending the service but, as he said, 'I don't like pageants. Pageantry does not appeal to me.' Nearer the truth, more likely, was that he was more affected than he cared to admit.

# Chapter 22

# THE GREAT HOUSE, BEAU ESTATE

'But Colin', said Lane Pettigrew, standing in front of a *haveli* in the old quarter of Seurat, western India, 'there's someone living here. If you take the pillars away, the house will fall down.'

'Nonsense', replied Colin. 'They're ravishing. I have to have them'. And so the pillars were, all four of them: tall and graceful, with spiral twists running diagonally from the flowered carved capitals down to the plinth. Colin ignored the woman's entreaties to leave her house intact, and dealt with her son and daughter-in-law, who needed the money.

Colin had decided that his final house would be authentic Indian, as opposed to pastiche, and that it would last with his 'treasures intact'. For his quest for genuine architectural features – columns, doors, and the like – he found Tizak Toddywalla to take him around Gujarat on a buying spree. Other columns and carved doors followed, including some pieces from a monastery in Ahmedabad where he and Lane were caught by a monk surreptitiously measuring the columns. In the end they were offered the whole place as the order needed the money to move into a brand new concrete house in preference to the eighteenth-century gem. Colin was a true trader. He might enter by the front door of the shop, but invariably ended up dealing in some warehouse at the back. Consequently he bought the unusual, and the best. The 'treasures' from Gujarat were then removed, packed in a container, and eventually turned up in St Lucia to await their inclusion in his new house.

But, as so often happened in Colin's travels, disaster struck. Speeding in a taxi through the Kutch desert on a minor road, he became incensed with the driver who was chewing betel-nut and, opening the door slightly as he drove along, spitting out the juice. As Colin insisted on the windows being open, great globules of red saliva flew back into the taxi and landed on his white trousers. Colin was enraged and told him to stop spitting. The driver refused, whereupon Colin leant forward and bit his ear, drawing a stream of blood. The man howled in pain, stopped, and ordered Colin and Lane out of the taxi, throwing their luggage after them, then drove off in a cloud of dust along the empty road. They were fortunate to be rescued by a passing bus after a short wait on the kerb.

All his life, Colin had rushed around at a frenetic rate – 'do keep up' had become his constant cry to others. A replacement hip restored his madcap pace when he began to slow. His health became of paramount importance. He had long since given up drinking alcohol, then eating red meat. He employed a personal trainer twice a week, as much for the conversation as for the exercise. But just as the tribulations of Beau and the effort of running Bang were beginning to take their toll, the perfect solution presented itself when May, the elder twin, became engaged to Anton Creasy, an IT expert. Colin came over to England for the wedding at Holkham, where Anne showed that she was equally capable of throwing a grand party as he.

After the wedding, May and Anton sold up everything in London and left their jobs to go out to St Lucia to take over Colin's entire operation. With 20:20 hindsight vision, it was an impossible situation that could not possibly have worked and it was doomed from the start.

Colin had always had a sneaking regard for Amy. He had admired her alternative approach to life – she was the first sibling to have a job and be financially independent when she worked variously on an Irish ferry and taught outward-bound skills on Snowdon. She loved the West Indies, and always had a rapport with the locals. May was more conservative, with a conventional job in a documentary film company.

The two girls had always had a difficult relationship with Colin. While they were both devoted to him, their love was not returned in the same manner. As May said of a later encounter:

I wanted to show him love, even though it was damned hard. I went through a stage of giving him huge hugs but this didn't last long as one day he turned to me and said, 'I just want you to know, I hate all this touchy feely business. It's all the fault of the Princess of Wales.'

Although they had the constant love and support of their mother and Barbara, the younger siblings – Christopher, May and Amy – found Colin's attitude towards them upsetting. He was irrational in his treatment of them, which made them as children constantly nervous of being around him, as they never knew 'when he was going to blow his fuse'.[cv] There were treats and expeditions, but these, like many a family holiday, were often spoilt by him throwing a tantrum. As Amy said: 'We were frightened of him as children. He was more into other children than us'.[cvi] They were jealous, too, of his treatment of others their age, such as Jade Jagger or Ariana Neumann, with whom he would take such trouble, and to whom he would give lovely presents. It was ever thus.

Being slightly older than his siblings and cousins, they would long for Colin's visits as he made them such fun. As his step-sister Emma Tennant wrote, 'The words "Colin is coming," whether said by a guest at our childhood home, or by a hopeful child, brought a wonderful sense of expectation, a kind of naughtiness which took its cue from childhood. Colin was one of us.'[cvii] Later, during the huge house parties at Glen when filled with Charlie and Henry's contemporaries, Colin was 'totally wonderful with them all. He was like the pied piper where the children would scream with excitement following him over the hill after picnics at Loch Eddy. He organised charades after tea for them or games, like sardines, all over the house.'[cviii] With the twins, when Colin was relaxed, he was very entertaining and great fun. Their childhood was certainly far from boring and conventional and both agreed that, in the end, the injustices were certainly a price worth paying.

In 1995 May felt that there was just a possibility that decamping to St Lucia might work. Colin was lonely and tired of the drudgery of running Bang; May wanted to strengthen her ties with him, and Anton was young and enthusiastic. But 'sadly no miracle occurred'. Colin simply would not let go of the reins. The 'honeymoon' period was short lived, and May and Anton lived in a strained and difficult relationship with Colin.

Naturally, Colin blamed them for the arrangement not working and detailed the causes in three full pages of a notebook. In his neat, precise hand, he complained that they were ungrateful, that the advice he and Kent gave was taken as interference, and that they wanted him to leave at the earliest opportunity:

If someone comes into a family business, of which they have no previous experience or knowledge (other than as a consumer or patron) they learn. If furthermore they have no experience of management they assist. To take over a long established business in a remote foreign country they must establish relations with the locals, and know their clientele.

Of course they made mistakes. Anton was sharp with the staff, earning the soubriquet 'Pharaoh', as in slave driver. Colin had always had a very good rapport with his local staff, not least because he turned a blind eye when they lied or robbed him, which he expected, and therefore built the thefts and falsehoods into the equation. Coming straight from England, Anton could not possibly have the same affinity with them that Colin had developed over fifty years in the Caribbean.

The former film director and restaurant critic, Michael Winner, had written up Bang in *The Sunday Times* over the years and he and Colin were as thick as thieves. But whatever May and Anton's faults and shortcomings, the most glowing of all his reviews of Bang was when they were running the restaurant. Winner wrote:

> Anton cooks. May does the office work. 'You must both show yourselves', I advised them, as if I knew anything about anything. 'You're charming, nice-looking people. Get out there and greet the guests.' The food was beyond belief excellent. We started with slices of grilled coconuts. Then beignets of tri-tri – little just-hatched fishes from the mouth of the river – followed by crawfish caught that morning in the stream that runs behind my suite in the Jalousie Plantation Hotel. With them was boiled green paw paw and christophene gratinée.

Being Michael Winner, he could not resist mentioning that amongst the many 'other' celebrities who had dined there were the Duke and Duchess of Gloucester, Stephen Spielberg, Nicholas Cage and Lord Falconer.

It could not last. Anton stood up to Colin, which made matters worse as he was not used to confrontation, and became vindictive. He would, for instance, telephone the cook, Deborah, to say that she was not needed when she was, so throwing the kitchen into turmoil. By the time May went home in the summer she was pregnant, and decided to stay there until the baby was born. Anton followed soon after and once again Colin, by his own choosing, was left to carry on his St Lucia life without them. Barbara Barnes, their erstwhile nanny and great friend of the family, never forgave Colin for his treatment of May and Anton. Undaunted by their departure, Colin became irrepressible when he took on new and exciting twin projects: to build the Great House in time for his eightieth birthday, and to finance both.

With Jalousie once again up and running, and yachts anchoring off, potential clients came to the Beau Estate. One such was the (then) Arsenal and England International footballer, Sol Campbell, of Jamaican origin, who immediately fell in love with the place. But yet again Colin's life reverted to a game of snakes and ladders. Sol said that he would buy a good and expensive lot, so taking Colin some way up the fiscal ladder. But all too soon he was 'bitten' by a snake and came tumbling down again. This time the 'snake' was in the form of UNESCO, who declared the Pitons a World Heritage Site of Special Physical Significance. Colin initially supported the programme, and donated 40 acres of steep land towards the scheme. But when the Government put an embargo on all development in the area while they decided how to interpret the preservation order, the whole of Beau was blighted. Tired of waiting for an alien's land-holding licence and planning permission Sol pulled out of Beau, taking his deposit with him.

Notwithstanding the loss of the Campbell money that Colin was counting on to build his house and to fund his party. He went ahead anyway with both. Catherine the Great could well have been describing him when she wrote: 'The fury to build is a diabolical thing – it devours money and the more one builds the more one wants to build. It is as intoxicating as drink.' Lane had drawn up a set of plans that incorporated all the architectural pieces they had bought together in India five years before, and work went ahead. Colin had already built the terrace and the base of his house, under which were three bedrooms and a kitchen, where he was already living and had guests to stay. Throughout his life, whatever his emotional or financial state, there was a true and genuine compassionate side to Colin. There were dozens of examples of his kindnesses, both small and large. Sarah Henderson, Anne's great friend, recalled Colin's thoughtfulness and generosity: 'I was very low after the death of a close friend. Colin heard about it and said that it would do me good join him in St Lucia, and that he would send me the ticket. In the end I could not go but it was so very kind of him to offer it.'

While the house was being built, again in coral blocks from Barbados,

Colin and Lane, accompanied by Kent, went off to India – they were to make four trips in all. There, with the help of Mitch Crites and Maharukh Desai, Colin furnished his house as it was being built. In Jaipur he ordered a cotton *dhurrie* to be woven specially for the grand salon in a colour from a 'dye that no one had used since the days of the Raj that came from the root of a small dry bush only found in the Rajasthan Desert'.[cix] He found mirrored walls and paintings from the nineteenth century: he bought large temple cabinets displaying all manner of Hindu gods. On a trip to London he remembered that he had seen a Victorian chandelier that was said to have been destined for the Indian market, but had never made it because of the Sepoy Rebellion, hence it had never been assembled. Colin paid £75,000 for it. It made less than a third of that in the Bonhams sale after his death.

The house was ready for Colin's birthday party, although he later regretted building it so quickly, as it gave him nothing exciting to do after it was finished. The house was one gigantic folly: impractical as it was impressive. Lane had cleverly worked in all the Indian architectural pieces. Even the poor woman in Seurat who lost the pillars to her house would have been impressed. Colin had chosen a particular grey-blue for the woodwork, picked out in silver leaf. His cipher, a baron's coronet with a large G, surmounted an Arabic text over the front door. Two pineapples, the symbols of hospitality, flanked the base of the heavily carved door linings. The hall was large and grand, dominated by the chandeliers and the coral wall sconces that had been made by Janine Janet for the hall in Tite Street. A mirrored frieze of black peacocks ran round the top of the wall below the cornice. It was Colin's clever idea to have all the lights in the house controlled from a central cupboard: he declared that 'the nineteenth-century effect was not spoiled by ugly electric switches'. The hall leads into the main salon with a chamber on either side. Colin had sent three St Lucian painters out to India to be trained in the art of mixing tempera. Using egg whites and pigment they painted all the walls a subtle silver-grey colour that gave them an extraordinary lustre. The salon was dominated by a dome in the centre. This was Colin's great mistake. He told Lane that he wanted an 'upturned boat', which was completely the wrong shape and size for the building. The inside of the dome was a natural haven for bats that roosted there nightly, consuming their fruit. Their droppings ruined the *dhurrie* and bespattered the chandeliers.

The right-hand chamber was supposed to be Colin's bedroom, in which he put the silver four-poster bed that he had given to Anne, but it was totally impractical to sleep in as the whole of the front of the house was open to the elements, and the sides were only protected by elaborate grilles. The other chamber contained the mirrored walls bought in Rajasthan. Shading the main salon was a deep portico with the six pillars from the Ahmedabad monastery. The wide terrace held a beautiful view of Jalousie Bay dominated by the Petite Piton, while the undulating land in front of the house was planted with grass, on which imported white Indian zebu cattle grazed, giving it a park-like feel.

There is a well-known maxim on Wall Street: 'Once is a trend, twice is a tradition, and three times is a commandment' and so it was a commandment for the thirty lucky family and friends who came out from England to celebrate Colin's eightieth birthday and were put up at Jalousie in a final deal with the hotel owners. As usual, there were parties galore all around Souffrière – dinner at Bang on the first night, a visit to Lane at his house on the estate the next night, then up to Fond Doux, where Lyton and Eroline Lamontagne hosted a fancy dress party. There the theme was 'dress St Lucian' or 'most like Colin'.

Throughout the week, various members of the family were summoned to the Great House. They went trembling only to find that they had been given a piece of special jewellery or some *objet*. The climax was the birthday party itself at the Great House, where the theme was Indian. Fifty sat down in two long lines and, once again, Colin's eyes sparkled with the elation he derived from giving others so much pleasure. But age was 'catching him'. As he said: 'Here in St Lucia, age is not a topic to dwell on. Like steak, there are categories – rare, medium and well done. Having reached the age of indiscretion I would rate myself as 'indigestible' but you can always eat the fries.'

The party at Bang during the birthday week marked the end of an era and, when May and Anton confirmed that they were definitely not returning, Colin closed it down. In another disastrous deal Colin sold Bang and the surrounding 4 acres with beachfront to Roger Myers, the entrepreneur who founded the Café Rouge chain and the new owner of Jalousie. Roger paid Colin just US$75,000 with 50 per cent of the profit of the resulting development. Colin was to see no more cash from the transaction as the development lay dormant for the rest of his life.

But worse, with the closure of Bang came intense loneliness for Colin. He had also lost his faithful companion, Frankie, his Jack Russell terrier.

Small and aggressive, Frankie would take on any dog, whatever its size. The day before the guests arrived for the birthday party, the tyke was badly mauled by a large dog, and subsequently died. He was buried in a blue and yellow sequined jacket of the St Lucia flag that Maharukh had had made for him for the party. Colin never saw the extent of his injuries, and greatly mourned his death. Estranged from the hotel (apart from collecting his breakfast from the dining room, where he chatted to the odd guest), and not having Bang, he saw virtually no one. Colin complained that he had once eaten dinner for ninety days in a row on his own; or what passed for dinner – eight Ritz biscuits pounded with a stone, mixed with a dollop of apple purée with some milk or yoghurt. Sometimes he added a banana if he managed to filtch one on his breakfast foray, or a bread roll. It was invariably eaten at about quarter to nine in the evening.

As Colin became frailer, so Kent became more and more indispensable. Kent continued to manage Beau, where the mother of some of his children, Mona, oversaw the day labourers. He drove Colin everywhere and was at his constant beck and call. In the late afternoon he would drive him to the sulphur springs, where both would wallow in the natural hot water. When Colin was ready to retire to bed, Kent would draw him a bath and when he had bathed, Kent would be on hand to pull him out. Every night after Colin had gone to bed, Kent would lie on the floor next door watching films on DVD before driving up the hill to his house in Morne la Croix. Kent was party to all Colin's thoughts, prejudices, likes and dislikes, which he would endorse.

Although he rarely admitted it, Colin missed Princess Margaret dreadfully. For fifty years she had inspired him in a way that allowed him to flower. He admired her greatly, and, of course, who she was, and consequently responded to her sharpness and quick wit. But when she died, that part of him died with her, leaving the last eight years of his life a sadder time. He did, however, have one white friend, Norman Brick, who lived on the other side of Souffrière. Colin found the former CEO of Eastman Kodak highly intelligent and very good company.

Family and friends would visit Colin from time to time, when they found him appreciative of their visit, but his hospitality sorely lacking. Once his favourite cousin, Zanna Johnston, and her sister-in-law, Alice Chancellor, went to stay. In her witty address at Colin's memorial service, Zanna described the visit:

Colin did not believe in kitchens. He thought that people with such amenities were ridiculously spoilt. In St Lucia there was no toaster, no oven, no grill. An electric kettle was just permitted. He ate very little, weirdly, and if possible only out of paper bags. And he disliked the sight of others eating. I experienced this phobia when I stayed with him in St Lucia. Fridges were allowed in that climate but were all empty save for ice and cranberries that Colin ate for breakfast.

On the first evening we all met at six on the terrace. By seven there had been no suggestion of refreshment. By eight there was no talk of food and at nine Colin said 'I must go to bed now!'

No breakfast for us as Colin ate the cranberries. I took a water taxi to a local store and bought tomatoes, cheese, bananas and a bottle of wine. That evening Colin spotted the salad that Alice had made with the cheese and tomatoes and said. 'You're not supposed to eat that. It's being kept.' When Alice told him that I had bought them myself he said with mischievous glee 'Very well then – but I've hidden the bananas.' After a week of starvation I fainted at Gatwick on my return.[cx]

The author sent some friends, Andrew and Annie Muir, to see Colin at his house. Colin liked them very much, as they warmed to him and his witty, well-informed conversation. Warned that drink would be lacking, they prudently brought their own bottle of wine. They invited him to lunch at their hotel the next day, where their enjoyable conversation ensued. Later, the author asked Colin how the visit went, whereupon he indignantly complained that the Muirs had not written to thank him. For what?

With old age came bitterness. He developed a further hatred for Mustique and its people – Kent disliked it too, describing it as 'paradise in prison'. Colin was resentful of the fact that he had no pension from the Mustique Company. There had been a move in the mid-1970s to make him responsible for all the public relations on the island, with a salary and an expense account, to which he was well-suited, but they simply could not trust him to keep to a budget. He had no recognition either for single-handedly opening that part of the Windward Islands to tourism, until the St Lucian Government made him a 'Goodwill Ambassador'. The post meant little and he did less in it, but it did give him a diplomatic passport and a certain caché. He was, however, inordinately proud when Anne was made St Lucia's Ambassador to the International Maritime Association.

There was high excitement for all when the Prince of Wales and the Duchess of Cornwall came to Soufrière and visited Lyton and Eroline at Fond Doux Plantation – for all, that is, except Colin, who had not been included in the official party to meet them. Anne had recently flown out to be with Colin and they decided to go to Fond Doux anyway. As the Royal couple arrived, the Duchess spied Anne in the bar sheltering from the rain. To Colin's intense delight, with her hands thrown in the air the Duchess shouted 'My God! I had no idea you were going to be here. When am I going to see you?' and beckoned Prince Charles to come over. Never one to miss a trick, Colin suggested that the Duchess take Anne on board their chartered yacht, Sir Donald Gosling's *Leander G*, for lunch. The arrangements were quickly made and Anne departed with the Duchess. The next morning Lyton telephoned Colin to say that he had been asked by the Governor General to send her apologies that he was not included in the official party and she was coming down to apologise in person. Apparently the Prince of Wales was annoyed that Colin and Anne, his particular friend and confidante, were on the island and he had not been told. Later Colin did have the grace to admit that without Anne he would have been completely 'ignored, or shall we say, side-tracked'.

However much Colin disapproved of Mustique he would always return if the invitation was grand enough – lunch with Mick Jagger or his neighbour, Tommy Hilfiger, or Felix Dennis – or any invitation that came with a charter flight. He did attend the Mustique Company's fund-raising dinner to celebrate its fortieth anniversary, although he naturally thought that the celebrations should have been delayed a year to celebrate the fiftieth anniversary of him buying the island. He found the whole evening beautifully organised by Dora Loewenstein, but the majority of the people very alien, and deplored the fact that other than the Prime Minister, Ralph Gonzales, there were no local people. He crept away before the dancing and the arrival of Prince William and Catherine Middleton, whose parents had taken a house above Macaroni Beach, who came in after dinner to dance at a reduced rate.

Every year Colin had a check-up during his autumn visit to London, and every year he came back with a clean bill of health, that was until 2008 when his doctor found that his PSA (Prostate Specific Antigen) was high. He recommended that Colin went to see Professor Kirby, a leading specialist in prostate cancer. Colin reacted to the news badly, believing that if it was known that he had prostate cancer 'no one would do business with him'. He made his appointment at the end of the day in the hope that he would remain unseen, and hid in a back waiting room. The subsequent biopsy revealed that he did indeed have the disease. It was, however, in the early stages. Because of his age surgery was not an option, so he went on a course of hormone therapy, with injections every three months to shrink the tumour. For a time the treatment worked well and kept him in remission so that he led a relatively normal life. For example, he greatly enjoyed the visit of Sheilagh and her son, his heir, Cody, to St Lucia. He took them to Trinidad to stay at the old Tennant plantation, Ortinola, which had been converted into a hotel.

On his next visit to London, Colin gave Francis Wyndham lunch. He confided in his cousin how lonely he was in St Lucia, particularly as Christopher, who had been staying with him, had a new girlfriend and had returned to London to be with her. When Francis saw Colin again later in the week, he told him of the visit he had had from his godson, Joshua Bowler. Joshua, a psychotherapist, had recently moved into a flat around the corner from Francis, which gave him the chance to become reacquainted with his godfather and lifelong friend of his mother, Henrietta Moraes. When his sister, Caroline, asked about their early childhood, Joshua went to discuss it with Francis, and it was then that Francis told him he was fairly certain that Colin was his biological father. Joshua was taken aback, but not totally surprised.

Colin had been to the Chelsea Arts Club New Year's Eve ball of 1954 in a party that included Francis and his friend, Henrietta Moraes (as she became). Colin left with her that night and took her back to Graham Terrace. From the note written on C. Tennant, Sons & Co. writing paper it would appear that the liaison lasted only what was left of the night:

> Darling Colin I've walked out in what is bound to be your bestest shirt, very pretty with blue stripes because [it] really would be too shaming with no shoulders like last night & a whitish sweater but will of course send them back – I've eaten the grapes. I loved last night – love
> Henrietta

Henrietta was the archetypal Bohemian artist's model and went on to become the muse of both Francis Bacon and Lucian Freud. Bacon's *Portrait of Henrietta Moraes* sold for £21.3 million, while Colin bought one of her by Lucian that he described as 'a pensive girl with a blanket wrapped round her shoulders, looking out the window at the ducks outside Lucian's studio'. Poignantly, it always hung in the study of each of his houses, but was finally sold with his other pictures by Freud. As Colin looked at it for over thirty years, he cannot have failed to wonder about her and her son.

Seven months after the brief liaison with Colin, Henrietta, heavily pregnant, married the actor, Norman Bowler. A boy, who was christened Joshua, was born in September, and was followed by a daughter, Caroline, the next year. Norman accepted Joshua as his own son, although he must have had his reservations as to his true paternity. He walked out of the marital home when Joshua was just two and a half. Although Joshua did see him spasmodically for a time in his early teens, there was no emotional bond between them. By that time Joshua had been fostered by Diana, wife of George Melly, the jazz singer and author. Only once did he remember his mother talking about Colin, when he was about 8 years of age. At 15, Henrietta took him to lunch with Colin at Tite Street, ostensibly to sound him out on the merits of his school, Frensham Heights. Joshua claims that Colin paid half of his school fees, the other half coming from the London County Council. However, in Dianna Melly's autobiography, *Take a Girl Like Me*, she wrote that Lady Caroline Blackwood paid for Joshua's sister Caroline to go to Frensham, and that 'Joshua didn't have a rich godfather, but we appealed to the head of Frensham and, backed up by letters from Richard Hoggart and Jonathan Miller, Joshua too was accepted, and without fees'.

Charlie became a close friend of Joshua's at Frensham Heights, and the friendship continued after they both left. Colin asked Joshua to come to Glen, as Charlie's friend, and Joshua remembers Colin being very solicitous towards him – far more than would be expected of the mere friend of his eldest son. At 18, Joshua went out to Mustique, supposedly to be Colin's personal assistant – a trying post in anyone's book. There, people made references to his paternity but, as Joshua said, 'I convinced myself that I was there simply as Charlie's friend'. In his early twenties he made the conscious decision to stop worrying about his parentage 'as it didn't mean anything', and to get on with his life, undaunted by the uncertainty. Then, thirty years later, he heard the confirmation from Francis that Colin was almost certainly his biological father and he decided to prove it either way, once and for all.

The safest and least contentious way was to have his and Caroline's DNA tested in a laboratory in Cambridge. Although Joshua was expecting it, when the result came back that they were indeed half-siblings, it came a considerable shock. It did, however, explain his disastrous relationship with Norman. He then wrote to Colin in St Lucia, but received no reply as Colin was already in England. Joshua then telephoned him. 'He [Colin] was really sweet. Very welcoming. He explained that Christopher had moved on, so "he was up for grabs".' Joshua replied that 'he too was up for grabs' and gratefully accepted Colin's invitation to spend some time with him in St Lucia. Over the few weeks he was there, Colin delighted in his company, talking endlessly of his family which was of course all new to Joshua. Colin admired his 'new' son's work in helping psychologically damaged servicemen and women. At Anne's insistence, they both took a DNA test in Castries – Colin's version going to Miami for analysis, whilst Joshua sent his back to the Cambridge laboratory he had used before.

Three weeks later Joshua telephoned Colin with what he hoped he would find good news – confirmation that he was indeed his biological son – it was later confirmed by the laboratory in Miami. Colin thought it 'quite magical. ... What better Christmas present could there be for an old bloke like me than a son and four lively grandsons?' When Joshua returned to St Lucia as an official offspring Colin, according to Joshua, 'was completely overcome with emotion'. Although frail, the timing could not have been better, for it gave him a new impetus, not least the 'enjoyable' publicity that surrounded the announcement after it was 'leaked' to *The Sunday Times*. Anne suggested, organised and paid for the party to introduce Joshua and his 'new' grandsons to his family at Glen. It was a tremendous success, and the young all took to each other famously. It could have been awkward for Anne – had she known Colin had fathered a son out of wedlock her parents would never have allowed her to marry him – but in her usual, calm and pragmatic fashion, she accepted it all. Having been married to Colin for fifty-four years there was very little left to surprise her.

For a long time, Princess Josephine Loewenstein had lobbied the Board of the Mustique Company that they should mark Colin's great contribution to the island in some way – preferably with a statue. She had known Colin well since her debutante days and they were distantly related on both sides of their families. She and her husband, Rupert, were frequent visitors to Glen and Mustique, although they only bought and extended their house there after Colin had left the island.

The idea for the statue ran and ran with each successive board meeting, until Josephine forced the issue. She interviewed many sculptors and finally whittled it down to Philip Jackson, in whom she recognised 'his ability to convey the human condition [in sculpture] through the skilful use of body language'.[cxi] She and Rupert asked Philip to lunch to meet Colin, who took to him instantly – the fact that he, Philip, was in the process of sculpting The Queen Mother was an added plus for Colin. The price was fixed and Josephine easily raised the money from amongst the house owners.

Typically Colin produced many photographs of himself in his younger days – more shades of Dorian Gray – but Philip wanted to portray him as he then was. After an initial session with Colin in his studio near Midhurst, where he took his own photographs and made many sketches, Philip went out and spent an entertaining week with Colin in St Lucia, to get to really know 'the inner man'. He then went on to Mustique to see where the statue was to be sited. Josephine wanted it by the airport, but that was not practical: Colin wanted it where 'he' could see the sea. In the end a site was chosen on a small hillock, a *collina*, in sight of the sea once a branch or two had been lopped off – Colin, of course, wanted the trees removed.

Philip's maquette was then approved by all, and he set too, making his one and a half times life-size sculpture of Colin. With the hat and base, it was nearly 12 ft high. Colin lent a set of his Indian clothes, a hat and a cane, and a brochure of Mustique as props. The end result was a truly marvellous sculpture. Colin was secretly delighted. All his life, he felt that he had missed out on any kind of honour – or even recognition – for his achievements, but this statue was something that would last for all time.

The unveiling was timed for early January, when the majority of the house owners who had contributed would be on the island. The Mustique Company sent a small charter plane for Colin, Anne, May and Amy: a larger plane came the next day with the St Lucia contingent, led by Kent, Lyton, and Deborah, his cook. Josephine made a little speech then pulled the blue cloth from the statue to great applause; whereupon Colin replied with an appropriate and witty riposte. The short ceremony was one of the highest points in his life.

Colin went back to London in the summer for more treatment at the Prostate Clinic, and to attend the ninetieth birthday of the Countess of Avon (Clarissa). There, he saw many of his old friends, who found him decidedly odd-looking. He had grown a rather long, and totally extraordinary, grey beard, no doubt for effect. He caught up with Amy, who had decided to go out permanently to St Lucia in the late autumn to do some restoration work on various of his pieces and to look after him – 'she needs me', Colin had said, 'but more importantly, I need her'. He also enjoyed seeing May and her young daughter, Honor, in the boutique hotel where he stayed in Notting Hill, when they were finally reconciled.

When Anne stayed with Colin in St Lucia in early August, he had become even frailer. Whilst there, she nursed him after he had picked up some infection and became very ill. But he soon made a remarkable recovery, and was on very good form. He was affectionate and tender towards he. They talked of their life together. Anne later recalling their time together admitted: 'He made my life. He taught me to look at things in a new light. Without him, I would never have flourished in the way I have.' Colin summed up their life together simply: 'It wasn't all bad, was it?' he said at the end. By the Wednesday he was so much better – even swimming in the sea – that Anne decided to return to England where she had a large house party for the Bank Holiday weekend. As they said goodbye at the airport, neither dreamed that this was their final parting.

The morning of Friday 27 August 2010 began much like any other day at the Great House. Colin made his own breakfast as usual, while his faithful cook and housekeeper, Deborah Cyril, padded around upstairs sweeping up the leaves that had fallen during the night and blown onto the terrace, and inside the salon. She was still greatly puzzled as, for the first time ever, Colin had telephoned her at 10 o'clock the night before and thanked her for all she had done for him over the past twenty-three years. She heard Kent arrive, and go down to see 'Mr Tennants' below. After a few minutes, she heard Kent shouting for her to telephone for an ambulance. She rang straight away and went down to see Colin unconscious, being cradled by Kent on the floor. He had had a massive heart attack. Kent had tried to revive him by pumping his chest, but to no avail. Realising that the ambulance would not reach them in time, if at all, Kent picked up the dying figure, hugging him like a child. Lovingly, he laid him in the front seat of his Jeep, and sped off towards the hospital. But he knew instinctively that it was too late, for Colin was already dead.

Kent was totally inconsolable as he lifted out the lifeless body of his friend of thirty years. He carried Colin around in his arms, sobbing over him for four hours, until the corpse was prised out of his arms and taken away to the mortuary. For four days Kent cried, resisting all attempts at comfort.

No Lord Glenconner had ever lived beyond the age of 83 years.

# ENVOI

According to Lane Pettigrew, 'Colin changed lawyers like others changed their shirts. They all thought him a prestigious client and were happy to take him on.' On the Sunday, the day after the funeral, at 10 o'clock on the dot, a large black pickup arrived with the latest advocate from Souffrière. He, Anne, Tessa, Sheilagh and the twins, with Eric Shaw, the New York lawyer who handled the affairs of Beau Estate, settled down around the open-air dining table. I was not party to the reading of the will, but observed from a distance. Less than fifteen minutes later, the lawyer was gone, leaving the family dumbfounded. Later, I learned why the will took just moments to read. It was a bombshell. Colin had simply left everything he owned to Kent with the words 'as he knows my wishes' as the only explanation of his actions.

After all he had done for Colin over nearly thirty years, nobody, least of all the family, begrudged Kent a handsome settlement from the will – but not everything. Colin had inherited his fortune from his family. He was atavistic to a fault, as those who had heard the endless tales of 'Gran Edith' and the Tennants creating the Industrial Revolution will testify. Having inherited vast wealth and possessions himself, it was only right that he should act merely as their custodian throughout his life and pass them on, intact, to his family. He did, of course, hand over Glen and its contents to Henry – as it turned out, the gift was more a liability and only exists today because of Tessa's injection of her own cash and careful management. As we have seen, Charlie signed over his inheritance of Glen on the proviso that the West Indian interests should go to him. Thus, Beau and all Colin's possessions there had already been pledged to Charlie and his heirs and so they could not morally be left elsewhere.

My immediate thought was that Colin had made such a controversial will so that people would talk about him for years to come, and thus never forget him. Lyton told me that, in St Lucia, once the wake is over, you are indeed forgotten. Certainly today, at the mention of Colin's name, it is always the will that is first discussed – in New York, Carolina Herrera was so upset by it that she could not begin to talk to me about our old friend. But on further reflection there has to have been more than mere 'remembrance' for Colin to create such a surprising will, and naturally there have been many theories as to why he came up with something so controversial.

There are those who believe the reason for the change was collusion between Kent and the lawyer, who took advantage of a frail and sick Colin. There was some doubt about one of the signatures, and there was talk of a missing page. Colin was well known for signing documents he had not read, but I think it inconceivable that, even in his state of ill-health at the time, he would not have carefully checked the few words of his last will. I personally believe that there was nothing untoward and the will that Colin signed was the one he dictated.

According to the August 2012 article in *Tatler* on Colin, the locals in St Lucia believe that he redrafted his will as he wanted Kent to see his creation of Beau finished as the 'last monument to his extraordinary vision'.[cxii] Colin had no illusions that Beau was not a success, and was desperate to sell it all himself. Also, he knew full well that Kent, competent as he was as his estate manager, was certainly not capable of heading up a US$30 million operation.

Over the last three years of his life, Colin made various tape recordings for his autobiography. Sandwiched between an account of the visit of the Prince of Wales to Souffrière and his thoughts on the sculptor Philip Jackson were his clear intentions on the redrafting of his will. The whole thing made perfect sense: he proposed to leave just the shares of Beau to Kent in escrow until it was sold, then to distribute the estate as per his direction – the exact phrase was *'as Kent knows my wishes'*. Anne was to be a co-executor. Colin specified that the bulk of his estate, including the majority of the bequests, was to go to Cody, with the remainder being distributed to individual members of the family. If this will was made with one of his previous lawyers, which is likely, it was superseded by the last, which he made just seven months before he died.

Although he obviously did not discuss it with Anne, she is firmly of the opinion that Colin, enfeebled with cancer, was 'too tired, too ill and too exhausted'[cxiii] to make a proper decision over his will, and so opted for the easiest solution – to leave everything to Kent so that he could then carry out his wishes explicitly. Anne knew that Colin wanted Beau to be kept in good repair until it was sold, and the villagers of Morne la Croix to be looked after. She therefore endorsed the sale of the contents of the Great House at Bonhams in London, as she knew that the money was to be repatriated to St Lucia for the good of the people and the estate.

While this is a totally plausible explanation and one in keeping with Colin's state of mind at the time, I believe that there is more to the conundrum. Colin had an ambiguous relationship with his family. He was deeply proud of Anne, and in particular her role as Lady-in-Waiting to Princess Margaret and the way she held the family together – even embracing Joshua and his sons by organising the gathering at Glen. But then some imagined slight would offend him and he would become annoyed with her. Sheilagh enjoyed a period when she was the 'chosen one', when Colin deferred to the advice of her partner, Gerry. Colin was inordinately proud of his grandson, Cody, and delighted in telling of how he was turning into such a 'fine young man' with a beautiful singing voice. But it did not last. As Colin told me, Sheilagh had upset him by a letter she wrote to him. The May and Anton saga started well and finished badly. Even Tessa, the consistent bright star in Colin's firmament, sometimes fell from grace through some trivial or supposed oversight. Only Amy and Christopher remained unscathed, partially because the latter constantly told Colin how much he loved him. As we have seen, Colin demanded much from his family and, however much they gave, it was never enough. Unlike Kent, who lived on the edge of Beau, the members of Colin's family had their own lives to lead so could not be at his beck and call as he demanded.

Like Robinson Crusoe and Man Friday, Kent gave Colin, in varying degrees, loyalty and affection for nearly thirty years and seemingly asked for little in return other than a small monthly salary. During Colin's lifetime, Kent received many large and material gifts – apart from the extensive travel, there was the land above Beau that was put in his name. There was the large house in Choiseul that was being turned into a small hotel and restaurant, with quarters for Colin and a room for Anne (it remains unfinished), and probably other houses around the town. Kent gave Colin his friendship, which was reciprocated, and I believe it is this closeness that is, most likely, the root cause of the change of the will.

To better understand the bond between Colin and Kent (which, as we have already established, was completely non-sexual) I contacted Professor Suzanne Stern-Gillet, Professor of Ancient Philosophy at Bolton University, and author of Aristotle's *Philosophy of Friendship*.[cxiv] Within her extensive reply she wrote:

> The relationship between Colin and Kent seems worthy to be described as a friendship, albeit not a friendship of equality. Although C came to be utterly dependent upon K, it seems that, at the beginning at least, K was more of a 'helper' than an equal partner.
>
> The fact that the relationship lasted 30 years is proof that it was firmly embedded into both men's lives and that neither was a 'mere instrument' for the other. It cannot therefore have been entirely a friendship of utility – or, if it started as one, it matured into something else.

Certainly Colin and Kent benefited in different ways from their relationship. As Kent admitted, he owed his entire education to Colin (even after extensive tutoring in London he is barely literate). 'He taught me everything – how to think, how to talk, I just listen to him and I learn.' Colin educated Kent to be his equal: there was nothing that Kent did not know about him and his past, his forebears, his relationships and thinking, including his current prejudices. In a way, Colin created Kent into an extension of himself. Further, with Kent, Colin could be entirely himself, secure in the knowledge of the forgiveness of true friendship, however he behaved. Kent was indeed loyal to Colin, and his shadow when abroad: 'I have to follow Mr Tennant around all day to make sure nothing go wrong. I keep watching all the time. I know he eccentric and that people don't understand him, but that's the way he is'.[cxv]

At the end of his life, Colin relied on Kent for literally everything. Living their own lives 4,500 miles from St Lucia, none of Colin's family could begin to fill that role (except Amy, who had planned to be with him, but he died before she moved).

As Professor Stern-Gillet points out, the wording in the will, 'Kent knows my wishes' is somewhat ambiguous 'insofar as it may mean either *give some of the money to my family* or *don't give anything to my family, however pressing their demands*'. She continues, 'What he [Colin] felt he owed K may have come to silence in his mind the obligations that he nonetheless recognised having to his family.' I am convinced that Colin left his entire estate to Kent simply as he wanted him to have it, and not to spite his family.

When I went to St Lucia to see Kent in March 2012, we sat in the salon of the Great House. After a few minutes he stopped talking and declared that it was too upsetting to talk about Colin in the house and we decamped to the fish market in Choiseul to continue our conversation. There he told me that the content of the will came as a total surprise to him: 'I didn't know Mr Tennant did that. He never told me, only he say to me, "When I die, you will miss me, but you will always be rich." That's what he say to me.' Kent says that he had no prior knowledge of the contents of the will. But he later complained in the *Tatler* article that Anne had not invited him to its reading. If he expected to be there (which of course was not normal for the reading of a family will), then he knew he was the sole beneficiary, but equally, had he known what was in the will, then he certainly would not have wished to be present at its reading amongst the family who were likely to be hostile towards him.

But knowing Colin's intentions of the draft will dictated two years earlier with the same phrase 'as Kent knows my wishes', I automatically assumed that these wishes in the final will were the same as the draft, that is, that the estate was to be held in escrow until it was sold and distributed with the residue in varying degrees to Cody et al. As Colin discussed everything in detail with Kent, Kent would unquestionably have been party to these wishes too. I have known and travelled with Kent for many years and found him a thoroughly decent fellow. He has been treated as a member of the family, an equal, virtually since his arrival. But since the reading of the will he has felt threatened by the family. He has 'gone to ground' and will not answer telephone calls or letters. The possibility of legal action scares him and he is wary of lawyers. Instead he takes to his small, open fishing boat over the weekends, going 50 miles out to sea for sunfish, kingfish and blue marlin. Kent also told me that the articles in the press and comments on the internet about him have made him suspicious, although the family have never said *anything* derogatory about him, in fact quite the reverse.

But just like Colin, Kent harbours grudges, real and supposed, and has built up a raft of prejudices. Although Kent masterminded the whole funeral, for instance, he blamed Anne that there was no State funeral for Colin. That is nonsense. I was there and, like the rest of the family, we were all swept along, believing we were doing the right thing by following Kent's arrangements. As Tessa says: 'The family want the best for Kent, as well as what is fair from the deep promises Colin made to Charlie. Since Colin's death, Kent's silence has been the most regrettable aspect of it all. I live in hope that it will end.'

The highly successful Bonhams sale of Colin's effects made £1.1 million, including buyer's premium – the inflated price of everything being entirely down to provenance. Even Colin's hat and cane made £4,000 against an auction estimate of £400–600. However, after the auctioneer's commission, transport, agents and lawyers' fees, along with various debts, there was barely enough left to keep Beau going, particularly with its obligations to the existing house owners. When I last visited Beau, the estate was neat and tidy, and the Great House was in good repair. The inheritance is substantial. There is Beau Valley, worth in the region of US$20 million and the Great House. If Kent was not aware that he was the sole beneficiary of the will, then Colin would not have given him specific instructions as to how he wished him to further distribute the estate. But Kent told me: 'In my heart, I will do exactly what Mr Tennant say', which sounds like good news for the family.

And so the story of Colin is set to run and run as the drama continues to unfold. But whatever the outcome, it cannot, and indeed should not, overshadow the memory of the man. In life Colin, with his agile, complex brain and generosity, gave untold pleasure, as his countless admirers around the world will all testify.

# THREE ASTRAL WOMEN

Without doubt, Colin was indeed the prime example of the sum of his ancestors, a meld of businessmen, aristocrats, scientists, writers and politicians, all heavily seasoned with the eccentric and the downright bizarre. From this genetic boiling pot he inherited many traits: 'with their good and bad points, as yellow and blue make green'. Throughout his life, Colin was obsessed with these forebears, particularly those on his mother's side of the family, whom he thought considerably grander than the industrial Tennants. Captive audiences were endlessly regaled about their grandeur and eccentricities, their wealth and accomplishments, so much so that his planned autobiography was mostly made up of them, rather than his own fascinating life. He strongly believed that he was most influenced by 'galaxies of astral females' within his family and, foremost amongst these, 'strong women tugging to influence him' was Colin's paternal grandmother, Pamela Grey.

Born in 1871, Pamela was the daughter of the Hon. Percy Wyndham, younger son of the 1st Lord Leconfield of Petworth fame, and Madeline Eden, granddaughter of Lord Edward Fitzgerald, who espoused the Irish freedom cause and died in prison. Pamela was incredibly beautiful and, with her two elder sisters, Mary (Lady Elcho) and Madeline (Mrs Adeane), was painted by John Singer Sargent. The triple portrait, *The Wyndham Sisters*, now hangs in the Metropolitan Museum in New York. Pamela 'had a wilful personality, and she considered her ancestry far superior to that of the Tennants. She saw her background not only as aristocratic, but also as romantic and sensitive'.[cxvi] She married Edward Tennant out of disappointment when her passionate love, the roué Harry Cust, married another whom the Duchess of Rutland had told him was bearing his child in order to keep him in the village as her lover. Edward was later ennobled in 1911 when Lord High Commissioner to the General Assembly of the Church of Scotland, taking the name of Glenconner after the Tennant farm in Ayrshire. His sister, Margot Asquith, declared that 'he lacked drive' but this dependable, somewhat dull, husband made a perfect foil to his mercurial and whimsical wife. For much of their married life they lived in a *ménage á trois* with his best friend, Edward Grey. Colin always maintained, but with no proof, that Grey was the father of his uncles, David and Stephen, but not of his own father, Christopher. Again, through close examination of the dates in the visitors' book from Wilsford, Colin was certain that his biological grandfather was Ivor Guest, who became the 1st Viscount Wimborne. Apart from Christopher, David and Stephen, there were two older siblings: Clarissa, known as Clare, and Edward, known as Bimbo, or more usually just Bim, the adored and talented favourite child and eldest son.

The siblings can only have been the envy of their Edwardian peers, being indulged and encouraged by their mother, however cloying the emotional hold she had on them all. Margot Asquith once remarked: 'I can't bear to see a woman draped in her children.'[cxvii] Instead of a strict nursery routine Pamela created a fantasy world, bringing fairy stories to life with tales of chivalry and their Wyndham forebears to stimulate their imaginations. Notwithstanding her husband's great wealth and newly ennobled position, she professed a love of the simple life, although practicality was never far away. When she took her children camping in a gypsy caravan on Salisbury Plain, for example, they were accompanied by countless retainers following just out of sight behind. The genes passed down from this grandmother included many of her fine qualities, but also two of her less attractive traits: she not only possessed a fierce and explosive temper but also an unrelenting and prodigious capacity to spend money.

Compared to his elder brother Bim, Christopher was marginally less emotionally exploited by their mother and managed to escape from her clutches quite early when, destined for the Senior Service and a month shy of his thirteenth birthday, he was sent to the Royal Naval College Dartmouth in Devon. There, home life ended too. He did well at Dartmouth, earning the report: 'Above average officer. Good power of command. Promises well'.[cxviii] He was 15 when the First World War broke out, but Midshipman Tennant had already joined the battleship HMS *Lord Nelson,* the flagship of Home Fleet. In early 1915 she sailed from Portland Harbour to the eastern Mediterranean for the Dardanelles Campaign.

There, on station, Christopher trained as a gunnery officer, working alongside the ratings manning a 12-inch gun in the bombardment of the Ottoman forts. As he was still under 16 years of age Christopher was forbidden to go with the boats in the landings of the Naval Brigade at Gallipoli, which certainly saved his life. His superiors found him: 'Above average. Very promising officer. Good at taking charge of men'[cxix] and definitely in line for promotion.

The *Lord Nelson* continued on blockading duty in the Eastern Mediterranean for the rest of the war, but on his promotion to Acting Sub-Lt. in July 1917 Christopher transferred to HMS *Castor*, a Cambrian class light cruiser and flagship of the Commodore of the Grand Fleet operating in the North Sea. When she was not patrolling there, *Castor* was engaged in convoy duty to Archangel in the White Sea. Colin always maintained that his father could never feel pain (he always eschewed anaesthetic at the dentist whatever the ailment), having become inured from his time on the bridge in sub-zero temperatures. Soon after his promotion, in March 1918, Christopher was transferred to HMS *Royal Oak*, a Revenge class battleship lying in the Firth of Forth. At the end of the war the *Royal Oak* escorted the German High Seas Fleet to their internment in Scapa Flow.

After the war, in January 1919, Christopher enrolled in The President's Course at Cambridge University (specially designed for Service officers) but he did not go up for this course, being needed at home. In September 1916, at the Somme, his elder brother Bim had been killed, along with nine other Tennant first cousins, leaving Christopher as heir to their father. He succeeded as the 2nd Baron Glenconner in 1920 when his father unexpectedly died after a small operation at the age of 61. When he left the Royal Navy Christopher was described as 'Above Average. Zealous, capable and promising officer' and was to remain so for the rest of his life.

Meanwhile, the life of the Pagets at Cranmore during the First World War had been very different from that of their friends the Glenconners. Pamela, and her elder sister Sylvia, devoted their energies to a flock of goats from which they made, and sold, considerable quantities of Camembert-type cheese which was even bought by the Ritz Hotel. Sylvia voiced her patriotism, so typical of the time, by writing:

*Englishmen go to the war,*
*They've done it so often before!*
*If you're wounded or killed, never mind,*
*So long as you leave a dead German behind.*

Sylvia's and Pamela's father and Colin's grandfather, Sir Richard Paget, always known as 'Artie' was a most remarkable person and a complete polymath. A barrister and a scientist, he became a major player in the Admiralty Board of Invention and Research, even experimenting on himself and his family to test his various theories. He had perfect pitch and was once lowered into the sea in the Firth of Forth, where he resurfaced humming the note of a captured German U-boat engine. These experiments eventually led to the invention of radar.

Artie became an expert in acoustics and language too, especially phonetics and 'the technique of vocalization'. He developed a sign language for the deaf and would block up Sylvia's and Pamela's ears to try out his system. Other experiments included filling their ears with treacle, honey or other viscous material from the breakfast table to test their power of hearing against a variety of substances. Artie even taught a dog to say a few words. A true Renaissance man, he was a gifted architect and an accomplished artist. Intensely musical, his children were brought up to sing and play a variety of instruments: he and Sylvia could not only hum and whistle at the same time; they could do it in four-part harmony.

Artie's children were brought up to be independent. When electricity came to Cranmore Sylvia, aged 9, wired the house. The Paget girls were encouraged to take risks: they climbed trees and were made to jump about the roofs of their home to 'improve their spirit', just as they were made to jump backwards off a bus going down Park Lane at 30 mph to demonstrate their father's theory that the force of the air behind them would counteract the fall. Sylvia married Sir Christopher Chancellor and had four children, the eldest being John, Colin's contemporary. He is the father of the actress Anna Chancellor. The other sibblings are Zanna, married to Nicky Johnston, Alexander, the erstwhile editor of *The Spectator*, and Theresa, who was married to John Wells. Besides Sylvia and Pamela, Artie and Lady Muriel had two other children. The long awaited son, John, the father of seven children that include Patricia and Liz, a former Lady-in-Waiting to Princess Margaret, and Angela. She married Sir Piers Debenham. When a Debenham relation of loose morals married, Artie said that it was an appropriate match considering that the family department store was called Debenham and Freebody.

Colin remembered his grandfather well although he felt, wrongly, that he was neglected by him. He conceded that: 'He was brilliantly clever, and many of his descendants were brilliant too. Facets of him have come out in me. For instance, he was very forward looking, and, in so far as I may be considered to be forward looking, that is where it comes from'. In fact Colin had much more in common with his grandfather. He not only inherited a deep love of theatricals, but also his ingenious and inquiring mind. On the downside Artie's reluctance to admit that he was ever in the wrong could well have been passed on to Colin through this gene pool.

Sir Richard's mother was Caroline Surtees, always known as Mozey. As Colin recalled, 'She lived in Hove during the war where she was reduced to eating loaves of 'National' bread that were made largely of chalk. She died aged 99 but not before becoming an appalling bore.' She inherited Dane End, an estate in Hertfordshire with a fine Elizabethan manor house and a village full of sub-standard houses. Every Christmas Waldron, her maid, would wheel Mozey in her Bath chair through the dreadful mud up to each estate cottage where the tenants would complain about their rising damp and rotting timbers. Waldron would listen sympathetically then shout into Lady Paget's ear trumpet: 'They say they are very happy m'lady!'

Known in the family as 'Gran Edith', Colin's other maternal great-grandmother was the Countess of Winchelsea and Nottingham, the daughter of Edward Harcourt and Lady Susan Holroyd. Edith and her brother Aubrey were brought up at Nuneham Park, a Henry Holland Palladian villa outside Oxford, complete with a 'Capability' Brown landscaped park. Part of Brown's grand plan was the erection of magnificent gates with a pair of lodges. One gatekeeper, who had a dozen children, enraged Harcourt in his carriage by keeping him waiting. When the man finally appeared he roared: 'I put you here to open the gate, not to propagate!'

Edith and Aubrey had a virtually feral childhood and consequently a perverse sense of humour. One of their better antics was to stick labels under exquisite pieces of porcelain. When guests admired these priceless treasures and turned them over to look at the maker's mark, they saw that the children had written: 'Slightly cracked, 3/6d'! Colin remembered being driven into Sleaford in a Victoria (a one-horse carriage) with the octogenarian Gran Edith to buy squeaky buns and whoopee cushions in Woolworths.

The child Edith's closest friend was Alice Liddell, the daughter of the Dean of Christchurch and model for *Alice in Wonderland* and *Through the Looking Glass*. Through her friend, Edith met the author, the mathematician and photographer, Charles Dodgson, better known by his pseudonym, Lewis Carroll. Alice had been constantly photographed by Dodgson and Colin found a small photograph of her at around 12 years of age. On the back Dodgson had written: 'A ghost flew out of the shadowy air and sat in the midst of her moony hair.' Colin once used the line as his own in an essay at Eton. His English beak, Dr Arland, wrote *Excellent* in red ink, never having praised his work before.

In 1875 Edith Harcourt married Murray, 12th Earl of Winchelsea and 7th of Nottingham. Throughout their married life, Edith led him a merry dance and kept him at bay by being, like her mother, a professional valetudinarian – Lady Susan even had a doctor living at Nuneham Park. On one occasion when a doctor was summoned, Gran Edith instructed her maid to tell him that she was too ill to see him and to come another day.

When her husband succumbed and died at the age of just 48, Gran Edith soon recovered and exchanged invalidism for an extremely active life. She took up painting and like both her parents (her mother was trained by Edward Lear) she displayed a real talent. It was Colin's mother Pamela who coined the term 'school of aunt' as they were 'not works of art but works of aunt!'

Living on her own and to a great age, Gran Edith's idiosyncrasies became eccentricities and considerable legend – 'those myths, familiar to every historian, which become invested with the dignity of truth through family tradition'[cxx] survive in the memory of her great-grandchildren. She spoke to her servants in Italian although they were all English, and kept a chameleon that she wore around her wrist like an ever-changing coloured bracelet. To feed it she would hold it by a window pane and watch it flick out its tongue to catch flies. It was puzzled when placed on a tartan rug and once went completely white when it fell into a milk pudding. There was no electricity in the house, no telephone and no car, and visits were difficult. At over 80 years of age Gran Edith taught Colin to walk on stilts and, at her annual village garden fête, she had a race for octogenarians. She slept on a camp bed in a tent in the garden where, armed with a fire bucket and a flit gun, she would creep around at night, seeing off prowling cats hunting birds.

Gran Edith had two children, George, Viscount Maidstone, who died aged 9, and a daughter, Lady Muriel Finch-Hatton who married Artie Paget, the two being Colin's grandparents. She was the second in his galaxy of 'astral females'. Born in 1876 and educated at home, Lady Muriel could not have been more different from her self-centred mother. She devoted her life not to her husband and children, but to philanthropic causes both at home and abroad. She had boundless energy, so much so that a relation coined the epithet: 'How lucky Lady Muriel, isn't in the plurial'.

Lady Muriel began by running the Southwark Invalid Kitchens which provided nourishing meals for the sick of the London borough, which flourished and expanded. By 1915 the charitable Lady Muriel abandoned her family (including John, her year-old son) and left for the Russian Front where, in the Dmitri Palace, she founded the Anglo-Russian Hospital for wounded soldiers. Her days and nights were full, but she still found the time to dine with the Yusupovs in the cellar where Rasputin had lately been murdered. Her work spread to the Ukraine where she established a number of field hospitals and food kitchens. Lady Muriel was indeed at the Front, the back, and everywhere in between, except Somerset and Cranmore. Just six months before the Bolshevik *coup d'état* she was ordered out of Russia. In her true 'Lady Catherine de Bourgh' manner (she was, after all, a great-niece of Jane Austen) she commandeered a train to take her staff and the British Consul, John Bagge, out of the country, even diverting the train to Pinsk to rescue seventy English governesses and Tomás Masaryk (later to become President of Czechoslovakia), whom she hid under the seat and covered with her long skirt. Once, when a Revolutionary pointed his rifle at her stomach and threatened to shoot her, Lady Muriel fearlessly brushed the barrel aside saying 'Nonsense' and handed him her suitcase to carry. Eventually they reached Vladivostok where they embarked on a ship to Tokyo and thence returned home via Washington DC, where she had an audience with the President and Mrs Woodrow Wilson. Her husband, Artie Paget, happened to be in DC at the time. When someone asked if he was related to Lady Muriel Paget, he meekly replied: 'Only by marriage!' After the Armistice, Lady Muriel continued to feed the starving of Europe. She died of cancer in 1938 at 61 years of age and was buried at Cranmore, greatly mourned.

The epilogue to this remarkable woman came in 1995 when Colin, accompanied by other members of the Paget family, went to St Petersburg to unveil a plaque in her honour at the Dmitri Palace, the site of her original hospital. Certainly Colin's love of parties and their organisation was inherited from her, but not her physical bravery. As he would say, he was more akin to the 'Earl Bishop', Frederick Hervey, 4th Earl of Bristol and Bishop of Derry, who declared that he was not brave, but certainly had an 'acute sense of self-preservation'. The third of Colin's 'astral women' was his mother, Pamela.

But the other story of Colin, the Tennant origins, go back to far humbler folk, for up to the middle of the eighteenth century, Colin's branch of the Tennant family had been mere subsistence farmers, eking out a living around the seaside town of Ayr to the south-west of Scotland. Successive generations struggled with poverty but, against this background of hardship and lack of education, they not only survived but prospered to become one of the richest families in the world.

*Appendix II*

# TENNANT'S STALK

The first Tennant of note was John of Blairston, who owned and operated a corn mill on the Doon River. His son, William, farmed close by at Brigend of Doon, on land that included the Auld Brig o' Doon immortalised in Burns' *Tam o' Shanter*. The land was poor, the hovel where he and his wife, Agnes, lived was even poorer, yet they managed to produce nine children. All six sons and three daughters miraculously survived. John, the eldest son, became a successful farmer; Robert and Thomas merchants in Ayr; Alexander an innkeeper; David a classics master and rector of the Burgh School in Ayr and the youngest, James, went to the West Indies. That branch of the Tennant family was clearly on the move.

John was tenant of Laigh Corton, the small farm that contained some of the best land in the parish of Alloway. As an innovative farmer, he prospered, but his real break came in 1769, when he was appointed factor to the Earl of Glencairn. With his family and some of his siblings he moved to a farmhouse near Ochiltree, where he managed the estate and farmed 130 acres on his own account. The farm was called Glenconner. He was remembered for his 'goodness, common sense and open heart'[cxxi] and was immortalised as 'Auld Glen' in poems by his close friend and neighbour, Robert Burns. But this was the time of great expansion in Scotland, of the Scottish Enlightenment with the great advancements in philosophy, engineering, architecture, medicine, agriculture, chemistry and sociology. There were the thinkers, the likes of David Hume and Adam Smith, chemists such as Joseph Black, who was working with James Watt on harnessing steam power, and architects like William and Robert Adam. It was a time of opportunity, and the Tennants embraced it.

John, or 'Glen' as he became known, had sixteen children (by two wives) of which the ninth child was Charles. In a letter-poem to the Tennants from Burns he is mentioned:

*And no forgetting wabster Charlie,*
*I'm tauld he offers very fairly'.*

As Burns pointed out, the 15-year-old Charles had apprenticed himself to a *wabster*, or weaver, in Kilbarchan not far from Paisley, the centre of the linen-weaving industry and in striking distance of Glasgow. Born on the farm at Laigh Corton in 1768, Charles was to rise from humble beginnings to become the founder and master of a mighty chemical empire, a great liberal reformer and, notwithstanding his rudimentary education, one of the most progressive thinkers of his time.

Charles was quick to learn the weaving trade, which at that time was particularly well-paid and skilled. With the collapse of the tobacco and sugar trades after the American War of Independence, together with the French Revolutionary War, all that was left commercially for Scotland was its linen industry. While the spinning of the yarn and the actual weaving process had advanced considerably with new inventions, what held up the manufacture of cloth was the bleaching of the finished article that had not changed since the time of Ancient Egypt. The method was to soak the linen or cotton in a weak alkaline solution (usually stale urine) then spread it in the open to whiten under the sun. As that part of Scotland is not known for its abundance of sun, the process could take anything up to eighteen months. The end of the operation was to soak the cloth in sour buttermilk. Clearly a chemical solution was required to keep pace with the developments in spinning and weaving. Charles saw this as his way forward and, in 1788, bought his own bleaching fields at Darnley to the south-west of Glasgow. There his hard work and dedication were recognised by his neighbour, William Wilson, who befriended the young Charles who later married his daughter, Margaret. The marriage was to last for forty-three years, and in that time she bore him nine children. Later, Charles was to team up with his brother-in-law John who, with his partner, the chemist Charles Macintosh (better known as the inventor of a waterproof fabric) produced alum used in the dyeing industry.

Throughout the eighteenth century, chemists (mainly from Sweden and France) had made a start on a chemical bleaching process, experimenting variously with vitriol (sulphuric acid), or a combination of slaked lime and chlorine, which was found to be too dangerous to use, and too expensive when stabilised in an alkali. Charles Tennant was convinced that the answer lay in a combination of chlorine and lime. After several years of experimentation, he was granted a patent for his 'chlorine liquor' that was created by passing chlorine gas through a suspension of lime and water. This was cheap to produce, stable, and did not harm the fabric. Another patent was granted for his bleaching powder (then called 'bleaching salt'), but it is still not certain if it was the Glasgow University chemistry graduate Macintosh, or the former weaver-artisan Tennant who actually came up with the invention. Most likely it was a combination of them both.

With the granting of the patent, Charles and his partners (including Macintosh and James Knox, his salesman), purchased some land beside the Monkland Canal, just north of Glasgow. Known as St Rollox after an obscure French saint, it was the perfect place to manufacture the bleaching agents, being close to a ready supply of lime and the junction of the Clyde-Forth Canal. From the beginning the company prospered, although there were the inevitable setbacks with cash flow, bad debts (principally when their Irish venture failed), and infringement of copyright. When the patent expired in 1815 after fourteen years, the partnership was dissolved and Charles bought out his former Directors.

Charles continued to expand the business. A man of independent spirit, great entrepreneurial skill and forward thinking, he stood alone. He developed further industries out of the by-products of the bleach, such as the manufacture of soda, and later soap. Whatever he needed by way of ingredients, such as sulphuric acid, he would buy in the raw materials and manufacture it himself at St Rollox. Soon, he would buy the source itself, as with the purchase of the sulphur mines in Sicily, from where he would transport the chemicals in his own specially equipped ships. As a result, a hundred years later, most of the munitions during the First World War were transported across the Atlantic by the Tennant shipping company. Manufacture also depended more and more on coal, so Charles backed the Garnick to Glasgow railway to bring coal from the Lanarkshire collieries to his factory. There were two steam engines, the *George Stephenson* and the *St Rollox*.

When he died on 1 October 1838, Charles' chemical empire was the largest and most important in the world. He was a great philanthropist and reformer, always mindful of the welfare of his 1,000 employees and the education of their children, and particularly his extended family. He died a very rich man, much loved and, to the end, totally unpretentious.

Charles Tennant had a worthy follower in his eldest son, John, who had been well educated in Glasgow, both at the High School and University, and thoroughly schooled in the ways of business. He had also inherited his father's philanthropic ideals. The chemical works produced life-threatening pollution to a large radius around an already unhealthy Glasgow. There were many complaints, rarely upheld, owing in part to the wealth of, and the employment given by, C. Tennant & Co. In a flash of inspiration during a sermon, John came up with what he believed to be the solution – to build a very tall chimney to take the offending gasses to be dispersed into the atmosphere. Work began on what was to be known as Tennant's Stalk, a majestic 435½-ft high chimney with a 40-ft diameter base. At three times the height of Nelson's Column, it was the tallest structure in the world. John's idea succeeded in that it improved the lives of those living around the chemical works, but failed as it carried the noxious fumes to a larger area, further away. Tennant's Stalk was struck by lightning in 1922 and was subsequently blown up, being unsafe.

At the age of 22, John took up with a Robina Arrol who is thought to have been an employee at St Rollox. 'Lovely and intelligent',[cxxii] she had lived with two others and had two children by one of them. She moved into John's house by the factory with a plaque on the front door engraved: 'Mr & Mrs John Tennant', tantamount to a civil wedding in Scotland. This rule of law by which marriage may be constituted by cohabitation with 'habit and repute' was only repealed by the Family Law (Scotland) Act in 2006. Notwithstanding his legal marriage, John appears to have kept her presence secret as, in the 1861 census, he is described as 'unmarried'. After the births of their three children, Marion, John and Charles, their mother disappeared without trace, and took no further part in their upbringing. John moved into his father's substantial house in Glasgow's fashionable West George Street. He hunted with the Renfrewshire Hunt and cruised in his large yacht, the *Ruby Queen*, on the Clyde and in the Western Isles. Mindful of the pollution caused by his works, he sent his children to a healthy Ayrshire to be brought up and educated. He was a generous benefactor, his anonymous gifts far exceeding his public ones, and 'many who flourished in later life owed their start or their success to his encouragement and practical help'.[cxxiii]

When John Tennant died in 1878, his son Charles inherited not only St

Rollox, by then vastly expanded from his father's day, but other chemical works in England, an underwriting interest in Lloyds, and several railway companies in Scotland, along with many other chemical-related companies, agencies and offices around the world. Charles also took over the sugar and cocoa plantations in Trinidad that John had received as a bad debt in 1857 that were to play such an important part in the later fortunes of the Tennant family.

Charles Tennant, a man in a hurry with the Midas touch, was a multi-millionaire by the time he was 25 years of age. He began his own road to riches by borrowing money from Gurney's Bank to buy the highly speculative shares in the Midland Railway. These soon paid off handsomely and he invested the profit in land grants in Australia, which again multiplied his capital and formed the basis of his fortune. His success came 'in part from an absolute self-assurance and confidence, boosted without doubt by the financial solidarity his family had already achieved'.[cxxiv] He married Emma Winslow, whom he met taking the waters at Malvern, the first Tennant to marry outside Scotland. It was an ideal marriage, he one of the richest men in the country, she frugal from an austere upbringing.

With his new bride, Charles looked to establish the Tennant family away from the grime of Glasgow. In 1853, at the age of 30, he bought an estate in Peeblesshire called Glen, a modest house nestled in the centre of 3,600 acres of rolling hills close to the town of Innerleithen. Charles was 'as fecund a producer of children as he was energetic for business'.[cxxv] The first four infants died young, then, at almost yearly intervals, came eight more children. The eldest surviving child was Pauline, known as Posie, who married Thomas Gordon Duff; Charlotte, known as Charty, married the 4th Lord Ribblesdale (immortalised in the famous portrait by John Singer Sargent); then Colin's grandfather, Eddy, who of course married 'la Belle' Pamela Wyndham. Laura, who married Thomas Graham-Smith, came next, followed by Francis, known as Frank. Frank married Anne Redmayne and it is through this union that Colin claimed kinship with the Manners family when their daughter, Kathleen, married the 9th Duke of Rutland. Colin loved to tell the story of when her brother, Mark Tennant, went to stay one Sunday night at Belvoir Castle. As there were only the three of them for dinner, he came down in black tie. When the Duke appeared wearing white tie, he admonished his brother-in-law for having such a sloppy valet for not packing the correct clothes. Mark protested that he did not have a valet, and that he thought that, as it was an informal family dinner, black tie would suffice, adding, 'Do you never wear a dinner jacket?' 'Very occasionally', replied his haughty brother-in-law the Duke, 'but only when I am dining alone with the Duchess in her boudoir!' He was talking about the man's sister.

After Frank came Laura, who married Alfred Littleton, the former Secretary of State for the Colonies and a great cricketer, then the formidable Margot who was married to the Prime Minister H.H. Asquith, later 1st Earl of Oxford, as his second wife. The youngest child was Jack. Charles later had three more daughters (the youngest was born when he was 80) when, as a widower, he married Marguerite Miles. All three girls married well, Peggy to Lord Wakehurst, Katherine to Lord Elliott of Harwood, and Nancy to Lord Crathorne. Nancy was the author of *Tennant's Stalk*, a comprehensive history of the Tennant family.

Although passionate about shooting, fishing, golf and estate management, Charles was never afraid to spend money on furnishing and decorating his house. He put together a fine, readable library, mostly English and French literature and biography, which he had bound in Morocco leather. His collection of paintings, mostly nineteenth-century landscapes and contemporary Victorian was, at his death in 1906, one of the finest in private hands. He favoured portraits and owned, amongst others, ten Reynolds, five Gainsboroughs, six Romneys and three Hogarths. There were collections of Meissen and Chinese porcelain too, along with fine furniture. Charles was a knowledgeable collector who delighted in his possessions, as his youngest son Jack so evocatively observed:

> The pains he took with the arrangement of his possessions was [*sic*] notable and was the embodiment of his desire for perfection. He enjoyed his possessions in a delightful and almost childlike way. Sometimes late at night we would find all the electric lights blazing in the big drawing rooms of Grosvenor Square and there was my dear old father gazing at his Sir Joshuas or Hoppners in rapt delight. 'Doesn't Lady Crosbie look splendid this evening?' he would say and he would rejoice in our fervid agreement.[cxxvi]

In a way there was much of Colin in Charles' collecting habits. He too would take great delight in his possessions but, as he would later claim, he

91. A star-studded line up with (right to left) Anne, the model Cheryl Tiegs, her husband Tony (son of Gregory) Peck, Dianne Brill (dubbed 'The Queen of the Night' by Andy Warhol) and another model, with Anne's sister, Carey, in between.

93. Utter and complete happiness, Colin at his 60th birthday party.

92. The arrival of Princess Margaret and the designer, Carl Toms. She is wearing one of his creations that Colin had made for her in India, which she described as the kind of dress she had 'longed for since the age of six'.

94. Princess Margaret adjusts David Linley's headdress of a white peacock on Raquel Welch at the Peacock Ball.

95. Jerry Hall and Prince Rupert
Lowenstein both suitably clad for the
Peacock Ball.

96. Henry Tennant and 'friend' take a hot
tub during Princess Margaret's party on
Macaroni Beach, the day after the great
Peacock Ball.

97. Cody Tennant, here aged 11, the
present 4th Baron Glenconner and 5th
Baronet at the wedding of his aunt, May.

98. The twins Amy and May representing
Great Britain at the International
debutante ball in Washington DC.

101. The exquisite French conus shell snuff box dated 1746, made by Barnabé Sagaret, Louis XIV's goldsmith, which appealed to Colin's eclectic taste. It was later sold to Wartski.

99. Colin was rightly proud of his creation, the kitchens at his restaurant, Bang. The façade had been modelled on Oliver Messel's set for the Broadway production of *The House of Flowers*. Colin always loved this pose.

100. Surprise! May appears as if by magic from a box at the opening of Colin's restaurant, Bang, so called as it was 'Bang between the Pitons' at Beau Estate, St Lucia. The restaurant was opened by Princess Margaret. Lane Pettigrew, Colin's architect and sometime partner, is on the far left.

102. Charlie finally found happiness when he married Sheilagh Scott. He had his father's flare for clothes with a leopard-skin waistcoat and Tennant tartan trews for his wedding in 1993.

103. *The Elastic Band*, Cletus and Marcellus, perform at a party at Glen before their appearance at the Edinburgh Festival Fringe. The family marvel at their performance behind: (left to right) Tessa Tennant (Henry's widow and chatelaine of Glen), Anastasia (Christopher's then wife), Sabine, Christopher, Anne, Amy, and Euan.

105. A female frigate bird extends her red gular pouch to find a mate on the Galapagos Islands, but only succeeded in attracting Kent and Colin during this display.

104. David Bowie and Iman at the party they gave after Christmas, 1990. Colin thought it 'dazzling & brilliant'.

106. For many years Colin and Michael Winner were 'thick as thieves'. The restaurant critic praised Anton and May Creasy's cooking at Bang in his column in The Sunday Times.

107. The front door of the Great House ajar showing the magnificent hall within. Carved in the architrave, from Gujarat, is a pair of pineapples, the symbol of hospitality.

108. The front elevation of the Great House, Beau Estate, incorporating the reclaimed architectural pillars and arches bought in India some years before. Colin built the house for his 80th birthday and thereafter regretted finishing it so quickly as it left him with nothing to do.

109. Anne, Colin and Cody. He was allowed out of school to attend his grandfather's 80th birthday.

110. Colin posing against one of the pillars from the monastery at Allamabad at the Great House, Beau Estate.

111. Joshua Bowler met up with Colin, his biological father, on his last visit to England at a boutique hotel in Notting Hill. Eccentric to the last, Colin supported a long beard that gave him the appearance of a Dutch Old Master painter.

113. Deborah Cyril, Colin's faithful house keeper and cook. She was greatly puzzled to receive a call from Colin the night before he died thanking him for all she had done for him over 23 years.

112. Princess Josephine Loewenstein unveils the statue of Colin, January 2010. She masterminded the whole project and commissioned the sculptor, Philip Jackson.

114. Kent Adonai, Colin's friend and factotum for 30 years, at the fish market at Choiseul, St Lucia. He has used a part of his inheritance from Colin to buy an open fishing boat.

115. Lady Muriel Paget, née Finch-Hatton. She devoted herself to the Baltic States and Russia, which she called 'my little countries' at the expense of her husband and children.

117. Edith, Lady Winchelsea in her peeress' robed with her daughters, Sylvia, Pamela (Colin's mother) and Angela.

116. A romantic view of St Rollox, the Tennant chemical works in Glasgow, 1844. 'Tennant's Stalk', the highest structure in the World at that time, can be seen in the centre.

118. Sir Richard Paget, Colin's maternal grandfather, was a real Renaissance man. His experiments with underwater acoustics led to the invention of radar.

119. Sir Charles Tennant, a passionate golfer, in his late seventies. Known as the 'Bart' after he was made a baronet, he considerably enlarged the family fortune and was responsible for the 'gentrification' of the Tennant family by establishing them at Glen, his estate in Peeblesshire.

121. Clare, Christopher (Colin's father) Bim and David Tennant outside a gipsy caravan. Their mother, Pamela Glenconner, believed in the simple life of holidays in a gypsy caravan, although a retinue of servants followed close by.

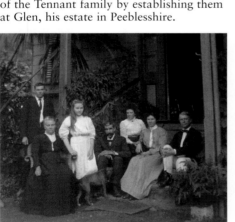

120. Eddy Glenconner (far right) on his first visit to the Ortinola Estate, Trinidad in 1906. The redoubtable Janet Stanhope Lovell (centre right) took over the management of the plantation from her father, 'Cocoa' Bain (with dog).

122. Pamela Wyndham, Colin's grandmother, was married Eddy, 1st Baron Glenconner, then Viscount Grey of Falloden. It is through her that the Tennants inherited their legendary beauty.

was too much of a dealer to hang onto them for long, while in his later years the desperate need for cash was too strong not to sell. Like his great-grandfather, Colin would take the same care in arranging everything in a room to show it off to its best advantage.

The finance for these treasures, houses and children came from Charles' genius for making money by shrewd and daring investment. Although a Director of C. Tennant & Sons at 20, he made most of his fortune from outside St Rollox, such as his involvement in the building of Dreadnought battleships. He had long since financed the sugar merchants Bernstein & Co, in Port of Spain in Trinidad. They in turn held the mortgages of the many estates that regularly produced 8,000–9,000 tons of sugar per annum. But the failure of the sugar crop of 1877 brought devastation to the island. Estates went bankrupt in the resulting slump and, when the final crash came, Charles took over the encumbered plantations. He could also have had the Pitch Lake, the largest source of asphalt in the world, but it was then of little use as paving roads with tarmacadam had not yet been invented.

Possibly Charles' greatest coup was to lead the consortium in the purchase of the Tharsis Mine in Southern Spain in 1866. The Glasgow chemist, William Henderson, had formulated a system whereby sulphur could be extracted from pyrites, otherwise known as iron sulphite or 'fool's gold', with a subsequent process for extracting copper. There was a superabundance of pyrites at Tharsis, which was made even more valuable when further experimentation produced a method by which pig iron could be extracted from the iron oxide residue, known as 'blue billy'. At that time C. Tennant & Sons owned 'the most important range of non-ferrous metallurgical patents in existence'.[cxxvii] A later patent was granted for the process whereby blue billy was transformed into mild steel, invaluable for shipbuilding. Charles formed The Steel Company of Scotland and, by 1900, was producing 1 million tons of mild steel a year.

Like his father, Charles invested in railways and railway building and was partially responsible for the building the Forth Bridge. He owned so much stock in the Chicago Great Western Railway Company that they named a very small town in Iowa 'Tennant' in his honour. He was further honoured with a baronetcy for his political services in 1885. Thereafter he was known as 'The Bart'.

Colin always told the tale of how when the widowed Sir Charles decided to remarry, his children were aghast, believing that, even at his age of 75, he would have more children to dilute their inheritance. So he handed over the bulk of his fortune to them and began anew, speculating in a gold mine. This is apocryphal as Sir Charles remarried in 1898 and the story of the Mysore Gold Mine began a full eighteen years earlier. Charles had heard from John Hunter Blair, a neighbour who had been in the Madras Civil Service, of an abandoned gold mine in Mysore and decided to invest in its restoration. In 1880 he formed the Mysore Gold Mining Company which, because of his track record, attracted great outside investment. For once a Charles Tennant project was not an instant success. When not an ounce of gold was recovered after four years, and with only £13,000 left in the bank, the shareholders moved to liquidate the company. But this was not Charles' way. With the support of just two others (Charles typically paid out the other investors at cost, so giving himself an enormous shareholding), he continued, finding a very small deposit at the last attempt. Charles had backed a chemist called Cassel, who developed an electronic process for extracting precious metals, but it proved so unreliable that it earned the sobriquet 'Cassels in the air!' Undaunted, Charles persisted with his own chemists who eventually came up with a process using cyanide and zinc filings which could extract 95 per cent, as opposed to 55 per cent, of gold from the ore. From 1889 on, profits from the mine soared – in eighteen years a 9d. share was worth £74 11s., a 1,988-fold increase on capital. Charles' interest in mining naturally led to explosives and, as a large investor in Nobel's Explosives Ltd., he was made Chairman of the Nobel Dynamite Trust Company, their holding company.

But nothing lasts forever, even in an organisation so structured as the Tennant empire. Charles had taken over St Rollox on the death of his father in 1878. Five years earlier a young German called Ludwig Mond offered him the 'Solvay system' a new and unproven method of producing of sodium-carbonate (washing soda or soda ash), the staple ingredient in the manufacture of paper, glass and soap. The Tennants, and the rest of the great chemical companies with their vast plants, were committed to the old system and were also making healthy profits from the by-products extracted from the waste. Rejected by Charles, Mond turned to another backer, John Brunner, and together they began to manufacture sodium-carbonate at his factory near Northwich in Cheshire. Within a decade Brunner-Mond were a serious threat to St Rollox and all the other producers still using sulphur in the old system. To combat the threat, Charles lowered the price of sulphur from his Tharsis Mines, then combined St Rollox with the other forty-eight major chemical factories in the land to form The United Alkali Company, with him as President. It was the largest conglomerate in the world. But these factories were already in deep decline and the Tharsis Mine was becoming worked out. Replacement mines were sought but Charles had lost his Midas touch.

Sir Charles died in 1906 at the age of 83, leaving, aside from the business, Glen and his considerable art collection, £3.5 million in cash – the equivalent of at least £1 billion today – which went to the eldest son, Eddy, with £1million going to the two younger brothers. According to family legend, the three siblings sat poker-faced and stony silent at the reading of the will, until the exasperated lawyer cried out: 'Well, ye might at least say thank you!' Elsewhere Sir Charles was deeply mourned.

However, twenty years after his death, the business genius of The Bart was fully recognised when United Alkali, Brunner-Mond, Nobel and British Dyestuffs were merged to form ICI, Imperial Chemicals Industries. Within those four companies, three enterprises – St Rollox, Nobel's Explosives and Cassel Company – had been founded or operated by Sir Charles. Colin was to sum up the Tennant wealth more simply: 'My great-grandfather invented the Industrial Revolution.'

But the story of the commercial Tennants does not end with the ICI amalgamation. In 1801 C. Tennant & Co established a London agency (C. Tennant, Son & Co.) for selling its own bleaching powder. From their offices in Upper Thames Street in the City the company soon expanded its operation by trading in its own right, exporting large quantities of chemicals and tallow (for candle-making) to Europe and the Colonies, as well as coal to the West Indies for shipping. When the Trinidad estates were added to the Tennant portfolio, these too came under the aegis of the London office. Benefiting greatly from Free Trade, C. Tennant, Son & Co. saw exports rise from £71 million to £200 million, while imports trebled to £300 million over the two decades from 1850. In the 1870s ferrous and non-ferrous metal departments were opened to handle the products of the Tharsis Mines and the Steel Company of Scotland and, through their expertise in this field, the company was instrumental in setting up the London Metal Exchange in 1877. After The Bart's death the chairmanship of C. Tennant, Sons & Co passed to his eldest surviving son, Eddy, who was joined by a distant Ayrshire Tennant cousin, William. But Eddy's interests lay elsewhere, mostly in the management of Glen and forestry. When Eddy died William became Chairman of the company and bought a large shareholding from Eddy's estate, as Christopher, Colin's father, was too young and inexperienced to take over. But some time later Christopher showed his mettle in the City and, quite unlike his father, 'immersed himself in the affairs of the firm'.[cxxviii] By 1928 William had recognised his worth and, in an extreme act of generosity, sold his majority shareholding back to the 'Glen Tennants'. Christopher took the firm forwards with careful and measured business sense over the next twenty-five years when Colin joined at the bottom, with a view to working his way up to finally take over when Christopher, retired. But in the end, it was not to be and the rest, as they say, is history.

$\mathscr{Notes}$

[i] Blunt, Sir Wilfred, *Lady Muriel, Lady Muriel Paget, Her Husband, and Her Philanthropic Works in Central and Eastern Europe*, London, 1962, p.261.

[ii] Gogarty, Oliver StJohn, *Rolling down the* Lea, Constable, London, 1950, pp.161–2.

[iii] Lady Glenconner, Elizabeth to author, London, 17 March 2011.

[iv] Pratt, Michael to author, letter, 10 April 1912.

[v] Hillingdon, Lady to author, Battersea, 19 November 2011.

[vi] Glenconner, Lord to Colin Tennant, letter, 8 February 1949.

[vii] *New York Times*, 1 June 1913.

[viii] Tennant, Colin to Pauline Pitt-Rivers, letter, 16 January 1950.

[ix] Hitchens, Christopher, *Hitch 22*, New York, 2010, p83.

[x] Smith, A.K. to Colin Tennant, letter, 27 July 1950.

[xi] Johnston, Susanna, tribute to Lord Glenconner, Traquair Church, 19 June 2011.

[xii] Blow, Simon, *Broken Blood, the Rise and Fall of the Tennant Family*, London, 1987, p.187.

[xiii] Vaughan, Roger, *Mustique*, New York/Mustique, 1994, p.34.

[xiv] Brock, Michael and Eleanor (ed.), *H.H. Asquith, Letters to Venetia Stanley*, Oxford, 1982, pp. 611–2.

[xv] Internet, 'Climbing the Esoteric Curiosa', *H. H. Asquith: Letters To Venetia Stanley.*

[xvi] Blunt, Wilfred Scawen, *My Diaries*, Vol. I, London, 1919, p.65.

[xvii] *Daily Express*, 19 March 1955.

[xviii] Hambledon, Lady (Patricia) to Colin Tennant, letter, 4 May 1949.

[xix] Payn, Graham and Sheridan Morley (eds.), *The Noël Coward Diaries*, London, 1982, p.236.

[xx] Dovkants, Keith, 'Dancing till break of dawn', *Evening Standard*, 11 February 2002.

[xxi] Amory, Mark (ed.), *The Letters of Anne Fleming*, London, 1985, p.140.

[xxii] Shawcross, William, *Queen Elizabeth the Queen Mother*, London, 2009, p.143.

[xxiii] Stuart, Hon. James to Lady Elizabeth Bowes-Lyon, 22 March 1922, RA QEQM/PRIV/PAL.

[xxiv] Bowes-Lyon, Lady Elizabeth to Beryl Poignand, May 1922 Glamis Archives CH.

xxv *Oxford Dictionary of National Biography*, online edition.

xxvi *The Sketch*, 9 May 1956, p.263.

xxvii Heald, Tim, *Princess Margaret, A Life Unravelled*, London, 2007, p.122.

xxviii Honan, Corinna, 'I had everything and threw it away', *Woman*, October 1976, p.10.

xxix *The Guardian*, 3 March 1953, p.9.

xxx Tennant, the Hon. Colin to Lord Glenconner, letter, 29 January 1953.

xxxi Tennant, the Hon. Colin to John Kiddle, letter, 10 June 1960.

xxxii Heald, *Priness Margaret, A Life Unravelled*, London, 2007, p.122.

xxxiii Peers, Captain Hugh, RN to author, email, 17 March 2012.

xxxiv Cartwright, A.P., *Gold Paved the Way*, London, 1967, p.305.

xxxv Staempfli, William to author, email, 10 February 2012.

xxxvi Crook, J. Mordaunt, *The Rise of the Nouveaux Riches*, London, 1999, p.239.

xxxvii Wilson, B., *Dear Youth*, London, 1937, pp.155–6.

xxxviii Staempfli, email.

xxxix Ibid.

xl Wilson, p.157.

xli Ford, Sir Edward to Colin Tennant, letter, 16 December 1965.

xlii Reading, Marquess of, to author, Cavalry and Guards Club, 10 April 2012.

xliii Girouard, Mark, *Sweetness and Light*, London, 1977, p.177.

xliv Chelsea Society Annual Report, 1962.

xlv Ibid.

xlvi Cohn, Nik, *Today There are No Gentlemen*, London, p.98.

xlvii Johnson, Peter to author, Filgrave, 6 May 2012 .

xlviii Pepys-Whitely, D., (revised James Hamilton), Oliver Messel entry in the *Oxford Dictionary of National Biography*, Oxford, 2004, online edn.

xlix Vaughan, Roger, *Mustique*, New York, 1994.

l Touche, Sir Rodney to author, email 9 March 2012.

li Vaughan, p.1.

lii Brown, Tina, 'What Colin Tennant does for Princess Margaret', *Tatler*, London 1976, p.79.

liii Honan, Corinna, 'I had everything and I threw it all away', *Woman's Own*, October 1976 pp.10, 14.

liv Castle, Charles, *Oliver Messel: A Biography*, New York, 1986, p.236.

lv Chamberlain, Jan, *Gourmet Magazine*, New York, October 1973, p.34.

lvi Llewellyn, Sir Roderick to author, Brooks's, 11 April 2012.

lvii Ibid.

lviii de Courcy, Anne, *Snowdon the Biography*, London, 2008, p.224.

lix Llewellyn, Sir Roderick.

lx Golds, John to author, email, 13 April 2012.

lxi Guthrie, Dr Randolph H., to author, telephone conversation, 24 April 2012.

lxii Touche, Sir Rodney to author, email, 9 March 2012.

lxiii Guthrie, Randolph H. to author, telephone call, 24 April 2012.

lxiv Tennant, Colin to Hans Neumann, letter, 22 June 1977.

lxv Vaughan, Roger, *Mustique*, New York, 1994.p.41.

lxvi Heimann, Maria Christina to author, New York, 2 March 2012.

lxvii Anon to author.

lxviii Tennant, Hon. Colin to HRH The Princess Margaret, letter, 2 February 1977.

lxix Campbell, Lady Jean to Colin Tennant, letter, 24 January 1955.

lxx Avon, Countess of to author, London, 26 June, 2012.

lxxi *Sunday Times*, 27 March 1977, p.23.

lxxii Rees, Peter to Lord Glenconner, letter, 10 September 1983.

lxxiii Palmer, Lord to Lord Glenconner, letter, 23 November 1992.

lxxiv Unknown (Simon), Lord to Lord Glenconner, letter, 23 November 1992.

lxxv Rouse, P.T. to Lord Glenconner, letter, 23 December 1992.

lxxvi Tennant, Colin to HRH The Princess Margaret, letter, 2 February 1977.

lxxvii Alexander, Hon. Brian, John Golds and Nevill Turner, *The Mustique Marketing Report*, October 1977.

lxxviii Alexander, Hon. Brian to author, email, 26 April 2011.

lxxix Wells, Mary, www.wowowow.com, 3 June 2009.

lxxx Lichfield, Earl of, *The Mustique News*, 'My Mustique', 1978.

lxxxi Alexander, Hon. Brian to author, email, 26 April 2011.

lxxxii Adams-Clark, Jane to Lord Glenconner, letter, 15 March 2010.

lxxxiii Harris, Keith to author, telephone call, 9 May 2012.

lxxxiv Ministry of Agriculture, Lands, Fisheries and Co-operatives, St Lucia, Veterinary and Livestock Division, post mortem report, 2 March 1993.

lxxxv Crites, Mitchell Abdul Karim, to author, telephone conversation, 28 June 2012.

lxxxvi Bonhams Catalogue 19567 'The contents of the St Lucian property of Lord Glenconner', 28 September 2011, lot 163, p.130.

lxxxvii Sotheby's Catalogue, 'Arts of the Islamic World', 14 April 2010, lot 189, pp.138–9.

lxxxviii Dunne, Dominic, 'It's a family affair', *Vanity Fair*, March 1987, p.101.

lxxxix Ibid., p.148.

xc Ibid., p.149.

xci Phillips, S.J., invoice, 6 September 1990.

xcii Walcott, Derek, *Litany to the Pitons*, quoted in Bourdeau, Laurent and Sonia Chaassé (dir), *Actes du colloque sites du patrimoine et tourisme*, Quebec, 2-4 juin 2010, p.801

xciii Mitchell, Sir James to author, Brooks's, 20 May 2012.

xciv Mahvi, Pascal, *Deadly Secrets of Iranian Princes, Audacity to Act*, e-book, 2010, p.343.

[xcv] Hockney, David to author, email, 8 May 2012.

[xcvi] Margaret, HRH The Princess, Countess of Snowdon to Lord Glenconner, letter, 25 February 1991.

[xcvii] *The Times*, 23 October 1996, p.21.

[xcviii] Johnson, Susanna, tribute to Colin Glenconner, Traquair Church, 19 June 2011.

[xcix] Bullman, Joseph, *The Man Who Bought Mustique*, Chanel 4 documentary, 2000.

[c] Clarke, Gerald, 'Lord Glenconner on St Lucia', *Architectural Digest*, August, 2002.

[ci] Davies, Hunter, *The Independent*, 25 March 1993.

[cii] Jaranti, Vikram, *Independent on Sunday*, 30 July 2000.

[ciii] Holden, Stephen, *The New York Times*, 9 May 2001, p.E4.

[civ] Redmond, Camilla, *The Guardian*, 3 August 2000, p.29.

[cv] Creasey, the Hon. May to author, email, 8 June 2012.

[cvi] Tennant, the Hon. Amy to author, 7 June 2012.

[cvii] Quoted in *The Esoteric Redux*, internet, 30 August 2010.

[cviii] Henderson, Sarah to author, Butlers Marston, 9 August 2012.

[cix] Pettigrew, Lane to author, Paddington Station, 25 May 2012.

[cx] Johnston, Susanna, address at Traquair Church, 19 June 2011.

[cxi] Kusunoki, Dr Sharon-Michi, www.philipjacksonsculptures.com.

[cxii] Melly, Diana, *Take a Girl Like Me, life with George*, London, 2005, pp. 46-7**

[cxiii] Dovkants, Keith, 'Paradise lost,' *Tatler*, August 2012.

[cxiv] Glenconner, Lady to author, London, 25 July 2012.

[cxv] Stern-Gillet, Professor Suzanne, *Aristotle's Philosophy of Friendship*

Llewellyn, Sir Roderick.

# Index